AF249060

RANGE ROVER
Owner's Handbook 1986 ON

Specification details set out in this Handbook apply to a range of vehicles and not to any particular vehicle. For the specification of any particular vehicle owners should consult their Distributor or Dealer.

The Manufacturers reserve the right to vary their specifications with or without notice and at such times and in such manner as they think fit. Major as well as minor changes may be involved in accordance with the Manufacturer's policy of constant product improvement.

Whilst every effort is made to ensure the accuracy of the particulars contained in this Handbook, neither the Manufacturer nor the Distributor or Dealer by whom this Handbook is supplied, shall in any circumstances be held liable for any inaccuracy or the consequences thereof.

Published by
Land Rover Ltd

A Managing Agent for Land Rover UK Limited
PUBLICATION No. LSM129 HB EDITION BB   © Copyright Land Rover 1985

Land Rover Limted
Lode Lane
Solihull
West Midlands B92 8NW
England

 # WARNING LABELS FITTED TO VEHICLE

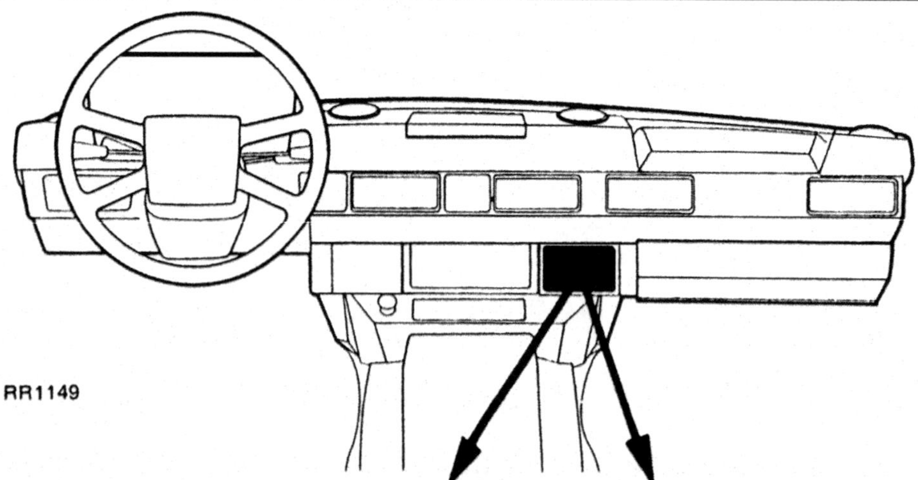

FOUR-SPEED AUTOMATIC GEARBOX MODELS

IMPORTANT — TRANSFER GEARBOX INFORMATION

ENGAGE DIFF LOCK BEFORE TRACTION IS LIKELY TO BE LOST. DISENGAGE DIFF LOCK AS SOON AS THE DIFFICULT SURFACE HAS BEEN CROSSED.

TO CHANGE TRANSFER RATIO, REDUCE SPEED TO BELOW 8 kph (5 mph), SELECT AUTO 'N', MOVE HIGH/LOW LEVER RAPIDLY TO REQUIRED POSITION, SELECT AUTO GEAR. ALTERNATIVELY, STOP VEHICLE, MAKE SELECTION AS ABOVE.

FOR MAXIMUM ENGINE BRAKING, SELECT AUTO '1', KEEP ENGINE RUNNING.

FOR FURTHER INFORMATION ON CORRECT DRIVING TECHNIQUES AND ROLLING ROAD OPERATION REFER TO DRIVERS MANUAL.

FIVE-SPEED MANUAL GEARBOX MODELS

IMPORTANT — TRANSFER GEARBOX INFORMATION

ENGAGE DIFF LOCK BEFORE TRACTION IS LIKELY TO BE LOST: WIDE THROTTLE OPENINGS SHOULD BE AVOIDED IN 1st AND 2nd GEAR LOW RANGE.

DISENGAGE DIFF LOCK AS SOON AS THE DIFFICULT SURFACE HAS BEEN CROSSED.

CHANGE RATIO FROM HIGH (H) TO LOW (L) ONLY WHEN THE VEHICLE IS STATIONARY.

FOR FURTHER INFORMATION ON CORRECT DRIVING TECHNIQUES AND ROLLING ROAD OPERATION REFER TO DRIVERS MANUAL.

WARNING: AIR CONDITIONING
THIS SYSTEM IS FILLED AT HIGH PRESSURE WITH A POTENTIALLY
TOXIC MATERIAL. FOLLOW SERVICE INSTRUCTIONS WHEN
DISMANTLING OR APPLYING EXCESSIVE HEAT, e.g. STEAM
CLEANING, PAINTING, ETC. SERVICING MUST ONLY BE CARRIED
OUT BY A QUALIFIED ENGINEER IN ACCORDANCE WITH
INSTRUCTIONS IN THE WORKSHOP MANUAL.

THIS PLUG
MUST NOT
BE REMOVED
WHEN ENGINE
IS HOT

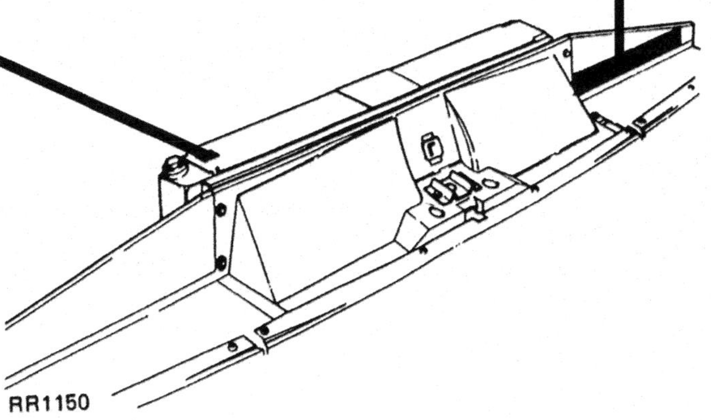

IMPORTANT
BEFORE JACKING VEHICLE·
1. ENGAGE DIFF LOCK (i.e. WARNING
LIGHT MUST BE ILLUMINATED PRIOR
TO SWITCHING OFF IGNITION)
2. APPLY HANDBRAKE
3. CHOCK WHEELS

RR1150

CONTENTS

CONTENTS

RANGE ROVER

THE FORMAL INTRODUCTION

1

Section Contents   **Page**

A quality product

Congratulations on receiving your new Range Rover, a quality product vaguely imitated by some but unmatched by any other vehicle. The manufacturer, Land Rover UK Limited, achieves high standards in the design and production of the vehicle to ensure reliability, safety and efficiency in operation.

These standards can be continued throughout the life of the Range Rover by proper maintenance and care from the operator.

The important first step in preventive maintenance, the Pre-delivery Inspection of your vehicle, will have been completed by your Dealer or Distributor who should also be contacted for advice, subsequent inspections or planned servicing requirements as recommended in this book.

Now it's up to you. Use your Dealer or Distributor and use this book to help you ensure a long, safe and efficient operating life for this highly mobile aristocrat.

The structure of this book

Generally it is assumed that the reader has no previous knowledge or experience in the operation of a Range Rover but is, of course, a qualified driver.

Therefore, the information in this book is presented to guide the reader progressively from reception of the vehicle through familiarisation with controls and instrumentation, starting and driving techniques, day-to-day running requirements and longer term maintenance with a 'Data' section at the end of the book.

Where specific information is sought, first consult the list of contents which will direct you to the relevant page or pages.

Models covered

This book covers a wide range of both petrol-engined carburetter and electronic fuel injection (EFI) models with either the manual or automatic gearbox. Two- or four-door versions, diesel models and various items of optional equipment are also mentioned.

Note however that all petrol-engined models feature electronic ignition using the Lucas 35 DLM8 distributor which is factory pre-set and should not be altered or disturbed. Any attention required on this item or on any aspect of the electronic fuel injection system used on some models must be referred to your qualified Range Rover Dealer or Distributor.

Now read on and enjoy real motoring!

Safety First
For the protection of yourself and others and the longer service life of your vehicle please heed the instructions carefully and note the **WARNINGS** and **CAUTIONS** that are given throughout this handbook in the following form:

 *WARNING: Procedures which must be followed precisely to avoid the possibility of personal injury or other damage.*

CAUTION: *This calls attention to procedures which must be followed to avoid damage to components.*

Note: *This offers advice or calls attention to methods which make a job easier to perform.*

In the interests of road safety, your attention is drawn to the following important safety hints.

Before driving, familiarise yourself with the layout and purpose of all controls, gears and switches.

Adjust the seat as necessary to achieve a comfortable driving position with full control over the vehicle.

Always start vehicle and operate controls from the driving position.

Always use the safety harness even for the shortest journeys. This is a legal requirement in the United Kingdom and many other areas.

Frequently clean the windscreen, rear and side windows to achieve clear vision. Use a solvent in the screen washer reservoir.

Maintain all external lights in good working order and correct setting of headlamp beams.

Maintain correct tyre condition and pressures. These should be checked at least each month, or more frequently when high-speed touring or under cross-country conditions, even to the extent of a daily check.

Ensure your speed is low enough for an emergency stop to be effective and safe under all road and vehicle loading conditions.

Under no circumstances should the ignition key be turned to the 'steering locked' position or any attempt made to withdraw the key whilst the vehicle is in motion.

When fitted, ensure the power take-off (pto) universal joints are shielded.

Before working on pto driven implements always disengage the pto and switch 'off' the engine.

 *WARNING: Do not carry unsecured equipment, tools or luggage which could move and cause personal injury in the event of an accident or emergency manoeuvre either on or off-road.*

 *WARNING: Always fully apply the parking brake when leaving your vehicle or it may roll and cause damage or injury. Also be certain to leave a manual transmission in first gear and an automatic transmission in 'Park'. On slopes and particularly in low range, ensure that the parking pawl of the automatic gearbox has fully engaged by gently releasing the brakes and allowing the vehicle to 'rock' into 'Park'. Never leave keys in the vehicle.*

 *WARNING: Under no circumstances should cross-ply and radial-ply tyres be mixed on this vehicle. Recommended tyre replacements are given in the Data Section.*

WARNING: Do not remove the expansion tank filler or radiator caps when the engine is hot, because the cooling system is pressurised and personal scalding could result.

WARNING: Many liquids and other substances used in motor vehicles are poisonous, they must not be consumed under any circumstances and must be kept away from open wounds. These substances include anti-freeze, brake fluid, fuel, windscreen washer additives, lubricants, battery contents and various adhesives.

⚠️ **Warnings for your safety**
Land Rover Ltd, do not recommend that any modifications be made to the suspension or steering system, as this could seriously affect the handling characteristics of the vehicle.

An illuminated brake warning light does not indicate that the parking brake is fully applied, only that the brake is not disengaged.

On a vehicle fitted with automatic transmission, never use the 'P' park position (gear selection) as a substitute for the parking brake. It should be used IN ADDITION to the parking brake.

The braking system is servo assisted only when the engine is running.

The steering system is power-assisted only when the engine is running.

Do not reach through the steering wheel to operate any controls.

Do not adjust the drivers seat while the vehicle is in motion, as this may result in the loss of vehicle control.

The head restraints should not be removed while the seat is occupied.

Do not carry passengers in the load space.

Do not drive with the tailgate open; poisonous carbon monoxide fumes can enter the vehicle.

Do not loosely store the load space cover in the vehicle. When not in use the cover should be stored vertically in the space provided directly behind the rear seat.

All tools should be correctly stored in their location after use.

It is advisable to restore the operation of the interior release handle when the child proof lock facility is not required.

Keep hands and clothing well clear of all moving parts.

Do not use reclaimed brake fluid, mineral oil or brake fluid that has been stored in old or open containers.

⚠️ *WARNING: The suspension levelling unit contains pressurised gas and must not be dismantled nor the casing screws removed. Repair is by replacement of the complete unit only.*

Do not remove any drain plugs while the fluid is hot, otherwise serious burns or scalding may be caused.

Where both wheel rim and tyre are marked 'TUBELESS', an inner tube must NOT be fitted.

Where wheel rim and tyre are not both marked 'Tubeless', and inner tube MUST be fitted.

Combat theft

Never leave your vehicle unattended with the key in the ignition switch. Always remove the key and lock all doors when leaving your vehicle unattended. Check that windows are secure and remove or conceal any items that might create the temptation to steal.

See also 'Ignition switch and keys' (Section 2) for further security measures.

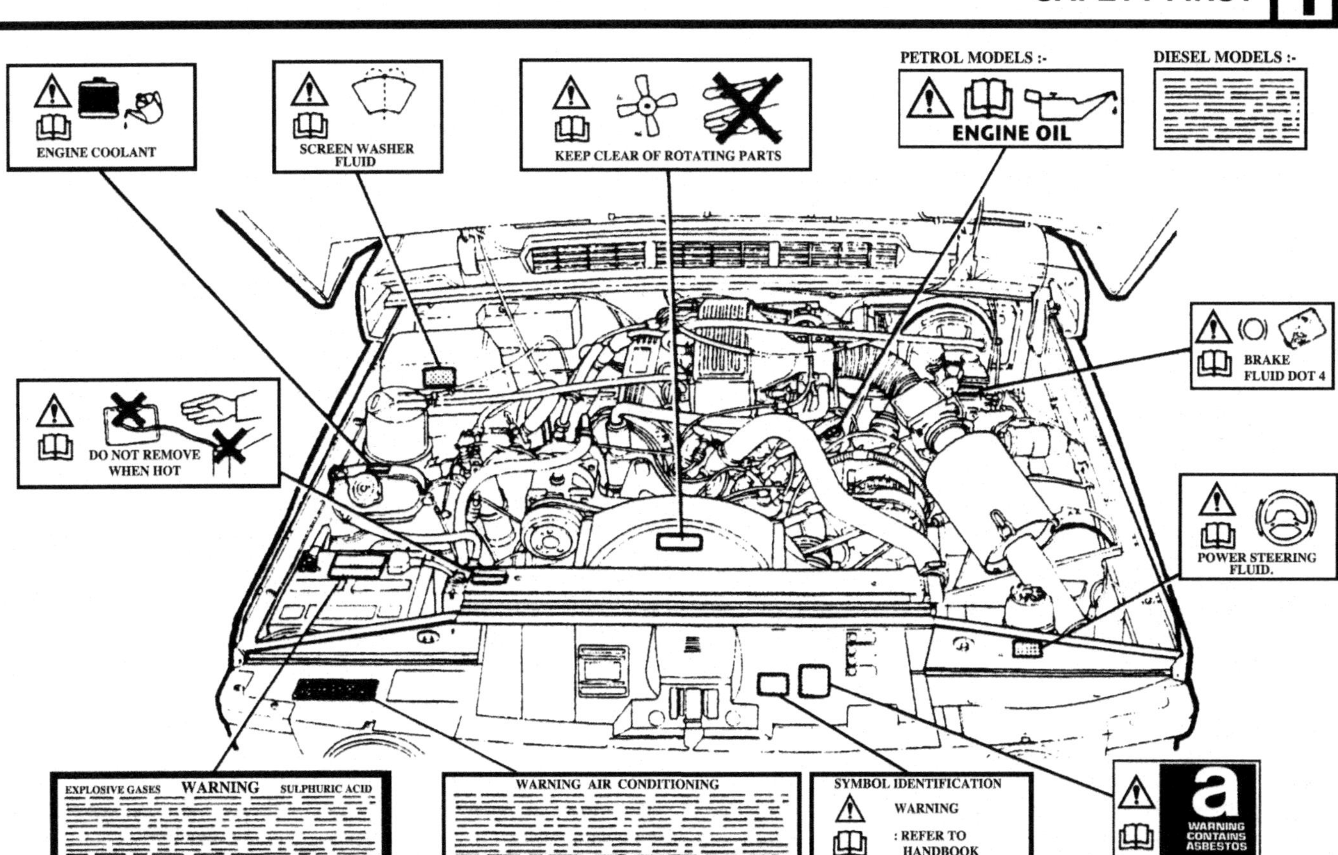

Fig. RR1256 - *Note; This illustration is for general guidance only as the position of components and the extent of labelling on the vehicle will vary between models in the range.*

MANUAL TRANSMISSION

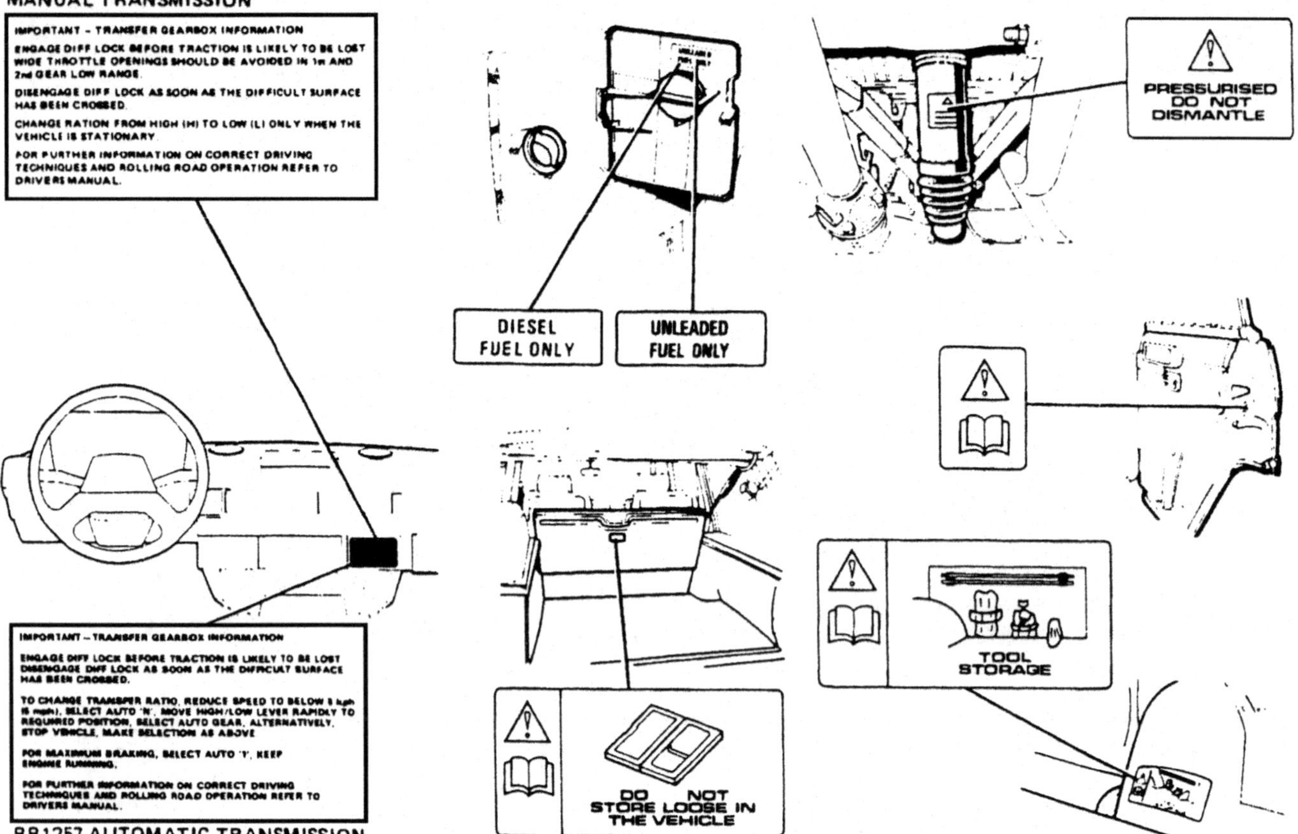

RR1257 AUTOMATIC TRANSMISSION

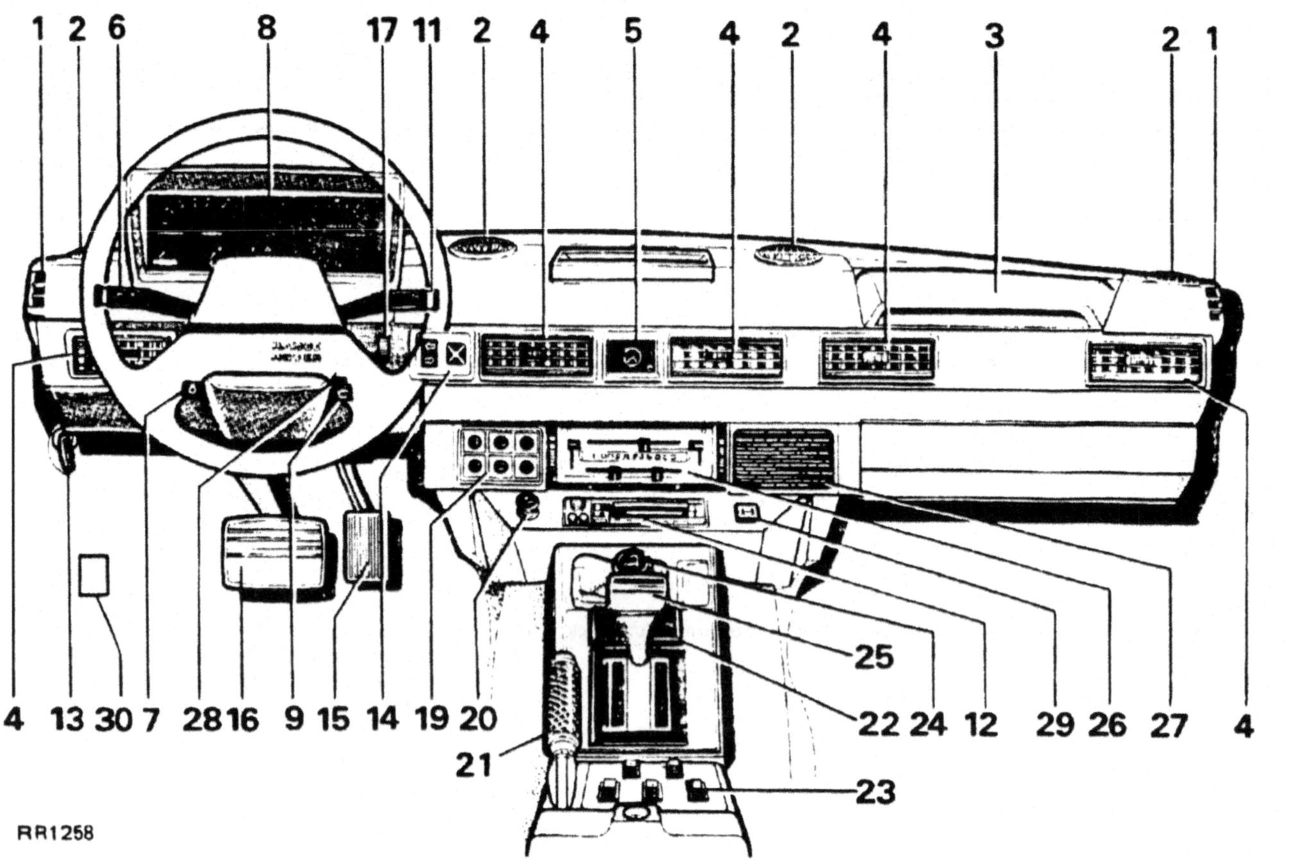
1 2 6 8 17 11 2 4 5 4 2 4 3 2 1
4 13 30 7 28 16 9 15 14 19 20 22 24 12 29 26 27 4
25
21
23
RR1258

Key to fascia layouts - Figs. RR1258 and RR1259

1. Front door side demister vent
2. Windscreen demister vents
3. Grab handle
4. Ventilation louvres (Two only on non-airconditioned model)
5. Clock
6. Headlamp dip, flash, direction indicators and horn switch
7. Main light switch
8. Main instrument binnacle
9. Rear screen wiper and screen wash switch
10. Cold start control (carburetter models only)
11. Front windscreen wiper and screen wash switch
12. Radio/cassette unit (optional) or pocket
13. Bonnet release handle
14. Electrically operated exterior mirror controls (optional)
15. Accelerator pedal
16. Foot brake pedal
17. Instrument illumination electronic dimming control
18. Clutch pedal (manual gearbox only)
19. Auxiliary switch panel
20. Cigar lighter
21. Transmission handbrake/park brake
22. Ashtray
23. Electrically operated window control switches (optional)
24. Transfer gear/differential lock lever
25. Main gear lever
26. Interior climate controls
27. Fuse box
28. Steering lock and ignition switch
29. Differential lock warning light

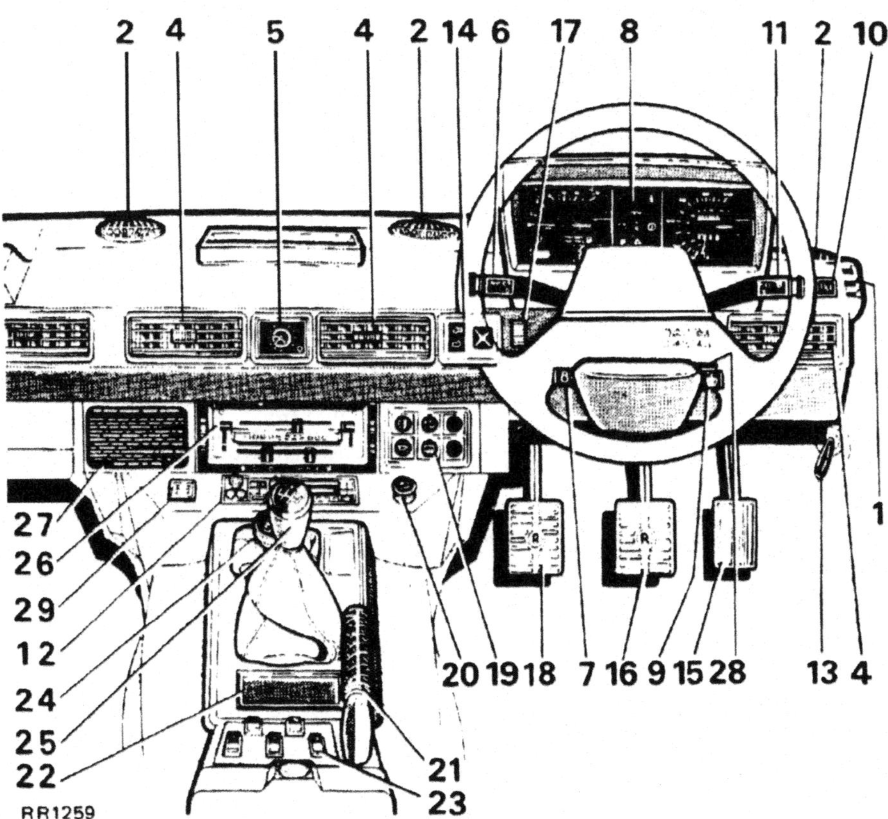

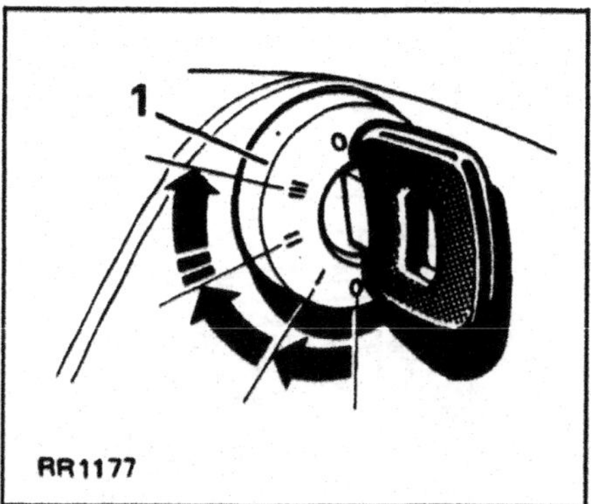

RR1177

Steering lock and starter switch Fig. RR1177

The four-position, key-operated switch (1) located on the right-hand side of the steering column, controls the mechanical steering lock, ignition, starter motor and, on diesel models, the heater plugs.

The steering lock/ignition starter switch and its electrical circuits are designed to prevent the ignition system and starter from being energised while the steering lock is engaged. Serious consequences could result from alterations to or substitution of the steering lock/ignition switch or its wiring. In no circumstances must the ignition switch be separated from the steering lock.

Switch positions:

'O' **Insertion or removal of the key is only possilble at this position;** Always remove the ignition key when leaving the vehicle unattended.
Removal of the key and movement of the steering to the straight ahead position will engage the steering lock.

To disengage the steering lock, the key must be inserted and turned clockwise. Slight movement of the steering wheel will assist in disengagement of the lock.

'I' **Steering unlocked, ignition off;**
Where applicable, radio/cassette unit, air conditioning motor, heater blower, electric window lifts and front and rear screen wipers can be operated.

'II' **Ignition switched on;**
Petrol driven models - all electrical circuits can be operated.
Diesel models - all electrical circuits switched on, heater plugs operating.

Leave the key in this position until the heater plug warning light (shown on the left) goes off, then turn the key to the next position.

'III' **Starter motor operates;**
The key will return to the position 'II' as soon as released.

⚠ *WARNING: Do not under any circumstances return the key to the 'O' position until the vehicle is stationary.*

⚠ *WARNING: Do not under any circumstances return the key to the 'O' position until the vehicle is stationary.*

To prevent the steering column lock engaging it is most important that before the vehicle is moved in any way i.e. for towing or coasting purposes, the ignition key must be inserted in the lock and turned to the auxiliary position 'I'.

If, due to an accident or electrical fault it is not considered safe to turn the key, the negative lead of the battery must first be disconnected.

Key numbers
For security reasons the key numbers are not stamped on the locks. Loss of the key for the ignition and steering column lock completely immobilises the vehicle. For this reason and because the keys are of a special design obtainable only from Land Rover Limited or authorised agents, dealers and spares stockists, two combined ignition and steering lock keys are supplied with each vehicle.

Owners and operators are advised therefore to take the following action:
(a) Immediately on receipt of the vehicle, record all the key numbers so that in case of loss, replacements can be obtained.
(b) Keep a spare combined ignition and steering column lock key away from the vehicle in a safe place but where it is readily accessible.

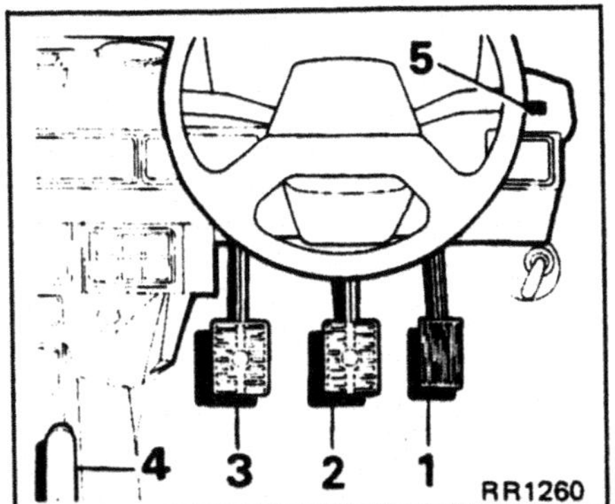

Steering

The hydraulic power-assisted steering is progressively geared. When steering straight ahead it is relatively low geared but becomes progressively higher geared as the steering wheel is turned.

CAUTION: Under no circumstances must the steering wheel be held on full lock for more than thirty seconds in any one minute, otherwise there will be a tendency for the oil to overheat and damage to the seals may result.

WARNING: Land Rover Ltd. do not recommend that any modifications be made to the suspension or steering system, as this could seriously affect the handling characteristics of the vehicle.

Pedals - Fig. RR1260

Clutch (1 - manual gearbox models only), brakes (2) and accelerator (3) pedals are the pendant type and function in the normal way. The brake and clutch operate hydraulically with servo assistance for the brakes.

To avoid needless wear of the clutch withdrawal mechanism do not rest the foot on the clutch pedal while driving.

On automatic models, the accelerator pedal, in addition to controlling engine speed, can be used to obtain a rapid downshift in the automatic gearbox (kickdown) by depressing it fully. As this results in excessive engine speeds, the downshift is automatically supressed.

Handbrake - Fig. RR1260

A drum-type handbrake, well protected from dirt and water, operates directly on the transfer box rear output shaft and is designed for parking use only. Maximum effect is obtained when the handbrake is used with the differential lock engaged.

The brake is applied by pulling back the lever (4). To release, pull the lever slightly back, depress and hold the release button while pushing the lever down to the limit of its travel.

Except in dire emergency, the handbrake must not be applied while the vehicle is in motion as this could result in transmission damage.

Cold start control, carburetter models only - Fig. RR1260

The cold start control (5) has two functions:

Pulled out approximately 14 to 16 mm (just over 1/2 inch) it increases the engine speed without mixture alteration.

Pulled out further the mixture is progressively enriched for cold starting. By turning the knob slightly in a clockwise direction, the control can be locked in any position. To ensure easy starting the control should initially be pulled fully out, summer and winter. After the engine has started, the control should be pushed in as soon as possible consistent with even running.

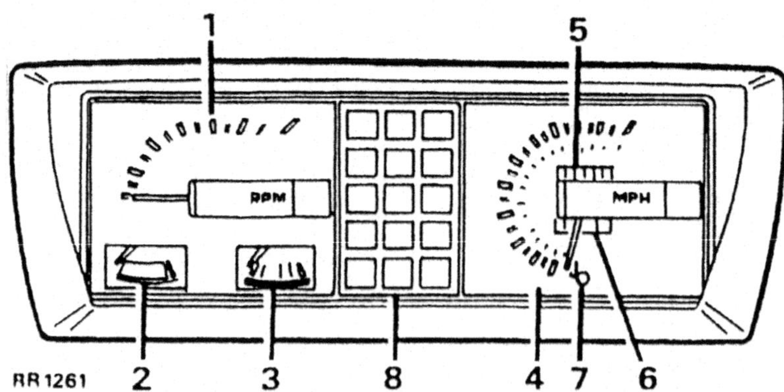

Main Instrument Binnacle - Fig. RR1261
Mounted on the top of the fascia directly in front of the driver, the binnacle houses the following easily-visible instruments:

The **tachometer** (1) indicates the engine speed in revolutions per minute. For normal road work, petrol engine speeds of between 2,000 and 5,000 rev/min and diesel engine speeds between 2000 and 3500 rev/min will be found to produce the most satisfactory performance from your Range Rover. Engine speed should never exceed 5,500 rev/min on petrol-driven models or 4,200 rev/min on diesel versions: these maximums should be considerably reduced during recommended 'Running-in' period (see the 'Driving and Techniques' section).

The **coolant temperature indicator** (2) needle should register in the mid-way area under normal running conditions. Should the needle travel to the hot (orange coloured) area during normal usage, the vehicle must be stopped and the cause investigated.

Fuel Gauge (3). With the ignition switched on, the needle will indicate the approximate level of fuel in the tank. Low fuel level is indicated when the needle position approaches the orange-coloured marker on the left of the gauge and is also indicated by illumination of a warning light in the centre panel. For fuel tank capacity details see the 'Data' section at the rear of this book.

The **speedometer** (4) is a mechanical instrument which also incorporates an **odometer** (5) showing total distance travelled and a **distance trip meter** (6) which can be reset to zero by depressing the button (7) projecting from the instrument face.

The **warning light central panel** (8) which will vary between diesel and petrol-driven models, uses symbols (shown on the following pages) which include an alternative for certain market requirements and a symbol for the high temperature of automatic gearbox oil where appropriate.

Binnacle Centre Panel Warning Lights

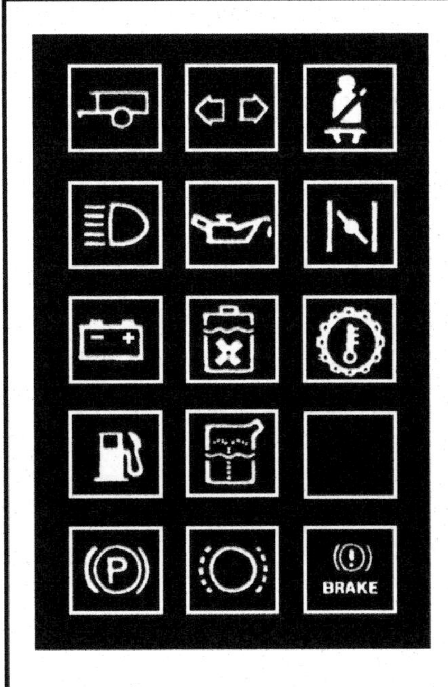

Note: *Warning lights are intended to be of assistance only in the operation of your vehicle and should not be solely relied on for evidence of malfunction.*

The driver's own judgement is important. If any malfunction is suspected, the vehicle should be stopped as soon as possible (consistent with road safety) and the cause investigated.

Trailer indicators

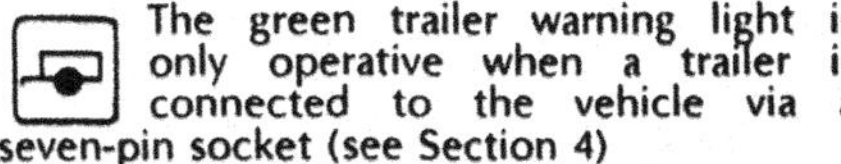

The green trailer warning light is only operative when a trailer is connected to the vehicle via a seven-pin socket (see Section 4)

The warning light will flash in conjunction with the vehicle indicator warning lights, thus demonstrating that the trailer indicator lamps are functioning correctly. In the event of a direction indicator bulb failure, the trailer warning light will **not** be illuminated.

Direction Indicators

Both green arrows flash in conjunction with the selected set of turn indicator lights. In addition the flasher unit is audible while the lights are flashing. Should a turn indicator bulb fail, the warning lights will **not** function and the flasher unit will **not** be heard.

Note: *Direction indicators and warning light should flash simultaneously when the hazard warning switch on the top of the steering column is operated.*

Seat Belt

The red warning illuminates and will remain on when the driver's seat belt is not fastened and the ignition is switched to the "II" position.

Note: *The seat belt warning symbol appears on all binnacles but will only illuminate when territory regulations require a seat belt warning system.*

Main beam

The blue warning light is illuminated when the headlamp main beams are in use; its purpose is to remind you to dip the headlamps when entering a brightly lit area, or when approaching other traffic. The warning light will also be illuminated when the headlamp flasher switch is used.

High or low engine oil pressure

The red warning light should always glow when the ignition is switched on. If the light remains on with the engine running, the engine must be stopped and the cause investigated.

Ignition

The red ignition warning light should glow when the ignition is switched on. If the light stays on when the engine is running, stop the engine and investigate.

Low coolant level

This red signal will remain illuminated when the coolant level is too low.

The fault must be rectified at the earliest opportunity but in the meantime care must be taken to ensure that the engine does not overheat.

Automatic gearbox oil temperature (where applicable)

If the vehicle is being worked hard in high transfer gear at low speeds, the oil temperature in the automatic gearbox will rise and cause illumination of the warning light. The driver must change to a lower gear to extinguish the light by selecting position **3**, **2** or **1**. If the light remains on, the transfer gear must be shifted into **LOW** (see details regarding use of the combined transfer gear/differential lock lever). If the light remains on with the transmission in low transfer, low gear, the vehicle **MUST** be stopped until the transmission oil temperature has fallen and the light extinguished.

Transmission (parking only) handbrake

Application of the handbrake with ignition 'on' illuminates a red warning light showing this symbol.

Fuel level

The green warning light will be illuminated when there is less than approximately 13 litres (approximately 3 gallons) left in the fuel tank. The light will remain on until the fuel supply is replenished. Intermittent flashing may occur when cornering before the low fuel sensing level is reached.

Low screenwash fluid level

Illumination of this red signal while the ignition switch is in the **'II'** position indicates reduction of the washer reservoir contents below approximately 1/4 litre (1/2 pint). The reservoir should be replenished at the earliest opportunity.

Cold start (petrol models) or heater plug (diesel models)

On carburetter models, the illumination of the amber warning light with this symbol will remind you that the cold start control is still out and should be returned to the 'off' position as soon as possible, consistent with even running.

However, the warning light will not be illuminated at the fast idle position, that is, the control pulled out approximately 14 to 16 mm (just over 1/2 inch).

On diesel models, this symbol will be illuminated to indicate that the heater plugs are warming up. During this period, the ignition key should be kept in the **'II'** position until the warning light is extinguished before turning the key to the **'III'** position to operate the starter motor.

Brake pad wear

 This light and symbol will be illuminated when the brake pads have worn down to the minimum permissible thickness and must be renewed.

Brake fluid pressure failure/handbrake applied

 With the ignition switched on, this signal will illuminate if the handbrake is applied or if there is a loss of fluid pressure (for leakage) from the braking system.

As a fail-safe precaution against total brake failure the brakes are operated on each wheel by a primary or secondary hydraulic system. Should one of the hydraulic circuits fail the other circuit will continue to function. This will result in increased brake pedal travel and effort.

Do not pump the brake pedal in an attempt to restore pedal pressure. If there is pressure failure in one of the brake circuits the cause must be investigated immediately.

Unless as a result of investigation you are satisfied that it is safe to proceed, you should leave the vehicle where it is and call for assistance. Even if you are satisfied that it is safe to proceed, extreme care should be taken and heavy braking avoided. In deciding whether it is safe to proceed you should consider whether you will be infringing the law.

Diesel models

Range Rover diesel models are fitted with a brake vacuum warning system which operates through the existing 'fluid loss' warning light on the instrument panel.

 This light operates if there is a leak in the hydraulic system or insufficient servo assistance. When starting the engine, the warning light may remain on for a few seconds until servo assistance is restored, this delay will be longer during cold weather.

 *WARNING: DO NOT drive the vehicle while the brake warning light is illuminated.*

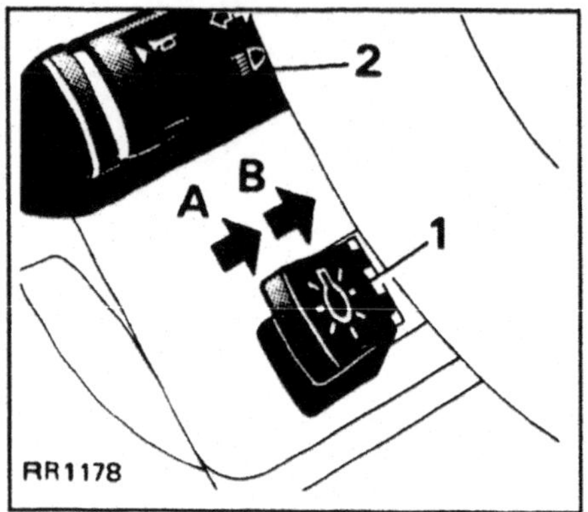

RR1178

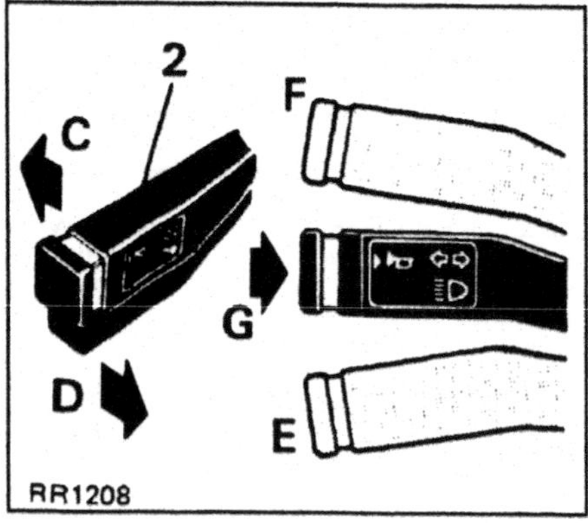

RR1208

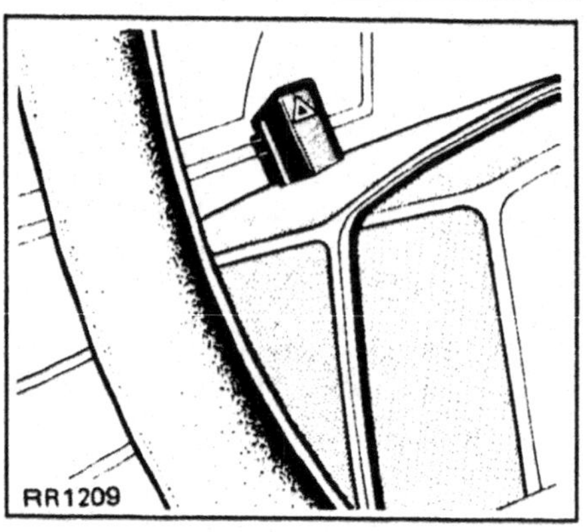

RR1209

Lights, direction indicator and horn - Figs. RR1178 and RR1208

Headlamps "Dim dip" lighting (UK only)
Vehicles manufactured after October 1st 1986, must comply with new lighting regulations which prohibit such vehicles being driven on side lights only. On Range Rovers, this is achieved by the addition of an electronic control unit in the lighting system, so that when the side lights are switched on with the engine running, low vlotage current is also supplied to the headlamp dipped beam circuit, giving dim dipped lighting. When the headlamps are switched on, full voltage is automatically restored, giving normal headlamp lighting.

Sidelights and headlights
Move the paddle switch (1) on the left-hand side of the steering column towards the driver (position **A**) to illuminate the sidelights (headlamp dim dip and sidelights UK only) and panel lights. Move the switch to position **B** to illuminate the headlights.

Headlight dip and main beam
Move the lever (2) away from the driver (position **C**) to switch on the headlight main beam. Flick the lever towards the driver (position **D**) to flash the headlights.

Direction indicators
Move the lever down (**E**) to indicate the intention to turn LEFT. Move the lever up (**F**) to indicate the intention to turn RIGHT. Hold the lever against spring pressure when indicating lane change.

Horn
To operate, press the end of the lever inwards (**G**).

Hazard warning - Fig RR1209
Press the switch to make all the direction indicators flash together as hazard warning lights; the RED light in the switch and the direction indicator light in the centre warning light panel will also flash. To switch off, press the switch again.

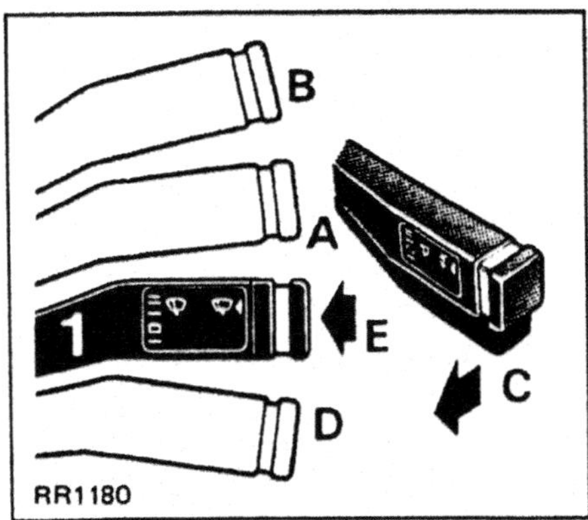

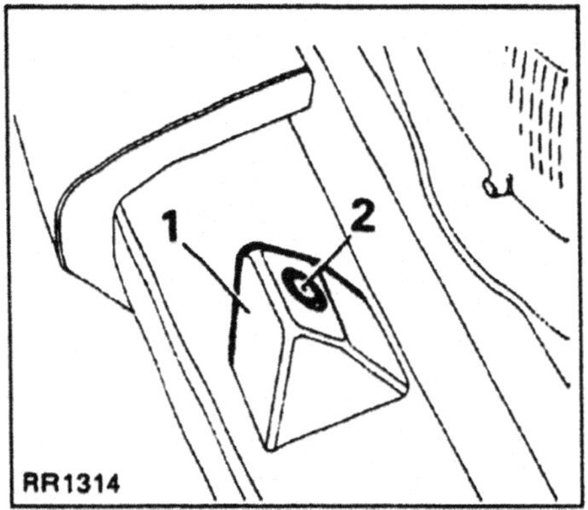

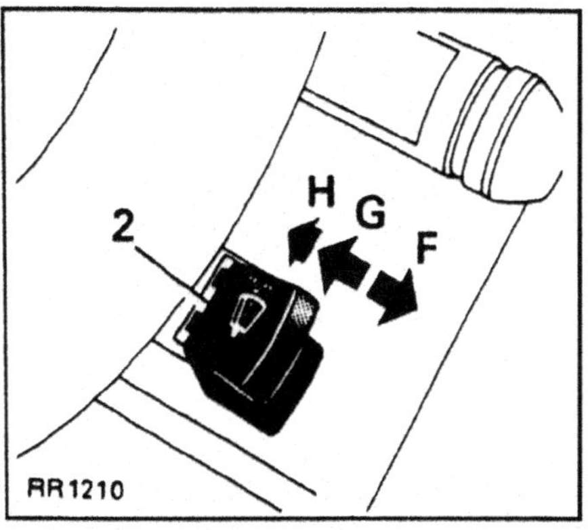

**Windscreen wipers and wash/wipe system -
Fig. RR1180**

*CAUTION: To prevent possible overload
damage to the linkage or the wiper motors in
either freezing or very hot conditions, ensure
that the blades are not adhering to the glass
before switching on the wipers.*

Raise the lever (1) to its first position (A) for
normal wipe and to its second position (B)
for fast wipe. Flick the lever towards the
driver position (C) to obtain a single wipe.
Move the lever down (D) to obtain
intermittent wiping. Always switch off and
allow the wipers to return to their parked
position before switching off the ignition.

Press the end of the lever inwards (E) to
obtain a windscreen wash and wipe. The
wash/wipe will continue for as long as the
lever is depressed. When released, the wash
will stop immediately but the wipers will
continue for a further five seconds
approximately. When selected, this sequence
will over- ride any other wiper function.

Headlamp wash - Fig. RR1314
If the headlamp washer facility is fitted
(optional), this will operate in conjunction
with the windscreen washer when the
headlamps are switched on in the dipped
position.
The headlamp washer jet units (1) are fitted
on the top of the front bumper, one in front
of each headlamp. The jet direction can be
adjusted with the aid of a needle inserted
into the orifice (2) which can also be cleared
with a fine needle or wire when necessary.

Rear windscreen wash/wipe - Fig RR1210
Move the paddle switch (2) away from the
driver (F) against spring pressure for a jet of
wash solution onto the rear screen, with a
wipe cycle which will continue for three
wipes after release of the paddle switch.

Move the paddle switch towards the driver
(G) against spring pressure to commence
intermittent wiping. Move the switch towards
the driver (H) against spring pressure to
cancel intermittent wiping.

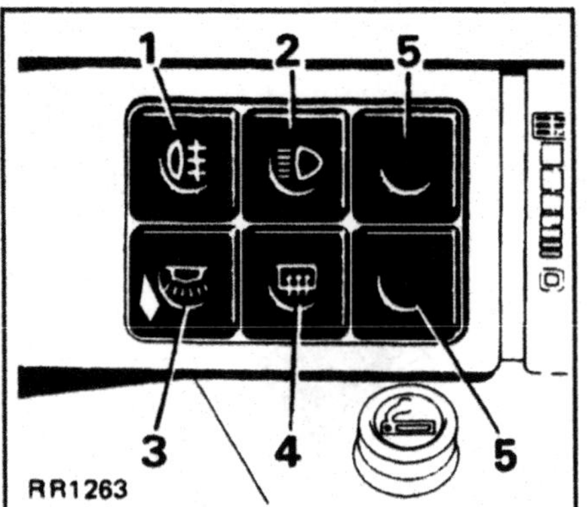

The **auxiliary switch panel (Fig. RR1263)** on the fascia has provision for six 'push-push' switches including two blank accessory positions. Relevant switches incorporate integral symbols which are illuminated when the vehicle lights are on.

The rear fog lamps and heated rear screen switches incorporate individual bulbs illuminated when each switch is operated.

Rear fog guard lamps

Operated by the switch **(1)** these lamps are operative only when dipped headlights are in use. The amber symbol in the switch will be illuminated when the fog guard lamps are on.

Auxiliary driving lamps

Used in conjunction with the main light switch on the side of the steering column, the switch **(2)** controls the two auxiliary driving lamps mounted in the detachable front spoiler fitted to some models of the Range Rover.

Interior roof and tailgate lamps

This switch **(3)** is provided for illumination of the interior roof and tailgate lamps when necessary with the doors closed. With this switch in the off position, interior lamps will be illuminated via courtesy switches when a side door or tailgate is opened. In relation to front side doors only, the lights will remain on for approximately 15 to 18 seconds after the last door is closed. However, the lights will be extinguished as soon as the ignition is switched on.

Heated rear screen

Press down the switch **(4)**. The amber warning light in the switch will be illuminated. The heated rear screen is only operative when the ignition is switched on.

A voltage sensitive switch is incorporated in the circuit to allow the heated rear screen and air conditioning to be used simultaneously under normal conditions.

However, should the total electrical loadings be such that the alternator cannot maintain adequate charge, for instance, when using all electrical services in a traffic jam, the voltage sensitive switch, will cut-out, rendering the heated rear screen inoperative. The switch will automatically cut-in again restoring the heated screen function as soon as conditions are favourable.

Note: The above also applies to the demister elements in the electrically operated outside mirrors (when applicable). These are controlled by the same voltage-sensitive switch.

Accessory positions

Two switch apertures are fitted with blank covers which are removable to facilitate the fitting of extra accessory switches if required.

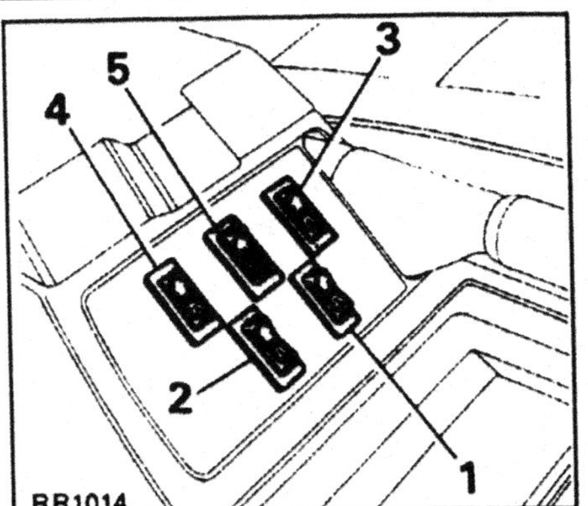

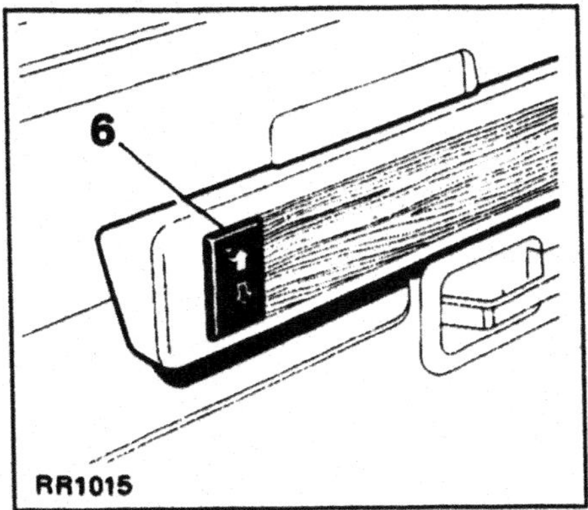

Electrically operated side door windows (where applicable) - Figs. RR1014 and RR1015

All side windows are operated from either front seat by four rocker switches fitted in the centre floor-mounted cover and controlling individual electric motors in each door.

1. Left side, rear window }
2. Right side, rear window } operating
3. Left side, front window } switches
4. Right side, front window }
5. Isolating switch - door fitted switches, rear windows.

Additionally, for the convenience of rear seat passengers, both rear side doors are also fitted with a rocker switch (6), integral with the door pull handles, which provides independent rear side window control.

Note: Windows are only operative whilst the ignition is switched on.

Operating switches (1 to 4)

To **lower** glass depress **front** of switch, to **raise** glass depress **rear** of switch.

Release switch as soon as window is fully open or closed.

Isolating switch (5)

To isolate **door fitted switches** on rear windows depress **front** of the central switch in the floor mounted cover. Use of the facility must be considered whenever children are present in the rear seats.

To restore independent rear passenger control depress **rear** of switch.

Rear side door window switch (6) - Fig. RR1015

Depress switch as indicated to lower or raise the glass.

CAUTION: Do not attempt to raise or lower a window when it is jammed by ice. Should a window be obstructed when being raised or lowered, a thermal cut-out will render the window inoperative. In this event, release the switch and remove the obstruction. The window can be re-operated after two seconds.

WARNING: Particular care should be taken that children are kept away from windows when raising or lowering is in progress.

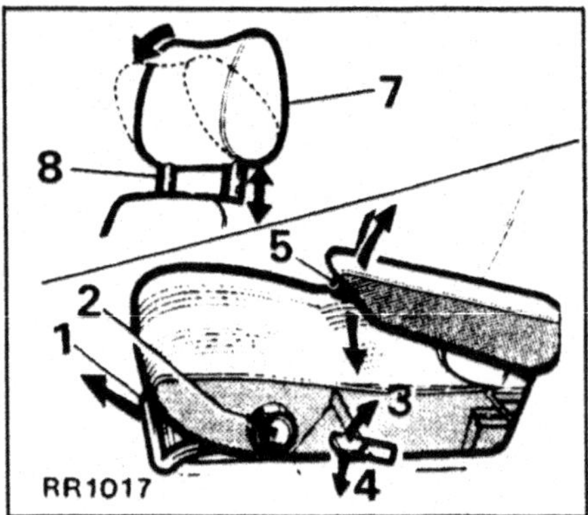

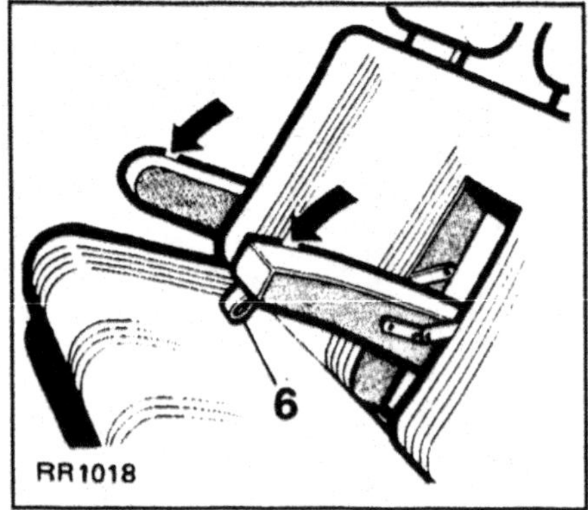

The new driver should adjust the seat as necessary to achieve a comfortable driving position to ensure full control of the vehicle and clear vision all round.

Reclining front seats, four door models - Fig. RR1017

The front seats have fully reclining backrests and in addition to fore and aft control can be adjusted for height.

Fore and aft adjustment

Lift the bar (1) and slide the seat forwards or backwards to the required position. Lower the bar to lock the seat in position.

Backrest reclining adjustment

Rotate the handwheel (2) to alter the angle of the backrest as required.

Height adjustment

Raise the spring-loaded lever (3) and retain in position. The **front** of the seat can then be raised or lowered to obtain the height and angle required. Release the lever to lock the seat in position.

Lower the spring-loaded lever (4) and retain in position. The **rear** of the seat can then be raised or lowered to obtain the height and angle required. Release the lever to lock the seat in position.

Folding armrests (where fitted) - Figs. RR1017 and RR1018

Two **adjustable angle** armrests are fitted to the **inner** side of the front seat backrests only. These complement the padded door pulls which provide an **outer** armrest facility.

Armrest angle adjustment

Pull the armrest down into position then turn the knob (5) in the end of the armrest to preset the angle required.

A **centre** and two **outer** folding **fixed angle** armrests are fitted to the rear seat backrest. These are provided with finger loops (6) for ease of operation.

Head restraints (where fitted)

The head restraint is designed to support the back of the head, **not** the neck.

To adjust

The head restraint (7) may be raised or lowered into one of three set positions and/or swivelled forward or rearwards as required.

To remove

Lift the complete unit from its retaining guides (8) in the seat back.

RR1019

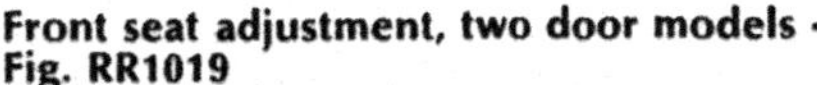

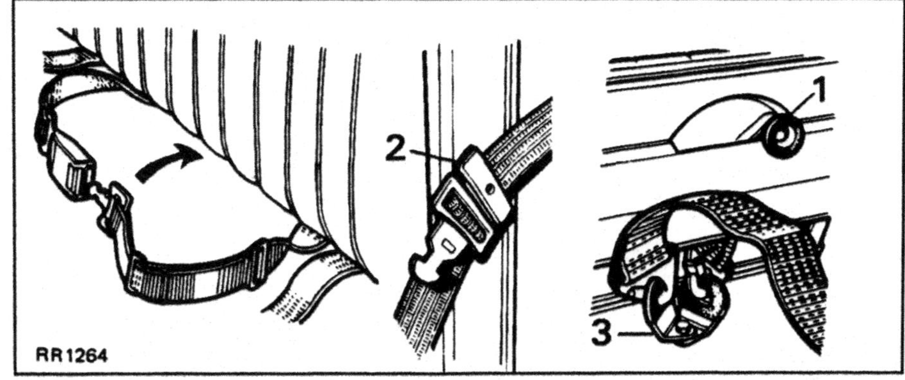

RR1264

Front seat adjustment, two door models - Fig. RR1019

Special safety type front seats (with fixed back rake) are fitted having the safety harness secured to anchorage points on the seat. Fore and aft adjustment of the front seats is controlled by lifting the locking bar (1) at the front of the seat cushion.

To allow easy access to the rear seat, the backrests can be tilted forwards by lifting the lever (2) on either the inboard or outboard side of the seat. The seats will then automatically move forward on runners to provide the maximum amount of space.

Non-split rear seats (where applicable) - Fig. RR1264

The backrest and seat can be folded forward to increase the loading area in the rear compartment, but first on four door models open both rear passenger doors. The seat is secured in the normally upright position by catches at each end of the backrest which can be released by use of the lever (1) at the rear centre of the backrest.

Protection of rear seat belts (where fitted)

Before folding down the rear seat back first ensure that the outer inertia type belts are correctly stowed in their clip holders (2).

To avoid damage to inner inertia type belts and static lap type centre belts mounted on the floor behind the rear seat, pass the four belts between the bottom of the seat back and the seat to the rear floor area as indicated.

Before erecting the rear seat ensure that all centre floor mounted belts are extended rearwards to prevent them from being trapped beneath the seatbase.

If the vehicle payload is likely to damage or chafe the belts in the rear floor area they should be removed temporarily. In this event unhook the belts from their respective floor mounted brackets by holding open the spring-loaded safety catch (3). After reconnection ensure that the safety catch fully returns to the closed position.

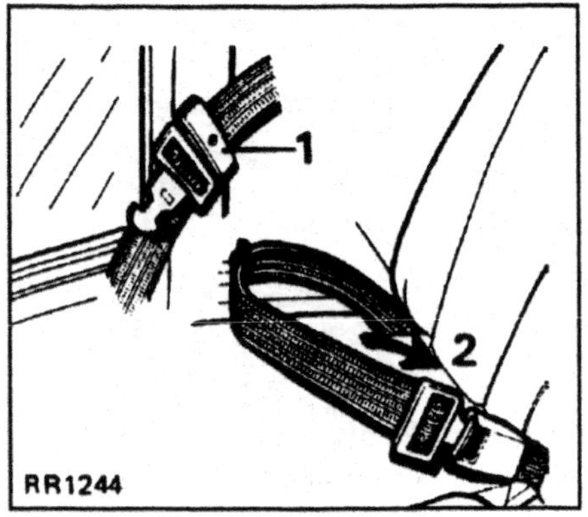

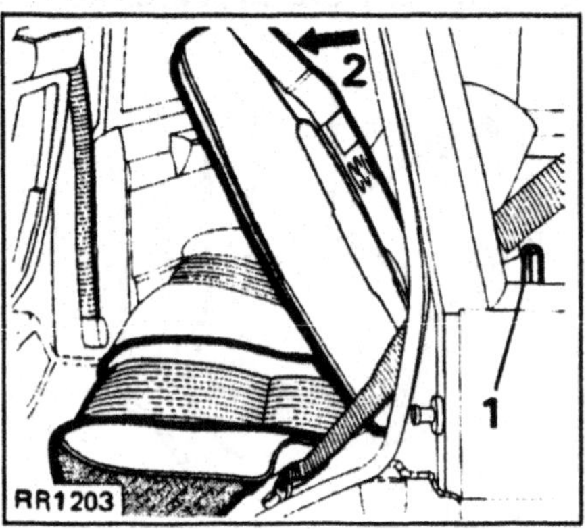

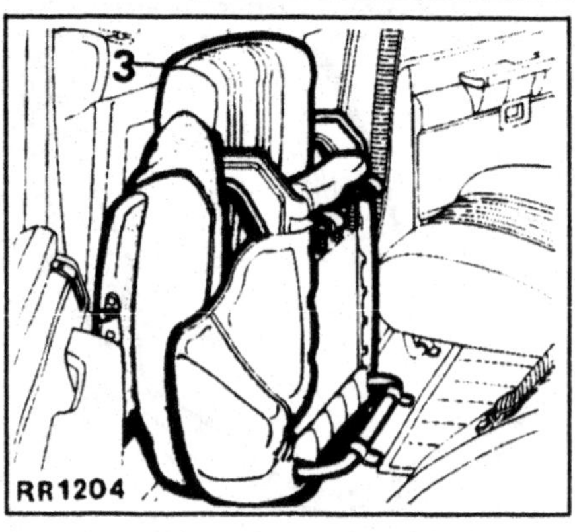

Split rear seating (where applicable)

One or both parts of the split rear seating can be either partially folded to provide a useful horizontal surface or fully folded forward to increase the rear load space.

Before folding either part of the seat, open the relevant rear passenger door (to avoid interference with the door furniture) and ensure that the inertia type outer seat belt is correctly stowed in the belt clip. (1 - Fig. RR1244).

To avoid damage to the lap-type centre-seat belts anchored to the floor behind the rear seat, pass the four belts carefully through the junction of the backrest and seat base as indicated (2) so that they are clear of the folding seat.

Folding the rear seat - Figs. RR1203 and RR1204

Both parts of the seat are secured in the normally upright position by a 'ring-pull' catch (1) at the window side of each backrest. Lifting the catch will release the backrest and allow it to be pushed forward (2) to provide a horizontal surface on the seat or to be folded forward with the seat into a vertical position at the rear of the front seat (3).

Before erecting the rear seat ensure that all centre floor mounted belts are extended rearwards to prevent them from being trapped beneath the seatbase.

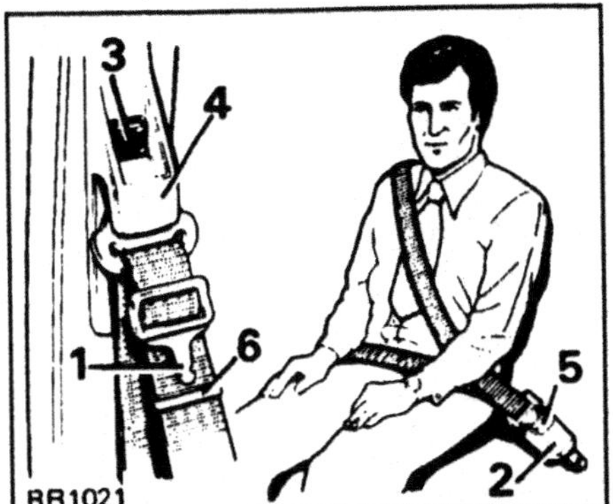

Inertia type front seat belts with shoulder level adjustment, four door models - Fig. RR1021

Seat belts fitted to both front seats are of the inertia real type designed for one-handed engagement.

Under normal driving conditions the reel will allow the harness to extend and retract to permit normal body movement without locking but will lock automatically in the event of hard braking or fast cornering.

No adjustment is required as the automatic retraction of the reel retains the harness at the correct tension.

Using the seat belt

Using the tongue (1) draw the belt out of the carriage on the door pillar until a loop is formed, then pass the arm nearest to the door through the loop.

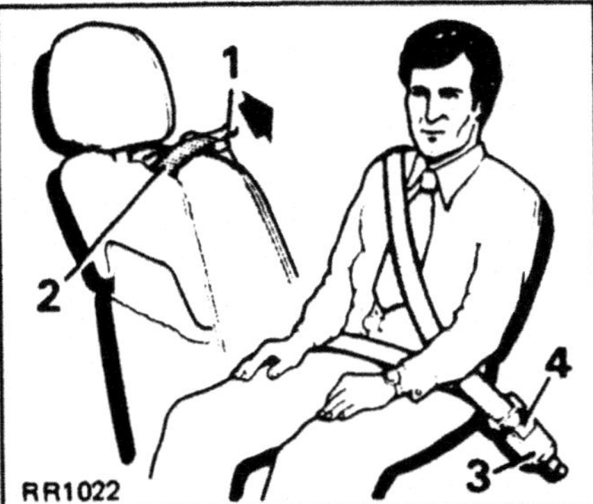

Pass the belt across the chest and push the tongue into the buckle unit (2) attached to the inner seat fixings. A positive 'click' will indicate when the buckle is safely locked.

⚠ WARNING: Seat belts are designed to bear upon the bony structure of the body and should be worn across the pelvis, chest and shoulder. Wearing the lap section of the belt across the abdominal area must be avoided. Belts should not be worn with the straps twisted.

Upper anchorage adjustment

Persons of different heights can readily make adjustment to raise or lower the harness as required in order to gain maximum wearing comfort. Adjustment can be made before or after the belt is fastened as follows:

Depress the release push button (3) and slide the carriage (4) fitted on the door pillar to the required position. There are five positions available and the carriage will 'click' into one of these when the push button is released. Ensure that the carriage is correctly located in one of the positions and that the push button has fully returned to its normal position before moving off in the vehicle.

Releasing the seat belt

To release the belt depress the button (5) on the buckle unit and allow the belt to retract fully into the carriage on the door pillar, manually assisting it for the last few inches. Position the slider (6) on the belt close to the door pillar bracket.

Inertia-type front seat belts, two door models - Fig. RR1022

Using the seat belt

Using the tongue (1) draw the belt out of its slot (2) in the top of the seat back until a loop is formed, then pass the arm nearest to the door through the loop. Pass the belt across the chest and push the tongue into the buckle unit (3) attached to the inner seat fixings. A positive click will indicate when the buckle is safely locked.

Releasing the seat belt

To release the belt depress the button (4) on the buckle unit and allow the belt to retract gently into the slot in the top of the seat back.

**⚠ WARNING: All vehicle occupants should wear their seat belts for maximum protection in the event of a collision or sudden stop.
Always protect the infant and child occupants of your vehicle with a restraint system designed especially for them and which conforms to motor vehicle safety standards.
Never leave a child unattended in your vehicle.**

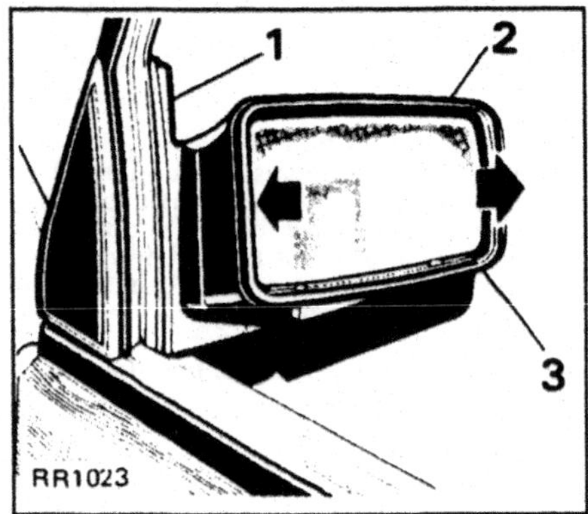

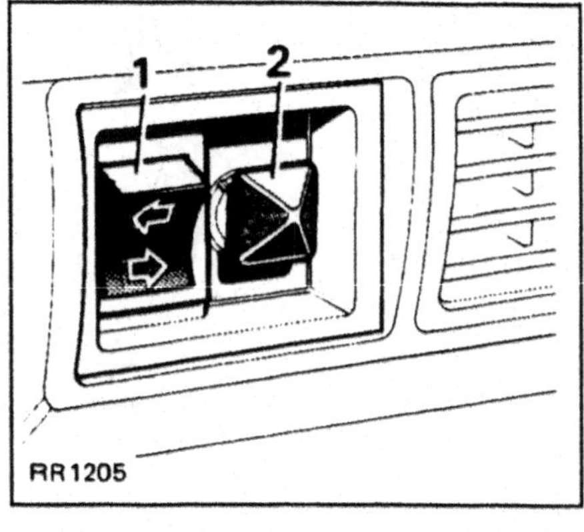

Exterior driving mirrors, four door model - Fig. RR1023
The mirror housing is hinged vertically (1) and should be set in one of the two fixed angle positions provided to suit the respective left or right side mirror location.

Additionally, for safety and convenience, the mirror housing (2) is designed to fold completely forwards or rearwards against the vehicle body.

Setting the mirror, manual version
The glass (3) angle is finely adjusted by moving it vertically or horizontally as required.

Exterior driving mirrors, two door models
Exterior mirrors are mounted on front doors. These mirrors may be manually swivelled to provide the required areas of vision.

Interior rear view mirror, all models
The required rear view is obtained by moving the mirror frame about its swivel; lens deflection for anti-dazzle night driving is obtained by moving the two-position spring-loaded lever, protruding from the base of the mirror.

Adjustment of electrically operated mirrors (Where applicable) - Fig. RR1205
The two-way switch (1) is used to select the mirror requiring adjustment i.e. pressing the top of the switch selects the left-hand mirror and pressing the lower part of the switch selects the right-hand mirror. The fingertip control (2) is then moved left, right, up or down to adjust the position of the mirror selected which will respond accordingly.

The mirror also incorporates a demist facility, activated by operation of the rear window demist switch.

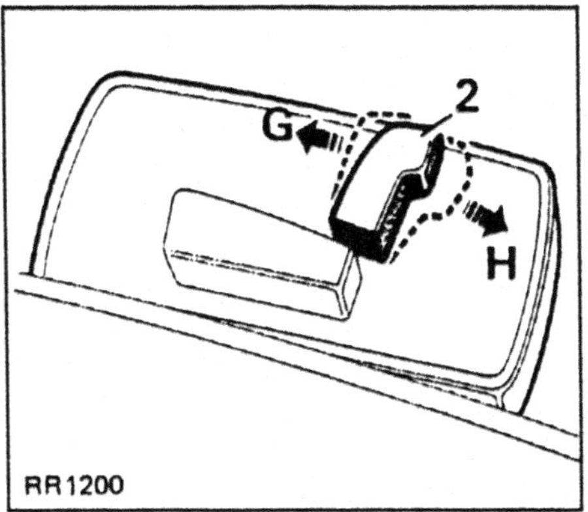

Electrically adjustable front seats (where applicable) continued

Backrest angle - switch (2) - Fig. RR1200
Decrease recline - switch to (G).

Increase recline - switch to (H).

Note: The fuse box and other equipment relative to the powered seating is housed under the left-hand seat. See Section 4 for fuse details.

Front seat adjustment, two door models - Fig. RR1019
Special safety type front seats (with fixed back rake) are fitted having the safety harness secured to anchorage points on the seat. Fore and aft adjustment of the front seats is controlled by lifting the locking bar (1) at the front of the seat cushion.

To allow easy access to the rear seat, the backrests can be tilted forwards by lifting the lever (2) on either the inboard or outboard side of the seat. The seats will then automatically move forward on runners to provide the maximum amount of space.

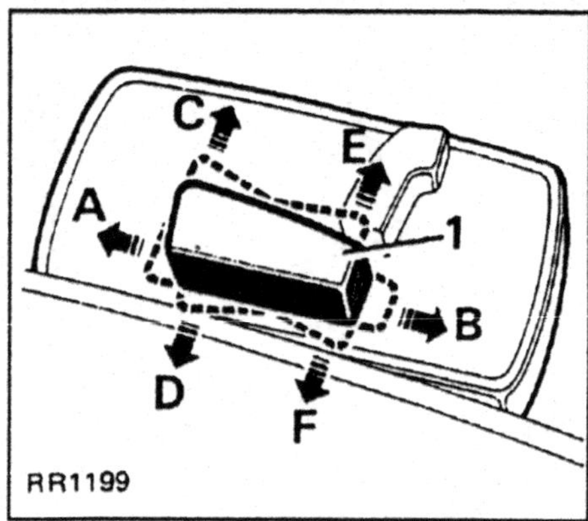

The new driver should adjust the seat as necessary to achieve a comfortable driving position to ensure full control of the vehicle and clear vision all round.

Electrically adjustable front seats (where applicable) - Figs. RR1199 and RR1200

Some models of the Range Rover are fitted with power-operated front seat adjustment controlled from switches mounted on the inboard side of each seat and shown above.

WARNING: To avoid the risk of loss of control and personal injury, never adjust the driver's seat or seatback while the vehicle is in motion.

Switches are operative only when
a) one of the front doors is open or
b) when the ignition is switched on.

As you will observe, the switch unit simulates the seat profile and is operated in the same manner as the seat movement required i.e. as follows:

Seat adjustment - Switch (1) - Fig. RR1199
Fore and aft - switch to (A) or (B).

Seat front up or down - switch to (C) or (D).

Seat rear up or down - switch to (E) or (F).

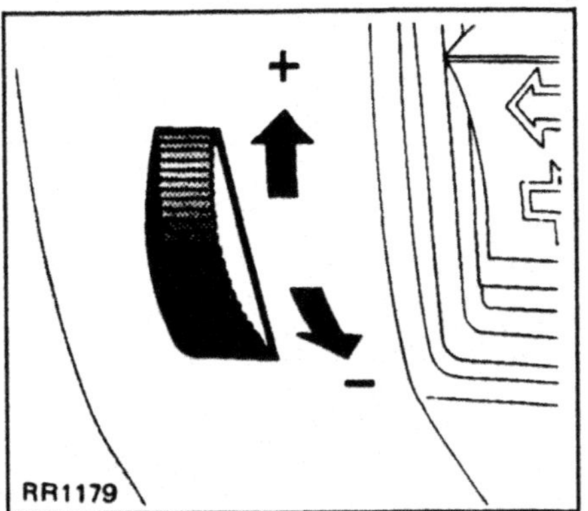

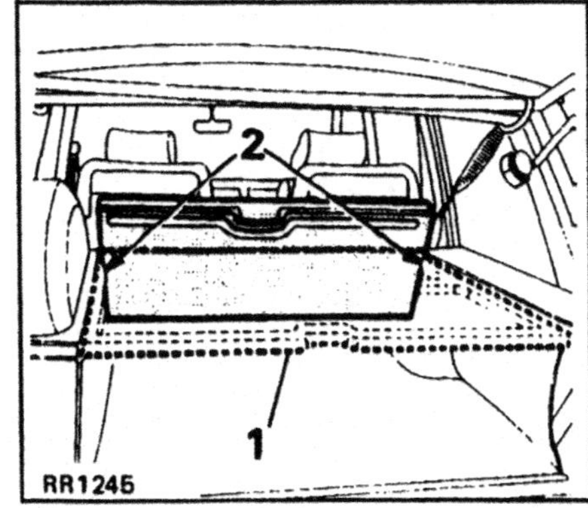

Instrument illumination electronic dimming control - Fig. RR1179

Rotate the control upwards to increase the intensity of instrument illumination and **downwards** to reduce intensity. The dimming control unit also controls the clock, heater and cigar lighter illumination.

Illumination of the radio/stereo unit panel is not influenced by the dimming control but is automatically dimmed when the vehicle lights are on.

Loadspace cover - Fig. RR1245

⚠ *WARNING: The loadspace cover is a simple lighweight item of trim not designed to support weight or to be used as a shelf behind the rear seats. Objects must not be carried on the cover as they may obscure vision and could become dangerous projectiles in the event of a sudden stop or collision. The cover is not intended to restrain luggage or loose items. Therefore all equipment, luggage or tools carried in the loadspace area must be secured to minimise the risk of injury from unsecured items in the event of an accident or emergency manoeuvre. When not required in its normal position (1), the cover can be folded and slotted into recesses (2) provided for its stowage behind the rear seating.*

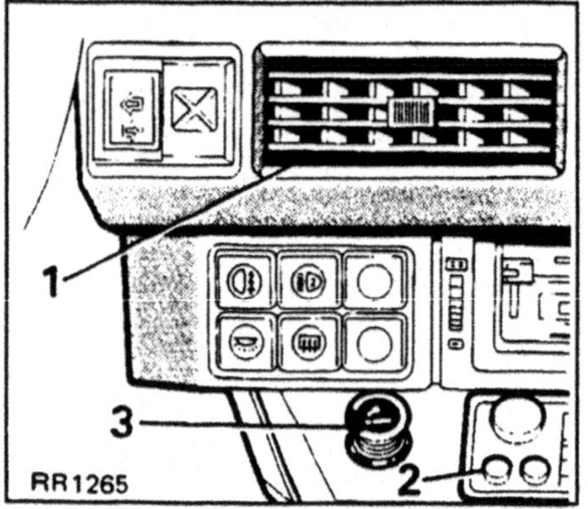

RR1265

RR1148

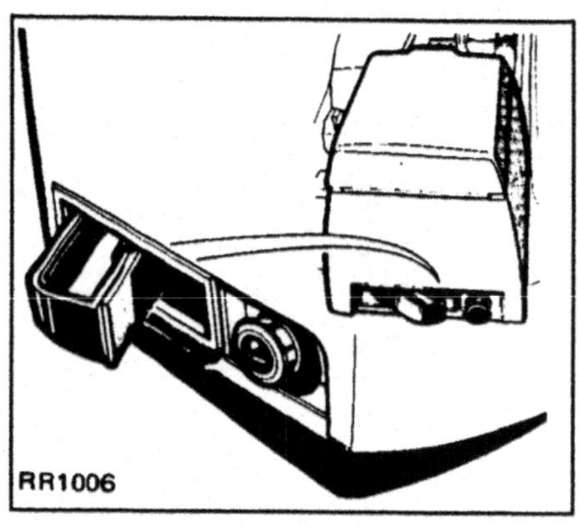

RR1006

Ventilation louvres (1) - Fig. RR1265

Fascia-mounted louvres can be set to provide fresh or recirculated air in the horizontal or near-vertical planes. The vanes of the louvres can also be opened or closed by use of the knurled adjuster in the centre of each unit to regulate the direction and amount of air flow.

Radio receiver (2)

All Range Rover models can be fitted with a radio receiver of the owners choice. An aerial and speaker units may already be fitted and there are leads incorporated in the vehicle wiring harness to facilitate installation.

Cigar lighter (3)

This is located to the side of the central storage pocket or radio housing. A second lighter is mounted on the rear face of the centre stowage box for the convenience of rear passengers. The units operate only whilst the ignition is switched on.

To operate, press in the button in the centre of the lighter unit. When ready for use the lighter will automatically partially eject and can then be withdrawn for use. When the side lights are on, the socket surrounding is illuminated to facilitate its location in darkness.

Clock - Fig. RR1148

The hands of the electronic clock mounted in the centre of the fascia may be set by depressing and rotating the black knob in the clock face.

Centre stowage box - Fig. RR1006

The centre stowage box can be used to store small items for the driver's convenience.

A cigar lighter, operating in the same manner as its front seat counterpart, and swivel-type ashtray are provided in the back of the centre stowage box for the convenience of the rear seat passengers.

Note: Useful stowage space, accessible from the front, is provided under both front seats except on electronic fuel injection models where the space under the right-hand seat is used to house the electronic control unit which should not be disturbed.

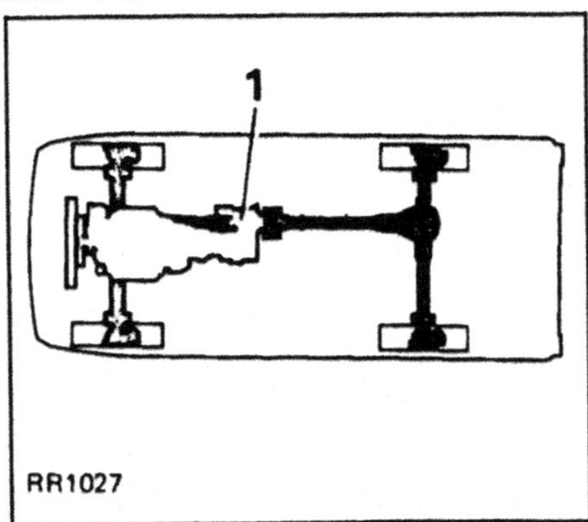

RR1027

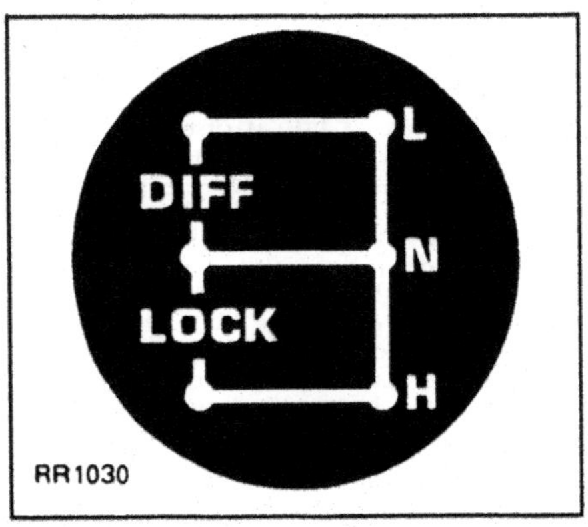

RR1030

Gearbox differential lock - Fig. RR1027

To allow the necessary variation of wheel speeds during cornering with permanent four-wheel drive, the Range Rover incorporates a third differential (1) between the drives to front and rear axles.

In conditions requiring maximum traction to both axles, ie, on snow, ice or any surface where the vehicle is likely to aquaplane, the gearbox differential unit can be locked so that both output shafts rotate at the same speed.

Use of the unit is more fully described in 'Driving techniques' Section 3 of this book.

Locking and unlocking of the differential is controlled through the combined transfer gear and differential lock lever.

Gearbox controls and ranges

The main gearbox of the Range Rover is augmented by a two-speed transfer box giving high and low ranges selected through a combined transfer gear and differential lock lever. Therefore the five-speed manual gearbox used in conjunction with the transfer gearing produces ten forward and two reverse speeds. In the same manner, the four-speed automatic box may be regarded as producing eight forward and two reverse speeds.

The low range should only be required where progress in the normal 'high' range is found difficult to maintain easily and safely or in any situation where heavy-load manoeuvring is necessary.

Combined transfer gear and differential lock lever - Fig. RR1030

The transfer gear lever controls the selection of the high or low gear ranges and the engagement of the differential lock. The lever, which is located immediately in front of the main gear lever, has the following positions:

Central right. Transfer box in neutral, **N**, centre differential unlocked. In this position drive cannot be transmitted to the road wheels regardless of the position of the main gear selector. Use this position for winching or power take-off (where applicable) and when being towed.

Fully forward and right L. Transfer gearbox low range engaged.

Fully forward and left L. Transfer gearbox low range engaged AND centre differential locked (warning light illuminated).

Fully rearwards and right H. Transfer gearbox high range engaged. This position is used for normal driving.

Fully rearwards and left H. Transfer gearbox high range engaged AND centre differential locked (warning light illuminated).

Centre left. Transfer box in neutral, **N**, centre differential locked. In this position drive cannot be transmitted to the road wheels regardless of the position of the main gear selector.

Note: On a new vehicle, transfer gear lever operation may be a little stiff until the gearbox is 'run-in'.

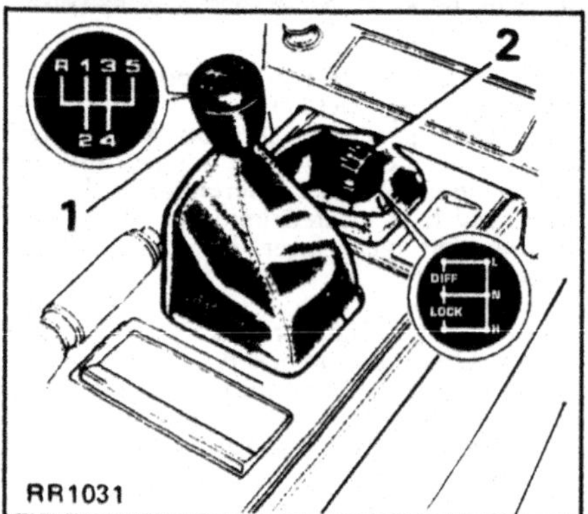

RR1031

Manual gearbox, main gear change lever - Fig. RR1031

In neutral, light-spring loads align the main gear lever (1) with the third/fourth gear positions to assist smooth gearchanging and to ensure selection of the required gear.

To select first or second gear, move the lever to the left against the spring and select the required ratio as normal. When changing between first and second gears, remember to continue to hold against the spring or the lever will return to the third/fourth position.

When changing from second to third gear, as second gear is disengaged, allow the spring to align the lever with the third position before engaging third gear.

To engage fifth gear, move the lever to the right against the spring and select the gear as normal. When changing from fifth to third or fourth gears, as fifth is disengaged, allow the spring to align the lever with the third/fourth positions before engaging the required gear. To change from fifth to second or first gear, allow the lever to return to the third/fourth position and move the lever towards the left against the spring as already described. Note that fifth gear is designed to reduce engine speed and thus improve fuel economy when cruising. Ensure that while it is in use the engine runs easily without labouring, otherwise use a lower gear.

Reverse is protected against inadvertent selection by an additional 'knock- over' spring load. To engage reverse, strike the lever as far as possible towards the left using the palm of the hand and move it forward to engage the gear. To disengage, pull the lever rearwards and allow the spring load to return it to its normal position in neutral.

It is recommended that, before driving away for the first time, the driver becomes familiar with the operation of the gear change by changing up and down through all ratios several times.

Use of the transfer gear lever on manual models - Fig. RR1031

CAUTION: Changing from high (H) to low (L), should only be attempted when the vehicle is stationary. Depress the clutch, pedal and push the lever (2) fully forward, release the clutch. Should there be any hesitation in the gear engaging, do not force the lever. With the engine running, engage a gear with the main gear lever and release the clutch momentarily, then return the main gear lever to neutral and try the transfer control again.

Changes from low (L) to high (H) can easily be made as follows without stopping the vehicle.

Depress the clutch pedal and release the accelerator pedal as for a normal gearchange. Move the transfer lever into neutral. Release the clutch pedal for 3 seconds. Depress the clutch pedal and move the transfer lever firmly to the 'high' (H) position. Then move the main gear lever to second gear and release the clutch pedal while depressing the accelerator to take up the drive smoothly. As the vehicle accelerates, change gear in the main gearbox in the normal way. This operation can be carried out smoothly and quickly after a little practice. Proper use of the gearbox range will ensure optimum efficiency and transmission component life.

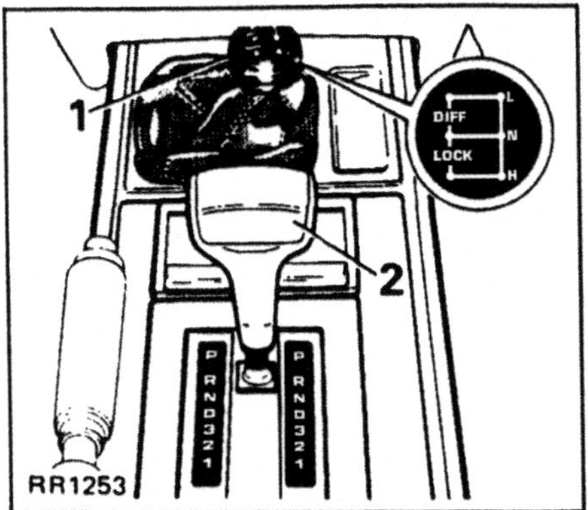

Use of the transfer gear lever on automatic models - Fig. RR1253
The transfer gear lever (1) controls the selection of high and low gear ratios and the engagement of the differential lock.

To change ratio from high to low, or low to high, proceed as follows:
1. Reduce the vehicle speed to below 8km/h (5 mph).
2. Move the automatic gearbox selector lever (2) to the **N** neutral position.
3. Just before the vehicle comes to rest, move the transfer gear lever rapidly to the required position.

To change ratio with the vehicle stationary, simply move the main gearbox selector (2) to the **N** (neutral) position before moving the transfer gear lever to the required position.

If the transfer gear cannot be engaged the following procedures should be used. Apply footbrake and handbrake, keep constant pressure on the transfer gear lever (1) in the the direction required and move the main gearbox selector lever (2) rapidly from Drive, through Neutral to Reverse and back into Drive until the transfer lever is shifted. Repeat the procedure if necessary.

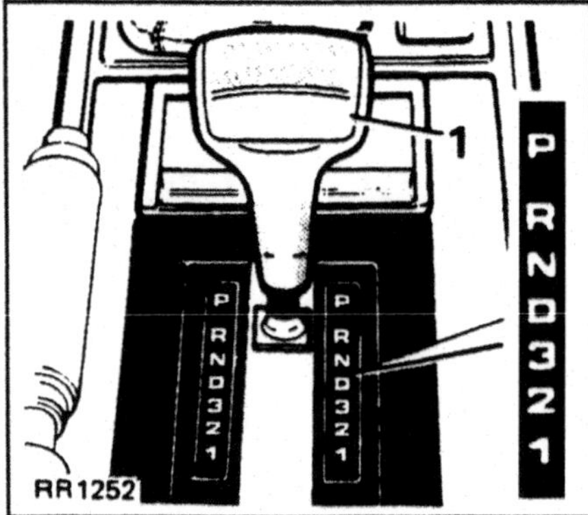

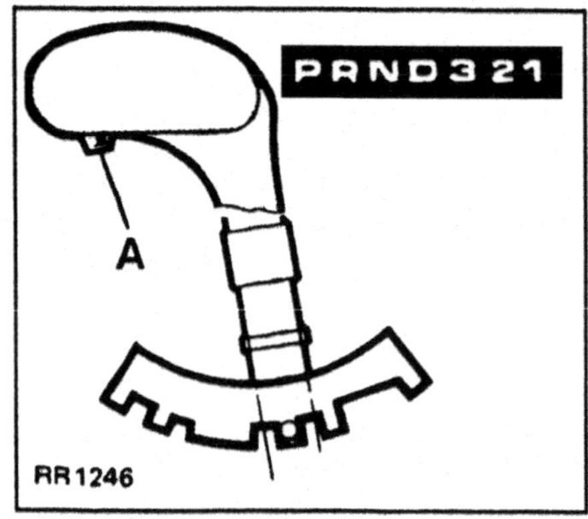

Main gear selector lever, automatic gearbox - Fig. RR1252

The gear lever (1) is mounted on the transmission tunnel. The upper face of the gear shift housing is marked with the symbols **P, R, N, D, 3, 2** and **1** which indicate the following functions:

P Park
R Reverse
N Neutral
D Drive - first, second, third and fourth gears
3 First, second and third gears only
2 First and second gears only
1 First gear only with engine braking

Note: If either '2' or '1' is selected from 'D' or '3' while the vehicle is travelling at high speed, third gear will immediately engage. Progressive deceleration will cause downshifts into second then first gear at the appropriate road speeds.

Selector operation - Fig. RR1246

The gear lever movement is restricted to facilitate selection. Those positions normally used in sequence are grouped together to prevent inadvertent engagement of **N, R, P** or **1**. The gear lever moves in a detented gate as illustrated.

Movement through the detents is effected by pressing in the button 'A' under the gear knob thereby releasing the spring loaded catch and moving the lever to select the desired gear. The lever will move freely between **D** and **3**. There is an additional stage of interlock protecting the **P** position from the **R** position.

WARNING: The handbrake or footbrake should be applied fully before selecting any of the forward or reverse drive ranges from a stationery position.

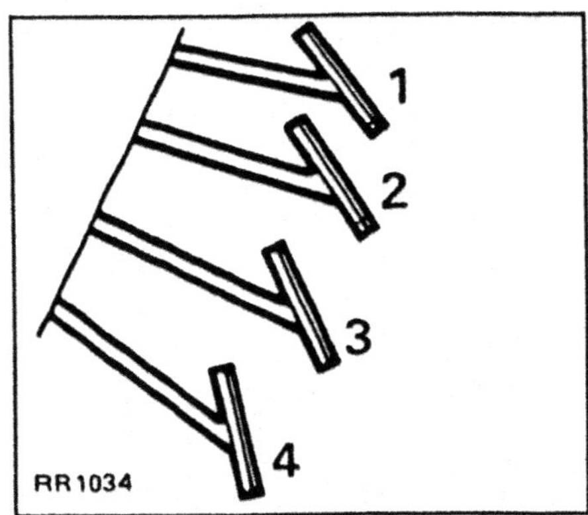

Accelerator pedal positions - Fig. RR1034

1 - Idle   3 - Full throttle
2 - Part throttle   4 - Kick down

Using the 'D' Drive range

The selector 'D' position provides full automatic up and down changes through all forward gears, depending on vehicle speed and accelerator pedal position. Use **'D'** for all normal driving on good roads. The gearchange points have been chosen to give best fuel economy during normal driving with moderate accelerator pedal positions.

With 'D' selected, **minimum acceleration from rest** will result in low road speed upshifts through first, second, third and fourth gears.

From rest, maximum acceleration - by pushing the accelerator fully down (kick down) - will result in delayed upshifts through the gearing

Intermediate acceleration from rest with 'D' selected will cause upshifts through first second, third and fourth gear. With practise these shifts can be made to occur at any required road speed betweeen maximum and minimum depending on how the pedal is depressed.

When in fourth gear below speeds of 84 kph (52 mph) a downshift (lower gear) can be obtained by pushing the accelerator pedal partly down.

To provide rapid acceleration for overtaking with 'D' selected, kickdown will cause a downshift into the lowest appropriate gear. When the accelerator is released from the kickdown position, normal changes - dependent on road speed and pedal position - will resume.

Above speeds of 69 km/hour (43 miles/hour), an automatic feature locks the torque converter in fourth gear, eliminating slip as a further aid to fuel economy.

Selector in position '3'

The '3' position provides automatic up and down changes between first, second and third gears only. For maximum acceleration, from stationary, kickdown will cause first, second and third gears to engage in sucession. When the pedal is released from the kickdown position, normal automatic changes between these three gears will be resumed. Fourth gear will not engage.

If '3' is selected from **'D'** while the vehicle moving at high speed, third gear will be engaged.

Selector in position '2'

The '2' position provides automatic up and down shifts between first and second gears only.

Positions '2' or '1' may be selected from 'D' or '3' at any road speed but, if the speed is high, third gear will be engagfed followed by second then first gear when the road speed has dropped to an appropriate level. From a standing start in '2', first gear will be engaged changing to second as the vehicle gathers speed. Once second gear has engaged no further upshift will occur unless '3' or 'D' is selected. Care should be taken not to overspeed the engine when the selector is in position '2' or '1'. The '3' or '2' position should be selected when driving in hilly terrain to avoid unwanted upshifts when the accelerator pedal is momentarially released.

'2' will give moderate engine braking downhill.

Selector in position '1'

The '1' position selected from rest will provide operation only in first gear. Therefore care should be taken to not overspeed the engine. The '1' position should be used when driving in very hilly terrain, particulary when towing a trailer, to avoid the engine labouring when driving uphill and provide the appropriate engine braking downhill.

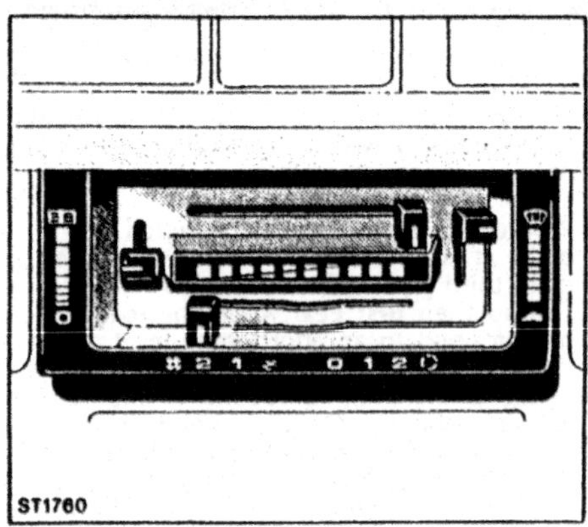

ST1760

Heating/ventilation unit — Fig. ST1760
The Range Rover has a combined fresh air and recirculating heating system which has been designed so that either system can be used separately.
The controls are operated with the following effect:

Air supply selector (lower horizontal slider)
The control has six positions which allow the selection of either fresh or recirculated air for routing through the system as determined by the setting of the other controls on the unit. Air supply selector positions are signified as follows:

At the extreme left position (2), a blower operates at full speed reducing to low speed as the selector is moved slightly right to the lower setting (1).

The blower is normally used when the vehicle speed is too low to provide sufficient fresh air by ram action alone.

The blower motor will only operate with the engine running or the starter key turned to the first position.

At this position, fresh air is allowed into the system by forward movement of the vehicle alone. The ram air intake grille is situated outside the base of the windscreen.

With the selector in this position, the entry of air to the system is completely cut off.

These two positions on the right-hand end of the lower horizontal slide control the operation of the recirculated air blower motor at low or high speed.

Internally recirculated air is normally used in heavy traffic conditions to avoid obnoxious fumes entering the vehicle, also for rapid heat build up inside the vehicle during cold conditions. The recirculation control is used with air conditioning to achieve maximum cooling and its use is also recommended in dusty conditions to prevent dust entering the vehicle.

Temperature control (upper horizontal slider)
The temperature of the air supply selected may be varied by movement of the slider between cold (blue area of coloured scale) and hot (red area). Warm or hot air will only be available when the engine has attained a suitable operating temperature.

Air distribution controls

Ventilation
The left-hand vertical slider position controls the amount of air supplied to the fascia ventilation louvres.

Maximum air is supplied when the slider is in the top position and reduces as the slider is moved down.

The supply is off when the slider is at the bottom of its stroke and this is the position recommended for use with air conditioning.

Screen/footwell
The right-hand vertical slider position controls the proportions of air supplied to (a) the windscreen and front side windows via the demister vents and (b) front footwells and the duct outlet under the rear of the centre stowage box.

Demisting

Mist often forms on windows when the humidity is very high.

Note: For maximum demist effectiveness, the fresh air supply should be used.

The right-hand vertical slider should be set to the top of its stroke for maximum air to the demist vents and the temperature control set to maximum heat position (as illustrated in Fig. ST1760).

RR1055

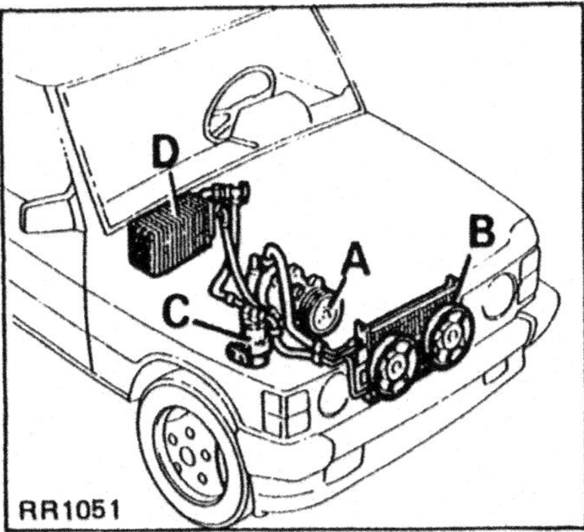

RR1051

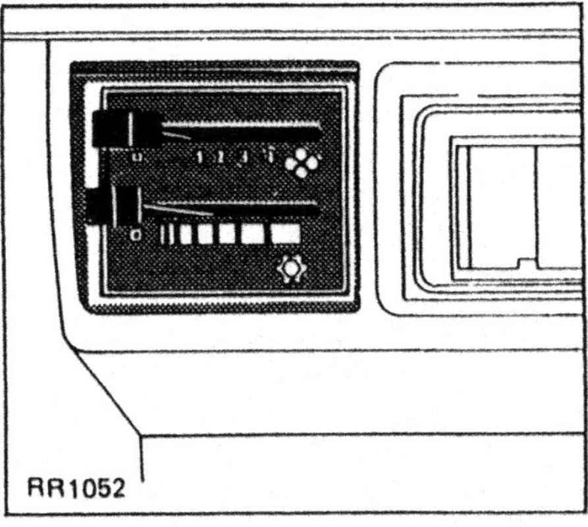

RR1052

Through-flow ventilation — Fig. RR1055

A through-flow ventilation system is achieved in the Range Rover by means of one-way air extraction vents (1) incorporated in both rear quarter panels. Each vent is automatically opened or closed progressively increasing or decreasing the amount of ventilation to suit interior conditions.

Air conditioning system — Fig. RR1051

Air conditioning equipment is a factory fitted option that can be included only during manufacture of the Range Rover.

The air conditioning system operates in conjunction with the vehicle heater to provide cooled and dried recirculated air.

> ⚠ *WARNING: The air conditioning system is filled at high pressure with a potentially toxic material. Follow service instructions when dismantling or applying excessive heat, e.g. steam cleaning, painting, etc. Servicing must only be carried out by a qualified engineer in accordance with instructions in the Repair Operation Manual.*

The system is made up of four separate units:

An engine-mounted compressor (A).

A condenser (B) mounted in front of the radiator.

A receiver/drier unit (C) located in the engine compartment.

An evaporator unit (D) mounted behind the fascia.

The four units are interconnected by hoses carrying refrigerant. The refrigerant circuit cools the evaporator which is connected to the ventilation system, and thus cools the air inside the vehicle.

Air conditioning control panel — Fig. RR1052

The installation incorporates temperature and fan speed controls mounted on the fascia inboard of the steering column and uses the ventilation distribution controls mounted in the central console.

Temperature control — lower slider

For maximum cooling in heavy traffic and for rapid initial cooling, the temperature control should be moved to the extreme right (cold) position. When the temperature inside the car becomes comfortable, the control should be moved back slightly to prevent the cooling coils from freezing.

Fan control — upper slider
The fan control should be adjusted to regulate the volume of air required.

Using the air conditioning
Set the heating/ventilation unit controls (Fig. ST1760) as follows:

Ventilation (left-hand vertical slider)
— to bottom of slide

Temperature control (upper horizontal slider)
— to extreme left of cold (blue) area

Screen/footwell (right-hand vertical slider)
— to bottom of slide

Air supply selector (lower horizontal slider)
— to ■ (off)

Set the air conditioning control panel (see Fig. RR1052) as follows:

Fan control
— to position 1, 2, 3 or 4 to give the amount of air required through the front fascia louvres

Temperature control
— to extreme right

When the temperature inside the vehicle becomes comfortable move the temperature control back slightly. This will prevent the evaporator cooling coils from becoming too cold and freezing-up.

Rapid cooling
Ensure that all exterior vents are closed.

Open a window.

Move the air conditioning fan control to position 4.

Move the temperature control to the coldest position.

After driving for several minutes, the hot air inside the vehicle will be expelled. Close the window, move the air conditioning temperature control back slightly and adjust the fan speed as desired.

Fresh air
Fresh air may be admitted into the vehicle by moving the lower horizontal slider of the heating/ventilation unit (Fig. RR1050) to one of its three left positions and moving the heater ventilation control slider upwards.

The air conditioning control, operated in conjunction with this function provides an effective means of removing excessive cigarette smoke or stale air whilst maintaining adequate cooling.

Highway driving
During a long trip when the temperature and humidity are extremely high, frost may form on the cooling coils of the evaporator. The unit is equipped with an automatic defrost system which normally will prevent this.

However, if the temperature control is maintained in the coldest position, the defrost system will not operate and the unit cannot supply adequate cold air.

Should this occur, move the temperature control slightly to the left and the fan control to position '4'. This will allow the defrost system to operate and provide effective cooling.

Use the heater in conjunction with the air conditioning.

Note: For maximum demist effectiveness, set the heater controls as described on the heating and ventilation page and, in warm weather, use the air conditioning system which acts as a de-humidifier. This will further assist demisting.

It is not necessary to use the system continuously, only when the misting persists.

Heating
During cold weather the air conditioner fan can be used to circulate warm air from the heater.

Move the fan control to the desired setting and move the air conditioning temperature control to the extreme left position.

For air conditioning maintenance, see the 'Service and Maintenance' section.

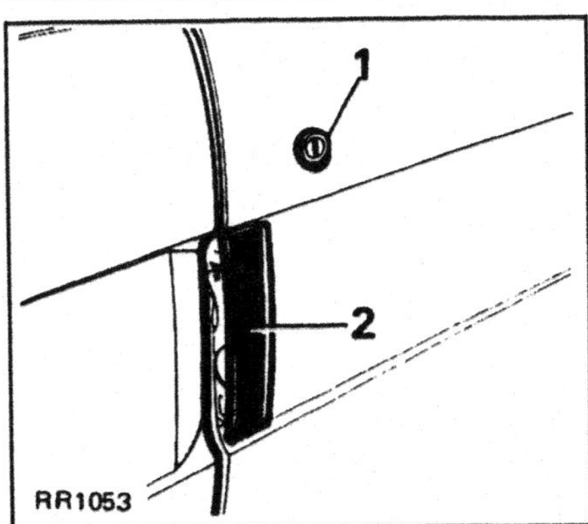

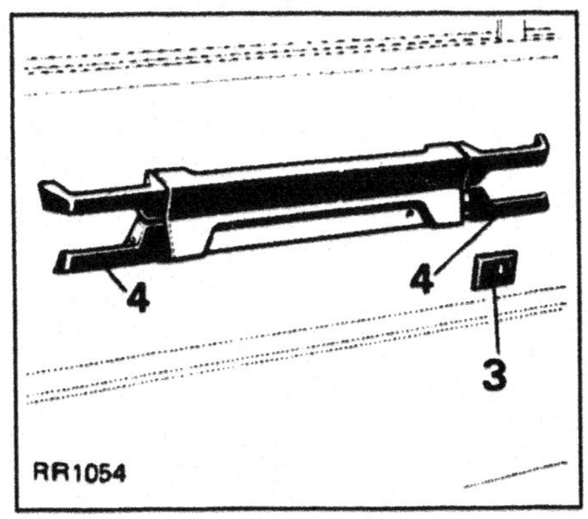

Door locks and controls, two-door models

Exterior operation - Fig. RR1053
To **unlock** a front door insert the ignition key in the 'private' lock (1), turn it **towards** the **rear** of the vehicle, return it to the **original** position and remove.

To **open** the door pull out the vertical door release handle (2).

To **lock** a front door the key is turned **towards** the **front** of the vehicle.

Keyless locking. To lock a front door from outside **without** using a key first ensure that the key is not left inside the vehicle. Slide the inside locking catch (3) **towards** the **front** of the vehicle.

Pull out the vertical door release handle (2) and, retaining it in the fully open position, close the door.

Interior operation - Fig. RR1054
To **unlock** either front door from inside slide the inside locking catch (3) **towards** the **rear** of the vehicle.

To **open** the door pull out either of the twin inside release handles (4). (The handles are located one at each end of the door for the convenience of the front and rear occupants).

Front door ventilator windows are controlled by a flush fitting safety type catch; push in the centre button to release and turn the catch **towards** the **front** of the vehicle.

The windows can then be opened to increase air flow through the vehicle (via the one-way air extraction vents incorporated in the rear quarter panels).

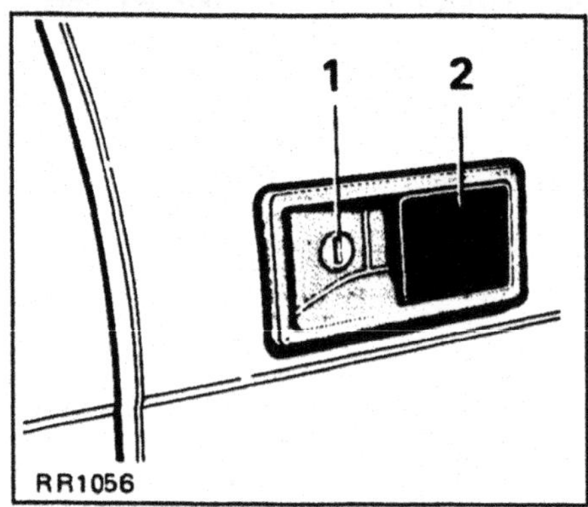

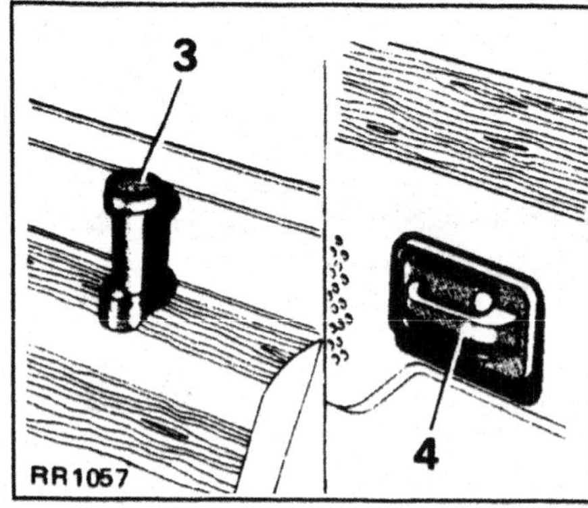

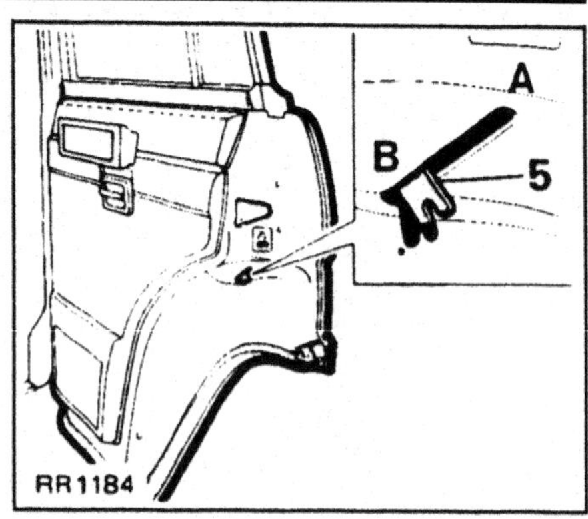

Door locks and controls, four door models

Exterior operation - Fig. RR1056
To **unlock** a front door insert the ignition key in the 'private' lock (1), turn it **towards** the **rear** of the vehicle, return it to the **original** position and remove.

To **open** the door pull out the door release handle (2).

To **lock** a front door, the key is turned **towards the front** of the vehicle then returned to the original position for removal from the lock.

To lock a rear door depress the inside sill locking knob (3).

Close the door and check that it is locked.

Interior operation - Fig. RR1057
To **unlock** any door from inside lift the sill locking knob (3).

To **open** the door pull out the inside release handle (4).

Electrically operated central door locking (where applicable)

Locking or unlocking the driver's **front door** from outside by key operation or from inside by sill knob automatically locks or unlocks **all four side doors and also the fuel filler flap** .

Rear doors can be independently locked or unlocked from inside by sill knob operation but are over-ridden by further operation of the driver's **front door** lock controls.

Note: The Children's safety lock for both rear door release handles can be preset mechanically, as described above.

Children's safety lock - Fig. RR1184. Both rear doors are fitted with an additional locking lever which renders the inside release handle inoperative. This is pre-set as follows:

Open a rear door. Move the small lever (5) which projects through the door shut face, to position 'A'.

To **restore** inside release handle operation move the lever to position 'B'.

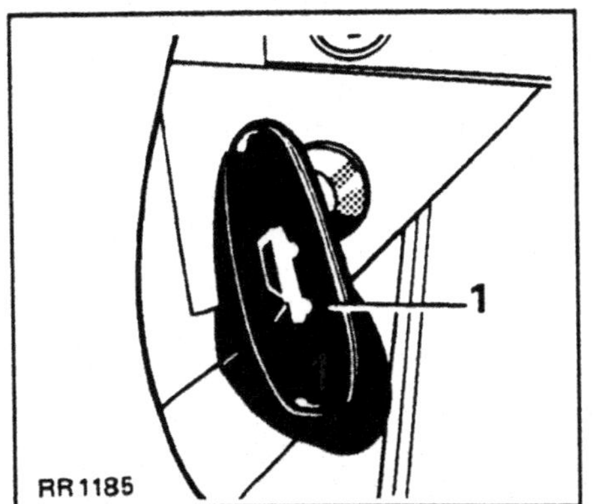

RR1185

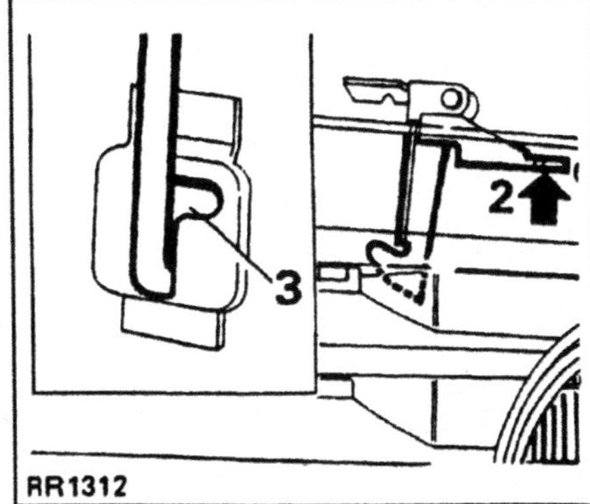

RR1312

RR1187

Bonnet lock control - Figs. RR1185 and RR1312

To open the bonnet, pull the control knob (1), located below the driver's side fascia. This disengages the locking plate and allows the bonnet to spring open sufficiently to provide access to the safety catch located at the front right-hand side of the bonnet (viewed from the front of the vehicle). Fingertip lifting of the lever (2) assisted by slight downward pressure on the bonnet will release the catch.

After release of the catch, the assisted lift feature of the bonnet allows it to be raised easily.

In the fully open position, the bonnet must be held by the support rod, which should be engaged in the slotted hole (3) in the centre top of the bonnet locking platform.

To close the bonnet, replace the support rod in its retaining clip on the underside of the bonnet, lower the bonnet to approximately 300 mm (12 inches) above the grille and allow it to drop into position.

If it is necessary to push down on the bonnet, do this with the palms of both hands on the front edge.

Tailgates - Fig. RR1187

CAUTION: Ensure that the rear screen wiper is in the parked (off) position before raising the upper tailgate, otherwise damage may occur to the wiper arm and motor. Do not operate the rear wiper when the upper tailgate is raised.

⚠️ **WARNING: Do not drive with the tailgate open; poisonous carbon monoxide fumes can enter the vehicle.**

The upper tailgate, which must be opened before the lower tailgate can be lowered, is released by depressing the locking button in the centre of the handle (1). The upper tailgate can then be raised to its fully elevated position, where it is supported by means of telescopic gas struts which also assist in raising the tailgate.

(Continued)

Tailgates (continued)

NOTE: The tailgate is not included in the central locking system fitted to some models. See 'Door controls - Four-door models' later in this Section.

The lower tailgate is an all-steel construction for greater strength. It is supported in the lowered position by means of folding stays. The lower tailgate latches automatically on closure and has an interior centrally located release handle.

DRIVING AND TECHNIQUES

Before starting
Check that the handbrake is on and that the gear lever is in neutral (manual gearbox) or the selector lever is in **'P'** or **'N'** (automatic gearbox).

Diesel-engined models
DO NOT use the accelerator pedal during the starting procedure; extra fuel for cold starting is automatically supplied by the injector pump. Also, the engine MUST NOT be run above fast idle until the oil pressure warning light goes off; this is to ensure that the turbo-charger bearings are receiving lubricant before being run at speed.

In cold weather, depress the clutch pedal while the starter motor is in operation to improve engine starting speed.

Petrol-engine models
Do not operate the accelerator pedal during initial starting. If the engine does not start within 5 to 10 seconds, fully depress the accelerator pedal and operate the starter for a further five seconds. If the engine still does not start, investigate the cause.

WARNING: Never start or leave the engine running in an enclosed unventilated area. Exhaust fumes contain carbon monoxide, a colourless and odourless gas which if inhaled may be fatal.

If the engine is cold, pull out the cold start control (if fitted) and turn the knob clockwise slightly to lock it in position.

The **electronic fuel injection (EFI) version** of the Range Rover incorporates a cold start injector which operates automatically whenever the engine temperature is below 35°C

Starter operation
Insert and turn the ignition key to operate the starter, release the key as soon as the engine is running.
The RED ignition and oil pressure warning lights will go out when the engine is running.
Do not operate the starter for longer than 10 seconds; switch off the ignition and wait 10 seconds before re-using the starter. If after a few attempts the engine fails to start, switch off the ignition and investigate the cause. Continued use of the starter will not only discharge the battery but may also damage the starter.

Note: *If an automatic gearbox is fitted, the starter will only operate when the selector lever is in 'P' or 'N' position.*

Starting a semi-warm, warm or hot engine
Depress the accelerator pedal to approximately one quarter of its travel and hold in this position. Insert and turn the ignition key to operate the starter, release the key as soon as the engine is running. As the engine speed increases gradually release the accelerator pedal until the engine runs smoothly.

Starting in cold conditions i.e. below minus 12°C (11°F)
Insert and turn the ignition key to operate the starter, release the key as soon as the engine is running. Do not depress the accelerator pedal while operating the starter.

Manual gearbox: Depress the clutch pedal while operating the starter and until the engine is running.

CAUTION: Automatic gearbox models: When the engine has started, BEFORE moving the gear selector lever out of 'N' or 'P' it is important that the handbrake or footbrake is firmly applied and the accelerator pedal is not depressed - otherwise the vehicle may move immediately the gear lever is moved to any of the drive positions (1, 2, 3, D or R). This is particularly important if the engine is cold because the engine revolutions will be faster than normal.

With a cold engine, the faster than normal engine speed may mean that more care is needed in manoeuvring the vehicle. Under these circumstances, the footbrake should be used to control the vehicle until the engine is warm and running at normal speed.

Warming-up
When the engine is cold, drive the vehicle as soon as the engine has started. Do not warm-up the engine by running it at a slow speed with the vehicle stationary.

Note - Diesel engines
Before stopping the engine, allow it to idle for 10 seconds to give time for the turbo-charger to slow down whilst oil pressure is available at the bearings.
Switching the engine off too quickly could leave the turbine rotating at several thousand revolutions without oil pressure.

Starting a vehicle which has a discharged battery

A Range Rover automatic gearbox model cannot be started by pushing or towing. In an emergency, use one of the following methods.

Electric Start - A vehicle with a discharged battery may be started in a number of ways, the easiest is by substitution of the battery. Where this is not possible due to differing size or terminal types a slave battery may be connected to the vehicle battery using booster cables.

Booster cables must be of sufficient capacity to carry starter motor current.

The slave battery must be 12 volt supply.

Use of Booster Cables - Fig. RR1049

Park the two vehicles with the battery locations adjacent, ensuring that a road hazard is not being caused, and that the two vehicles do not touch.

If it is impossible to place the vehicles together remove the battery from the 'donor' vehicle and place it on the ground adjacent to the immobilised vehicle.

Carry out the following instructions.

Remove the vent caps from both batteries and place a cloth over the open vent wells.

Ensure that all electrical accessories are switched off.

Connect one booster cable from the positive (+) terminal on the slave battery to the positive (+) terminal of the discharged battery.

Connect the other booster cable from the negative (-) terminal of the slave battery to the negative (-) terminal of the discharged battery.

 **WARNING: Do not connect positive (+) terminals to negative (-) terminals.**

Where applicable, start the engine of the donor vehicle and let it idle for a few minutes, then start the engine of the vehicle with the discharged battery in the normal manner. When the engine is running normally, disconnect the booster cables, first removing the cable from both positive (+) terminals and then the one from both negative (-) terminals. Ensure that no contact is made between either cables or the vehicles.

Remove the cloths covering the battery vent wells and dispose of them safely. Replace the vent caps.

The battery and charging system should be checked for condition by your Dealer.

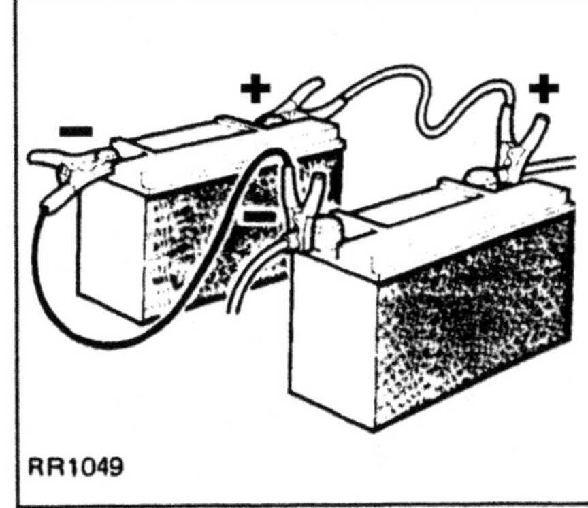

RR1049

Engine Restart

If the engine stalls for any reason whilst the vehicle is moving, it cannot be restarted by selecting a low gear. In addition, overrun braking and steering assistance will be lost.

Therefore the vehicle should be brought to rest as quickly as possible consistent with traffic conditions and overall safety.

The gear selector lever must be moved to **N** and the engine restarted in the normal way. Steering assistance will resume as soon as the engine starts and, by moving the gear lever back to its original position, normal drive and over-run braking will be restored. If the engine refuses to restart after two attempts, the cause of the engine stalling must be investigated.

These engine fault diagnosis pages have been compiled for your general assistance in an emergency.

Checking of any part of the electronic ignition or fuel injection systems must be referred to your Range Rover Dealer or Distributor.

WARNING: *The electronic ignition system involves very high voltages. Inexperienced personnel and wearers of medical pacemaker devices should not be allowed near any part of the high-tension circuit.*

Symptom	Fault	Remedy
Starter will not turn engine (headlights dim)	Battery low in charge, often causing the solenoid to chatter	Charge battery and check charging system
	Defective battery	Renew battery
	Corroded battery cables or loose connections	Clean battery connections or renew battery cables. Tighten battery and starter-motor connections
(Headlights bright)	Starter jammed	Free starter
	Defective starter solenoid	Renew
	Defective starter	Renew
	Defective starter switch	Renew
Engine turns slowly but will not start	Battery low in charge	Charge battery and check charging system
	Defective battery	Renew
	Corroded battery cables or loose connections	Clean and secure battery connections
	Poor engine-to-chassis earth strap connection	Clean and secure connection
	Defective starter	Renew
Engine turns normally but will not fire	Ignition fault	Check for spark at plug lead. Note above warning
	Where no spark is observed at plug lead	Consult your Dealer or Distributor
	Where spark is observed at plug lead	Carburetter models: With engine cold, check mixture control operation. If necessary, assist with gentle finger pressure - a drop of oil on the butterfly spindle may help. Loosen petrol-pipe union at carburetter. Switch on ignition for electric pump. Check if petrol is being delivered. Electronic fuel injection models: Consult your Dealer.
	No fuel to carburetter	Remove petrol-tank cap and check for fuel (fuel gauge may be inaccurate)

Symptom	Fault	Remedy
Engine backfires violently, kicks back or bangs through carburetter	Ignition timing faulty	Consult your Dealer
	Damp distributor cap and leads	Dry thoroughly and check firing order
Engine fires, but fails to keep running	Ignition or fuel fault	Refer to order of checks for 'Engine turns normally but will not fire', with special emphasis on mixture control, plug condition and continuous HT spark at plug lead
Carburetter models		
Engine stalls when idling (engine cold)	Mixture control throttle-stop requires adjustment	Adjust
	Mixture control not operating correctly	Check mixture control operation
Engine stalls when idling (engine hot)	Engine idle speed too low	Adjust idle speed
	Mixture control stuck in operation	Check mixture control operation at carburetter
	Carburetter flooding	Adjust fuel level or float setting to specification. Clean needle valve
	Intake vacuum leak	Check manifold, carburetter mounting, any connections to manifold and vacuum advance. Also check butterfly spindle and bosses; if worn, seek advice
Engine has rough idle	Fouled or improperly gapped spark-plugs	Clean and adjust plug gaps or renew plugs
	Incorrect ignition timing	Consult your Dealer
	Intake vacuum leak	Check manifold, carburetter mounting, any connections to manifold and vacuum advance
Engine stalls on acceleration	Mixture control not functioning properly, or improperly adjusted	Check mixture control operation at carburetter with engine cold
	Insufficient fuel supply to carburetter	Clean needle valve and jets. Check float level
	Air-cleaner element dirty	Clean or renew filter element. Conform to recommended maintenance schedule
	Carburetter has a seized piston	Polish piston and cylinder with dry or petrol-damp rag. Check that correct oil is used in dash-pot and top up to the required level
Engine has poor acceleration	Incorrect ignition timing	Adjust
	Intake vacuum leak	Tighten or renew faulty gaskets
	Insufficient fuel supply	Clean needle valve and jets. Check fuel
	Accelerator linkage out of adjustment	Check that full throttle on the pedal is also full throttle at carburetter. Adjust as necessary.

Fault	Probable cause	Remedy
Failure to start	Fuel tank empty	Fill tank and bleed air
	Obstructed fuel lines	Purge fuel lines
Fuel	Fuel filter clogged	Renew filter and bleed system of air
	Fuel line leakage	Check all fuel line connections for tightness
	Air in fuel system	Bleed fuel system
	Faulty fuel pump	Renew pump
	Clogged air cleaner	Clean or renew filter
Electrical	Discharged battery	Check electrolyte and recharge
	Loose cable connection	Tighten battery terminals
	Faulty starter switch	Renew starter switch
	Faulty start	Renew/repair starter
	Faulty glow plugs	Renew glow plugs
	Faulty injection pump solenoid valve	Check electrical supply. Renew solenoid valve
Starts and stops	Obstructed fuel lines	Purge fuel lines
	Fuel filter clogged	Renew filter and bleed system of air
	Air in fuel system	Bleed fuel system
	Low idle speed	Check and adjust minimum engine rev/min
	Faulty fuel pump	Renew pump
	Clogged fuel tank breather	Clear fuel tank breather
Poor engine performance	Insufficient fuel to supply to injectors	Check for fuel leaks, air in system, clogged fuel filter, wrong type of or contaminated fuel
	Valve clearance out of adjustment	Readjust valve clearance
	Faulty injection pump timing	Check/adjust pump timing or consult Dealer
	Injector fault	Renew injectors
Exhaust smokes badly	Injector fault	Test/adjust injectors
	Faulty injection pump timing	Check/adjust pump timing or consult Dealer
	Clogged air cleaners	Clean/renew filter
	Oil sump overfilled	Drain to proper level
Engine overheats	Low coolant level	Fill the cooling system to the correct level
	Faulty water pump	Repair/renew pump
	Water leaks	Check hoses, fittings, plugs and radiator
	Faulty temperature gauge	Renew gauge
	Low oil level	Fill to proper level
	Clogged cooling system	Drain and flush cooling system
	Incorrect timing	Readjust timing

Running-in
The importance of correct running-in cannot be too strongly emphasized, for during the first few thousand miles of motoring, all working surfaces of the power train are 'bedding in'.

Progressive running-in of your new Range Rover has a direct bearing on reliability and smooth running throughout its life.

The most important point is not to hold the vehicle on large throttle openings for any sustained periods. To start with, the maximum speed should be limited to 80 to 95 kph (50 to 60 mph) on a light throttle and this may be progressively increased over the first 2,500 km (1,500 miles).

Manual gearbox models
Do not use a gear which is too high for the vehicle speed and travel conditions involved; it is preferable to select a lower gear and use more revolutions rather than allow the engine to labour at low speed.

Do not use the clutch pedal as a foot rest. Keep the left foot well clear of the clutch pedal while the vehicle is in motion.

Range Rover driving in general
Do not engage the differential lock while there is any suspicion of wheel spin. The lock should be engaged before driving on to any surface where traction may be lost at one or more wheels.

Do not engage the differential lock for road surfaces that do not require its use.

Do not use the handbrake while the vehicle is moving - except in an emergency.

Do not allow the engine to labour in too high a gear.

Do not overload the vehicle for sustained cross country work. Reduce the payload by 90 kg (198 lbs).

Do not wrap your thumbs round the steering wheel as severe steering kick back over rough ground may result in personal injury.

Do not coast with the engine switched off as the brake servo and steering assistance will not operate. The brakes will still function but more foot pressure will be required.

Do not rely on the handbrake to hold the vehicle if the brake linings have been subjected to immersion in mud and water (See 'After wading' details later in this section).

Do not continue to drive an automatic Range Rover if the transmission oil temperature warning light comes on. If this should happen, either position 2 or 1 should be engaged on the main gear selector lever and if this fails to extinguish the light low range should be engaged. If the warning light remains on in low range, the vehicle must be stopped and the engine left running with the main selector lever in neutral until the transmission oil cools down and the light is extinguished.

Note: The warning light should illuminate only under very hot arduous conditions. If the light comes on under normal driving conditions on a regular basis, the cause should be investigated.

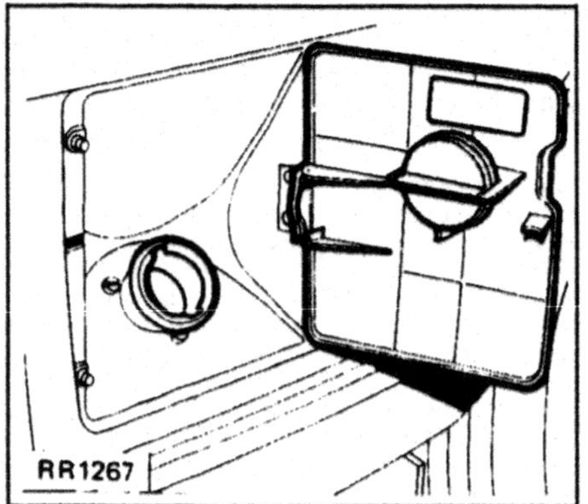

RR1267

RR1036

Unleaded petrol
Petrol with minimal quantities of lead is now available in certain territories. Range Rover V8 engines are designed to operate satisfactorily on leaded or unleaded petrol of the same octane rating. However, since the most commonly available *unleaded petrol* is 91 octane (R.O.N.) it is only suitable *for low compression (8.13:1) V8 engines.*

Fuel filler - Fig. RR1267
The fuel filler is located in the rear right-hand wing and is covered by a hinged flap. The flap is locked and unlocked by the central electrically- operated door locking system on models fitted with this feature. Two-door models are fitted with a lockable filler cap.

Fuel recommendations
Use fuel specified. No advantage will be gained by use of higher octane fuels.

CAUTION: *Do not use oxygenated fuels such as blends of methanol/gasoline or ethanol/gasoline (e.g. 'Gasohol').*

WARNING: DO NOT fill the tank completely and park the vehicle in direct sunlight or high ambient temperature, as this would cause the fuel to expand and escape through the breather pipe to the ground.

Saving fuel
Fuel consumption can be influenced by two major factors:
* How you maintain your vehicle.
* How you drive your vehicle.

To obtain optimum fuel economy, it is essential that your engine is correctly tuned and that the vehicle is maintained in accordance with the recommendations given in this Handbook.

Items such as ignition timing, the condition of plugs, air cleaner element, tyre pressures and wheel alignment can have a significant effect on the fuel efficiency of your vehicle.

Above all, the way in which you drive can radically affect fuel consumption.

The following driving hints will help you to save fuel.
* Ensure that the tyres are inflated to the correct pressures.
* Avoid fast starts; accelerate gently from rest.
* Do not drive in the lower gears longer than is needed.
* Decelerate gently and avoid sudden and heavy braking.
* Anticipate obstructions, road junctions, sharp corners or traffic lights and adjust your speed accordingly well in advance.

DRIVE GENTLY - SAVE FUEL

PASSENGER CAR FUEL CONSUMPTION ORDER 1983 No.1486 (80/1268 EEC)

	RANGE ROVER - FUEL ECONOMY					
	Simulated urban cycle	Constant speed 56 mph	Constant speed 75 mph	Simulated urban cycle	Constant speed 90 kph	Constant speed 120 kph
	mpg	mpg	mpg	L/100 km	L/100 km	L/100 km
Fuel injection versions: 5 speed manual model - with front spoiler - without front spoiler	15.4	27.2	20.9 20.4	18.3	10.4	13.5 13.9
4 speed automatic model - with front spoiler - without front spoiler	14.6	26.2	20.2 19.7	19.4	10.8	14.0 14.4
Carburetter versions: 5 speed manual model - with front spoiler - without front spoiler	14.3	26.4	20.9 20.2	19.7	10.7	13.5 13.9
4 speed automatic model - with front spoiler - without front spoiler	15.2	24.8	18.9 18.4	18.6	11.4	14.9 15.4
Diesel version: 5 speed manual model	25.5	34.1	24.4	11.0	8.3	11.6

Important note

The results given here do not express or imply any guarantee of the fuel consumption of the particular Range Rover with which this information is supplied. The vehicle itself has not been tested and there are inevitably differences between individual vehicles of the same model. In addition, this vehicle may incorporate particular modifications. The driver's style, road and traffic conditions, and the standard of maintenance, will affect the vehicles consumption.

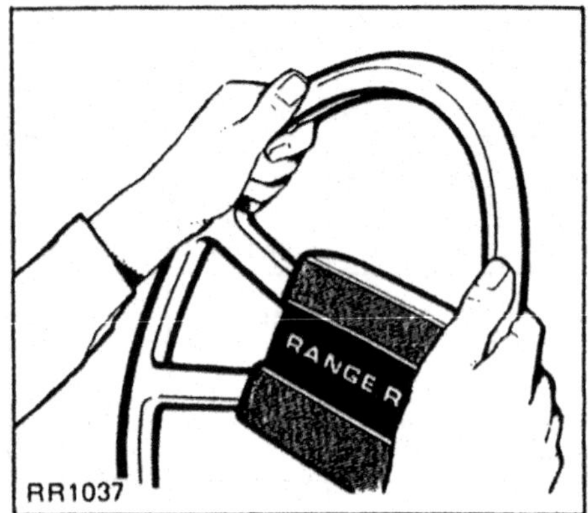

Driving techniques

The combination of gears available to the driver of the Range Rover is designed to cope with many variations in terrain and vehicle load conditions. To assist drivers, the following pages contain illustrated examples of various driving conditions and instructions on selecting the most suitable combination of gears to obtain maximum wheel traction and efficiency. These instructions are intended as an introductory guide; proficiency can only be achieved by experience.

Use of gear ranges

Use high range for all normal driving on good roads and surfaces. Low range can be used for cross-country and rough terrain driving, or for moving heavy loads.

The two ranges may be used progressively when changing up, if conditions demand.

As an example of how the full progressive range of the gearbox may be used, consider a vehicle which is heavily laden or towing a heavy trailer and which is required to pull away from a standing start up a steep gradient. With the transfer gear in 'Low' position, the vehicle will pull away in first gear and, on the manual gearbox model, gear changes for the first four gears can be made in the normal way with the main gear lever. On automatic models of course, the gearbox will provide the necessary changes to suit road speed and throttle position.

When road conditions are suitable, the high range may be brought into operation as described in Section 2.

Match engine speed to the gear selected

Before traversing a difficult section, select low range, differential locked and a suitable gear. For most purposes, second or third is satisfactory on manual gearbox models and '1' or '2' on automatic models. Remain in this gear whilst crossing and use care when applying the accelerator pedal as a sudden power surge may cause wheel spin. Unlock the differential as soon as practicable.

Riding the clutch — Manual gearbox

Keep the foot away from the clutch pedal. The practice of resting the foot on the clutch pedal should be avoided. Apart from premature clutch wear a sudden bump could cause the pedal to be depressed too far, disengaging the drive and causing the vehicle to go out of control.

RR1274

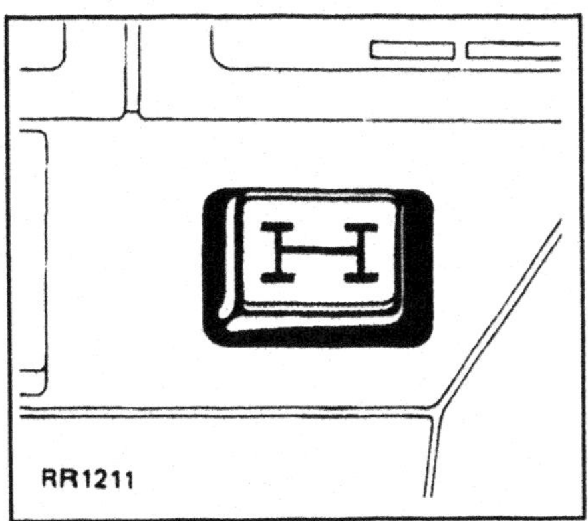

RR1211

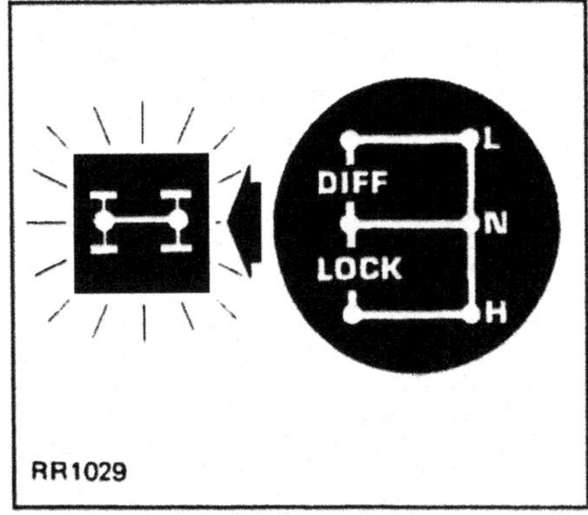

RR1029

Using the differential lock
In conditions requiring maximum traction to both axles, i.e. on snow, ice or any surface where the vehicle is likely to lose adhesion, the gearbox differential unit can be locked so that both output shafts rotate at the same speed.

Locking and unlocking of the differential is controlled through the combined transfer gear and differential lock lever.

The control can be operated while the vehicle is travelling without wheel slip and in a straight line, or while it is stationary. The differential should be locked before driving in slippery or doubtful surface conditions (Fig. RR1274).

Engagement of the lock with one or more wheels slipping will cause damage to the transmission.

Differential lock warning light - Fig. RR1211
This amber warning light, located at the side of the radio console, will be illuminated when the differential lock is engaged.

If the warning light (**Fig. RR1029**) remains on, this indicates that the transmission is 'wound-up'. The vehicle must be stopped and reversed for a few feet to 'unwind' the transmission; the warning light will then be extinguished and the vehicle can be proceed.

Note: *If, after reversing the vehicle, the light remains on, consult your dealer as soon as possible.*

Under certain conditions a slight delay may be experienced before the differential becomes locked, with subsequent warning light illumination. This delay is a built-in safety precaution and ensures that gears are correctly aligned before differential locking commences.

There may also be a delay after the differential lock is dis-engaged.

Braking
Keep the application of the brake pedal to a minimum. Braking on wet or muddy slopes can induce sliding and loss of control.

Use of engine for braking
Before descending steep slopes, stop the vehicle and engage first gear low range with the differential locked. While descending the slope it should be remembered that the engine will provide sufficient braking effort to control the speed of descent, and that the brakes should not be applied as this may cause the trailing wheels to lock on loose or slippery surfaces resulting in loss of control. Although vehicles fitted with automatic transmission have adequate engine over-run braking, remember that the effect of the torque convertor combined with the higher first gear in the automatic gearbox will result in a slightly faster descent than would be experienced with manual transmission.

Driving on soft ground
Where conditions are soft, such as marshy ground or sand, reduced tyre pressure (see Data Section) will increase the contact area of the tyres with the ground. This will help to improve traction and reduce the tendency to sink. **Tyre pressures should of course be brought back to normal when such situations have passed.**

Note: The detachable front spoiler and auxiliary driving lamps fitted to certain models should be removed before travelling over any terrain which might cause ground contact damage to the spoiler. Details of removal are given in the 'Running Requirements' section 4.

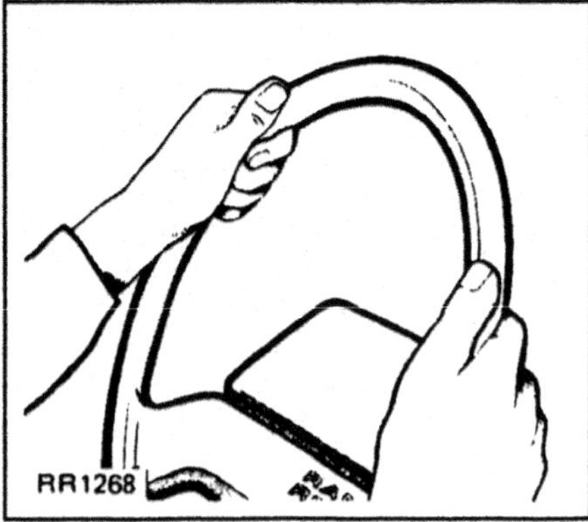

Rough rocky tracks
Although beaten rough tracks can be negotiated in normal drive, it is advisable to lock the differential if there is excessive suspension movement likely to induce wheel spin.

As the track becomes rougher and more rocky, low range may be necessary for easier control of the Range Rover. Do not hold the steering wheel with the thumbs inside the rim. A sudden violent kick of the wheel could damage or even break the thumbs. Grip the wheel on the outside of the rim (as shown in Fig. RR1268) for all cross-country travel.

Climbing steep slopes
This will usually require the use of low range with the differential locked. Select the 'D' position on the automatic main gearbox or second or third gear on the manual main gearbox.

Should the slope be slippery, use the highest gear that the engine can manage without labouring and stalling. If the vehicle fails to climb a slope but does not stall, the following procedures should be carried out. Hold the vehicle on the footbrake and engage reverse gear as quickly as possible. Release the brakes and allow vehicle to reverse down the slope whilst ensuring that both feet are clear of the brake and clutch pedals. **Do not attempt to turn the vehicle around while it is on the slope.** If the vehicle stalls on the slope, hold the Range Rover on the footbrake, then proceed as follows:

Manual gearbox models. Engage reverse gear and remove the feet from both clutch and brake pedals. Start the engine whilst in gear and allow the Range Rover to reverse down the slope, using only the retardation effect of the engine for braking.

Automatic gearbox models. Select 'N' or 'P', restart the engine and select reverse gear. The engine must be restarted before reversing down the hill as there will be no braking effort from the gearbox unless the engine is running.

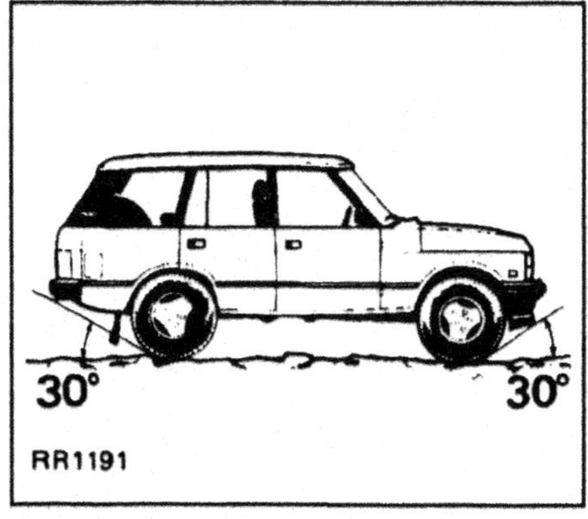

On a slippery slope never use heavy braking to check speed while reversing as this will almost certainly result in the locking of the front wheels and loss of directional control.

When back on level ground, or where forward traction can be regained, then a possible faster approach will give the extra momentum which will often enable the slope to be climbed successfully.

Negotiating a 'V' shaped gully - Fig. RR1269

This should be tackled with caution since steering up or down the gully walls could lead to the vehicle becoming trapped on the bank or on an obstacle such as a tree or rock.

Ground clearance - Fig. RR1191

Be aware of the need to maintain ground clearance under the chassis and a clear approach and departure angle. Avoid existing deep wheel ruts, sudden changes in slope and obstacles which could interfere with the chassis, differential or spoiler and auxiliary driving lights (where applicable).

Note: If the front spoiler (fitted to certain models) is removed, the approach angle is improved by 12°.

Rutted and existing wheel tracks

Generally the tendency is to over-steer the vehicle under these circumstances, resulting in the vehicle being driven on left- or right-hand lock in ruts. This should be avoided as it produces drag at the road wheels and can be dangerous, causing the vehicle to veer off the track the moment the front wheels reach level ground or find traction.

Allow the steering to follow the rut where possible and remember to keep your thumbs on the outside of the steering wheel.

Crossing ridges - Fig. RR1270

Bearing in mind the ramp break-over angle and the action of the differential, select a path so that the conditions under each wheel of the same axle are similar. This principle should be applied both in avoiding dissimilar ground surfaces and in assessing the correct angle of approach to an obstacle as as to avoid the wheels being lifted off the ground.

Approach a ridge at right angles so that both front wheels go over together. If approached at an angle, traction can be completely lost through diagonally opposite wheels leaving the ground.

Crossing a ditch - Fig. RR1271

Ditches should always be crossed at an angle so that three wheels maintain contact with the ground assisting the passage of the fourth wheel through the ditch. If approached straight on, both front wheels will drop into the ditch probably with the chassis and the front bumper trapped on opposite sides of the ditch.

Traversing slopes - Fig. RR1275 Traversing a slope should be undertaken having observed the following precautions:

(a) Check that the terrain is firm under all wheels and that the ground is not slippery as this may result in the vehicle sliding off the slope.

(b) Check that the downhill wheels are not likely to drop into a sudden depression in the ground as this will suddenly increase the angle of tilt.

(c) For the same reason ensure that the uphill wheels, do not run over rocks, tree roots, or similar obstacles.

(d) Any load carried in the back of the vehicle should be evenly distributed as low as possible and made secure. A sudden shift of load while traversing a slope could cause the vehicle to overturn. Passengers in the rear should sit on the uphill side or, in extreme conditions, vacate the vehicle until severe slopes have been negotiated.

RR1272

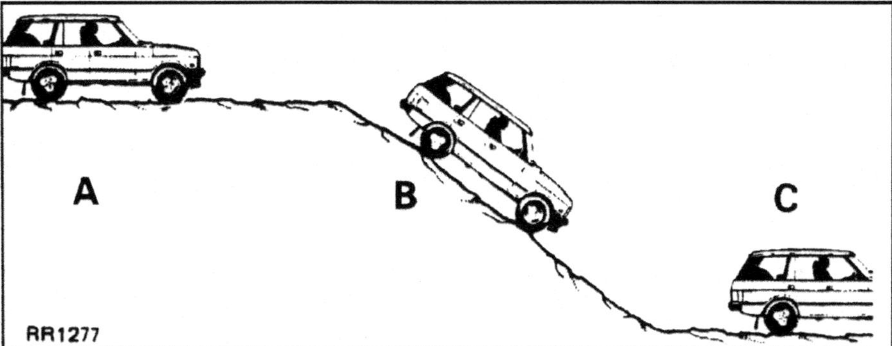

Wading - Fig. RR1272

The maximum advisable wading depth is approximately 0,5m (20 in). Before wading make sure the flywheel/converter housing drain plug is in position, (see Maintenance Section) and if the water is deeper than 0,5m removing the fan belt will eliminate the risk of the cooling fan spraying water over the ignition system and air cleaner. If, for various reasons, it is not possible to remove the fan belt, a sheet of plastic or other water resistant material draped in front of the radiator grill (to prevent any water from passing through) will reduce the risk of saturation of the ignition system.

After wading

Remove any plastic sheets placed in front of radiator.

Drive the vehicle a short distance and apply the footbrake to check that brakes are fully effective.

⚠ **WARNING: Do not rely on the handbrake alone to hold the vehicle once the transmission brake has been subjected to mud and water, on a manual gearbox model, apply the handbrake fully and leave the vehicle parked in first gear. On automatic transmission models, select the park (P) position and ensure that the parking pawl is fully engaged by momentarily releasing the brake to allow proper location of the pawl. Then fully apply the handbrake before leaving the vehicle.**

Refit the fan belt and remove the flywheel converter housing drain plug. If the water was particularly muddy it is possible that the radiator may be blocked with mud and leaves and this should be cleared immediately to reduce the risk of overheating.

If deep water is regularly negotiated it would be wise to check all transmission oils for signs of water contamination after each trip. Oil contaminated with water can easily be recognised by its milky appearance.

Descending steep slopes - Fig. RR1277

Stop the vehicle at least its own length before the slope and engage low range with the differential locked. Select position '1' on the automatic main gearbox or first gear on the manual main gearbox. Check gear engagement before moving off. Do not use heavy braking or operate the clutch pedal (where apllicable) during the descent - the engine will limit the speed and the vehicle will remain perfectly under control while the wheels are turning.

If the vehicle begins to slide, accelerate gently to maintain directional stability. As shown above in Fig. RR1277

(A) Stop at least a vehicles length before the slope. Select first gear on the manual main gearbox or position '1' on the automatic main gearbox and engage low range with the differential locked.

(B) After checking gear engagement, move forward and descend using engine retardation.

(C) When conditions permit, unlock the differential and resume normal driving.

Driving in soft, dry sand

It is generally advisable to select low range before driving over soft dry sand to avoid the risk of being unable to continue after stopping in these conditions for a change from high to low range.

When conditions are soft, reduced tyre pressures will increase the contact area, help improve traction and reduce the tendency to sink but first consult the 'Data' section 6 of this book for the pressures recommended and remember that pressure reduction will also reduce ground clearance.

Tyre pressures must be returned to normal immediately after driving in such conditions.

Manual Gearbox models - Select a gear, lock the differential and stay in that gear.

Because of the drag of the sand, the instant the clutch is disengaged the vehicle will stop.

Automatic gearbox models -on coarse firm sand, select **'D'** high range with the differential locked. On fine soft sand, select **'D'** low range with the differential locked.

Restarting on soft sand

When stopping your vehicle in sand remember that re-starting while facing up a slop is almost impossible and you should therefore park on level ground, or with the vehicle facing down hill.

In order to avoid wheel spin, a standing start is best achieved by the selection of second or third gear (manual gearbox) or 'D' (automatic gearbox) and low range with the differential locked. The minimum necessary accelerator pressure should be used to produce forward motion.

Exercise care in applying the accelerator pedal as sudden power will induce wheel spin and cause the vehicle to dig itself deeper into the sand.

If forward motion is lost do not try to accelerate out of trouble as this can only make things worse. Clear the sand from the tyres and ensure that the chassis and axles are not touching the sand.

If the wheels have sunk deep into the sand it will be necessary to lift the vehicle using an air bag or high lift jack and then build up the sand under the wheels so that the vehicle, when lowered, will be on level ground. If a restart is still not possible it may be necessary to place sand mats or ladders beneath the wheels.

Ice and snow

Range Rovers are, of course, used extensively in snow and icy conditions. The driving techniques are generally the same as driving on mud or wet grass.

Select a high gear on the manual main gearbox or position 'D' on the automatic main gearbox, high range with the differential locked and use only sufficient engine revolutions to just move the vehicle forward without labouring. Avoid violent movements of the steering wheel, using the brakes with extra care and only if necessary.

Snow chains

Chains may be fitted to the Range Rover rear axle to provide increased traction during extremely adverse heavy snow conditions.

Never fit chains to one wheel only, always fit snow chains in pairs to the rear axle only, and ensure the gearbox differential control is in the LOCKED position.

Remove the snow chains immediately the road is clear of snow.

Lost traction

Should the vehicle become immobile due to loss of wheel grip, the following hints could be of value.

Avoid prolonged wheel spin; this will only make matters worse.

Try to remove obstacles rather than force the vehicle to cross them.

If the ground is very soft, reduce tyre pressures if this has not previously been done.

Clear clogged tyre treads.

Reverse as far as possible or as far as deemed necessary so that the momentum reached in going forward again may get the vehicle over the obstacle.

Brushwood, sacking, or any similar 'mat' material placed in front of the tyres will help in producing tyre grip.

If possible, jack up the vehicle and place material under the wheels. Great care must be taken when doing this to avoid personal injury.

See also 'Vehicle Recovery' information at the end of this section.

Towing - Fig. RR1273
It is the driver's responsibility to ensure that all regulations with regard to towing are complied with according to the territory in which the vehicle is operated. All relevant information should be obtained from an appropriate motoring organisation. See also 'Trailer socket facility' in section 4.

Towing efficiency depends upon several factors:-

Towing stability.

Weight of the vehicle contents including passengers. When part of the weight is transferable, loading the towing vehicle will generally improve the stability of the combination.

Altitude: Engine performance is progressively reduced above altitudes of 300 m (1,000 feet).

For trailer stability (two-wheel trailers) the maximum load imposed in the vehicle tow bar (nose weight) should not exceed 75 kg (165 lb).

See recommended maximum laden trailer weights specified in Data Section.

When preparing the vehicle and trailer the following procedures should be adhered to:

Adjust vehicle tyre pressures as recommended in the Data Section.

Adjust trailer tyre pressures as recommended by the trailer manufacturer.

Where appropriate, balance the trailer and the vehicle, both unladen, so that with the trailer level the drawbar is at the same height as the hitch point on the vehicle.

As a general guide, there is no need to use low range when towing normal trailers, caravans and such in normal conditions.

For abnormal loads or conditions, if the towing vehicle is fitted with a manual gearbox, move off in second or third gear low range and increase the speed to 25 - 30 km/h (15 - 20 m.p.h.).

Depress the clutch pedal and release the accelerator pedal as for a normal gearchange. Move the transfer lever into neutral. Release the clutch pedal for 3 seconds. Depress the clutch pedal and move the transfer lever firmly to the 'high' (H) position. Then move the main gear lever to second gear and release the clutch pedal while depressing the accelerator to take up the drive smoothly. As the vehicle accelerates, change gear in the main gearbox in the normal way.

On Range Rovers fitted with automatic transmission the following procedure should be followed:

Move off in low range with the main gear selector in **'D'**.
Accelerate to approximately 8 km/h (5 m.p.h.) then move the main gear selector into neutral.

Move the transfer lever rapidly from low range into high range.

Re-select **'D'** with the main gear selector.

It is advisable to practise the above procedures with the vehicle stationary before attempting them with the vehicle moving.

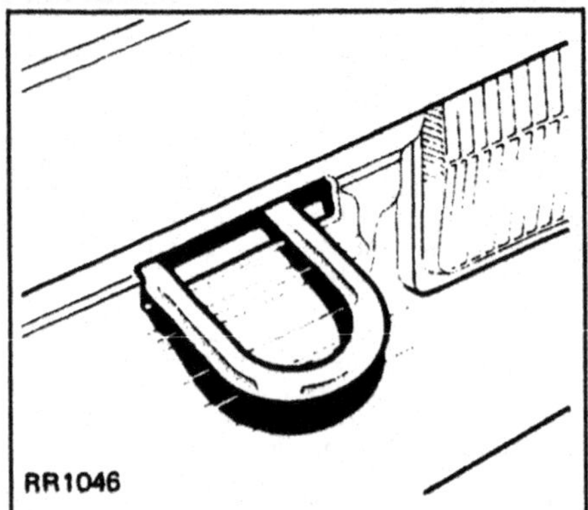

RR1046

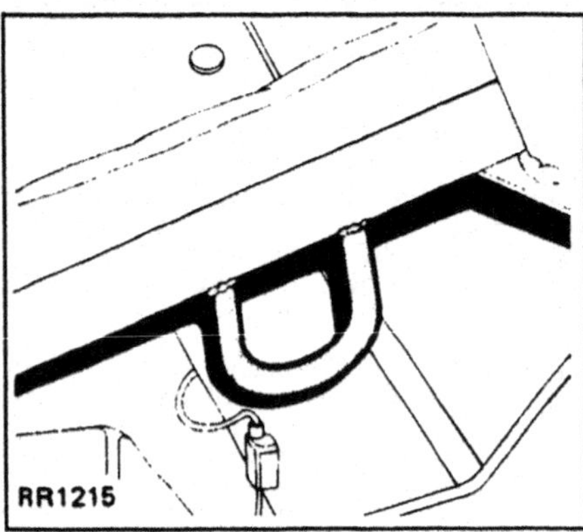

RR1215

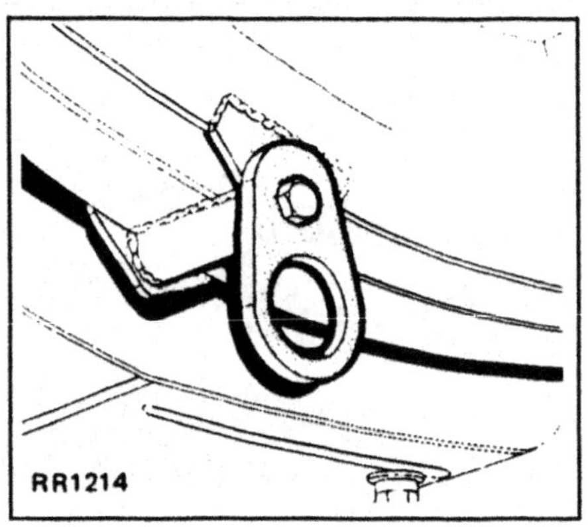

RR1214

Vehicle recovery - towed

If the vehicle should suffer a breakdown or accident damage and it becomes necessary to make a towed recovery, it is essential to adhere to one of the following procedures depending on the type of tow to be undertaken.

This is because the Range Rover has permanent four-wheel drive and is fitted with a steering lock.

Towing the Range Rover (on four wheels)

Set the main gearbox in neutral and set the transfer box in neutral with differential unlocked. Turn the ignition/steering lock key in position 'I', to release the steering lock.

Secure towing attachment to the vehicle connection (Fig. RR1046).

Release the handbrake.

CAUTION: The vehicle tow connection (Fig. RR1046) should be used only in normal road conditions and "snatch" recovery should be avoided.

⚠️ **WARNING: Unless the engine is running, brake servo and steering effort cannot be maintained. This will result in a considerable increase in pedal pressure being required to apply the brakes.**

Transporting the Range Rover on a trailer

Lashing eyes are provided on the front (Fig.RR1215) and rear (RR1214) chassis members to facilitate the securing of the vehicle to a trailer.

When the vehicle is properly located and secured on the trailer, the Range Rover's main gearbox selector should be set to neutral and the handbrake firmly applied before transportation commences.

Suspended tow by breakdown vehicle.

The propeller shaft must be disconnected from the axle to be trailed.

Note: Before removal, the propeller shaft flanges should be marked to allow accurate refitting to the original position.

If the front axle is to be trailed it will also be necessary to turn the ignition steering lock key in position 'I' to release the steering lock.

*CAUTION: The steering wheel and/or linkage **MUST** be secured in a straight ahead position but the steering lock **MUST NOT** be used for this purpose.*

The vehicle can then be attached to the breakdown vehicle and raised for towing.

RUNNING REQUIREMENTS

In addition to the Routine Maintenance described in this book, the following information details the running requirements necessary to maintain the overall efficiency of the Range Rover.

Methods of carrying out these tasks are fully described and illustrated in this Section or in Section 5 'Service and Maintenance'.

For specified tyres and pressures: for recommended lubricants, fuel, coolant, hydraulic fluid, and quantities of fluids required, see Data section.

Battery
The battery is designated 'Maintenance Free' and should require no topping up for a period of 3 years in temperate climates and 1 year in hot climates. See 'Service and Maintenance' section for more details.

Daily or Weekly Checks in Normal Highway Operating Conditions

Check and if necessary top up:

- Engine oil.

- Gearbox oil.

- Cooling system.

- Brake fluid reservoir.

- Windscreen washer reservoir.

- Power steering reservoir.

For safety, check the following:
Operation of exterior lights.

Operation of horn.

Operation of warning indicators.

Operation of screen wipers and all washers. Keep washer bottle filled with water, adding recommended solution (or methylated spirits) when necessary to prevent freezing.

Condition of driving mirrors.

Tyre pressures and tyre condition.

Special Operating Conditions
When the vehicle is operated in extremely arduous conditions or on dusty, wet or muddy terrain, more frequent attention should be paid to all servicing requirements.

Additional Daily or Weekly Attention Dependant on Operating Conditions:

Check/top up transfer box oil.

Check steering rubber boots for security and damage.

Check brake and clutch fluid levels: consult your dealer if any fluid loss is suspected.

Clean brake discs and calipers.

Lubricate front and rear propellor shaft grease points and front sliding joint. Under tropical or severe conditions, particularly where sand is encountered, the sliding joints must be lubricated very frequently to prevent ingress of abrasive material.

Every week and every maintenance inspection check tyre pressures and inspect tyre treads; under arduous cross-country conditions the tyre pressures should be checked much more frequently, even to the extent of a daily check.

Monthly
Renew gearbox oil.

Renew transfer box oil.

Check air cleaner element and renew every 6 months or as necessary.

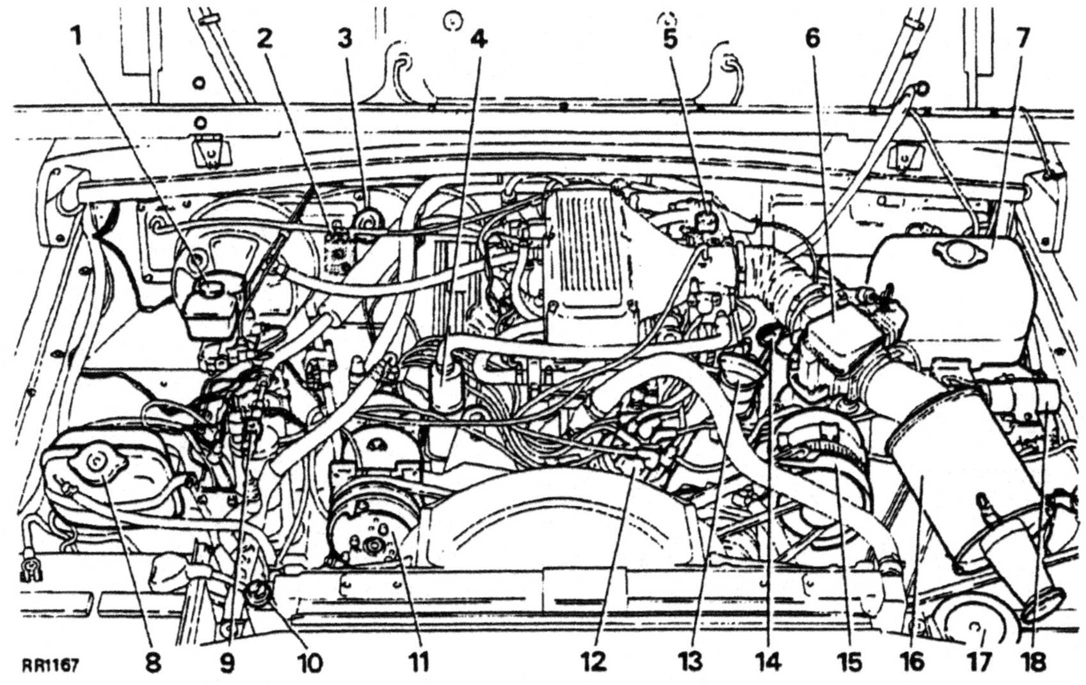

Fig. RR1167 - Under bonnet components of the electronic fuel injection, automatic transmission Range Rover with air conditioning.

1. Brake fluid reservoir
2. Clutch fluid reservoir (manual model only)
3. Automatic transmission fluid dipstick
4. Breather flame trap
5. Engine crankcase breather
6. Airflow meter
7. Front and rear screen wash and headlamp wash reservoir
8. Engine coolant expansion tank
9. Air conditioning receiver dryer sightglass
10. Radiator filler plug
11. Air compressor
12. Electronic distributor
13. Engine oil filler cap
14. Engine oil dipstick
15. Alternator
16. Air cleaner
17. Power steering fluid reservoir
18. Constant energy unit

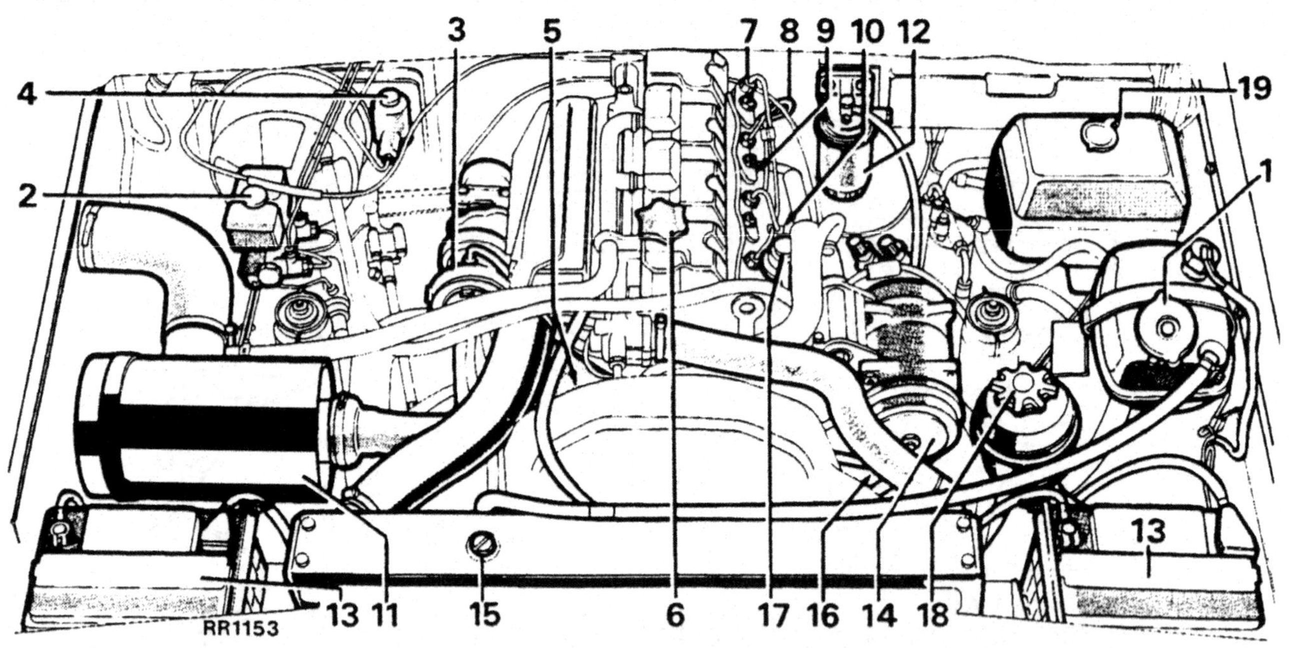

Engine Compartment.

1. Coolant filler cap.	5. Oil filter cartridge.	10. Fuel lift pump.	15. Coolant Filler Plug.
2. Brake fluid reservoir.	6. Engine oil filler cap.	11. Air cleaner.	16. Alternator.
3. Turbo-charger.	7. Injector.	12. Fuel filter.	17. Fuel injection pump.
4. Clutch fluid reservoir.	8. Engine oil dipstick.	13. Battery.	18. Power steering reservoir.
	9. Glow plug.	14. Air conditioning compressor.	19. Screen washer reservoir.

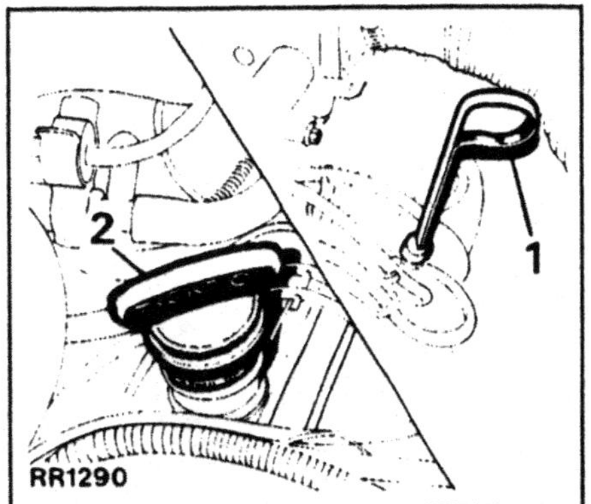

RR1290

RR1155

Petrol Engines

Check/top up engine oil level - Fig. RR1290
Position the vehicle on level ground and allow the oil to drain back into the sump.

Withdraw the dipstick (1), at left-hand side of engine; wipe it clean, reinsert to its full depth and remove a second time to take reading. The oil level should not be allowed to fall below the 'LOW' mark on the dipstick.

Add oil as necessary through the screw-on filler cap (2) marked 'ENGINE OIL' on the right-hand front rocker cover. Never fill above the 'HIGH' mark.

Diesel Engine

Oil level checking and topping up - Fig. RR1155
Withdraw the dipstick (1) and wipe the blade clean.

Reinsert the dipstick fully, then withdraw it and check the oil level indication, which must be between the 'MAX' (top) mark and 'MIN' (bottom) mark.

To top up, remove the filler cap (2) and top up the engine with new oil, then repeat the checking and topping up procedure until the oil level is correct. Do not overfill. Do not forget to replace the filler cap.

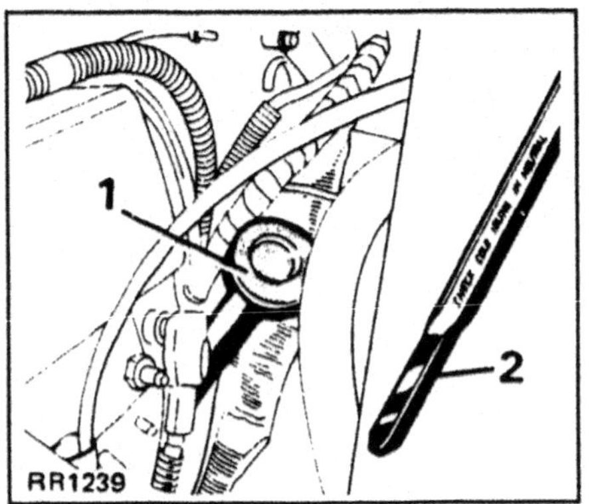

RR1239

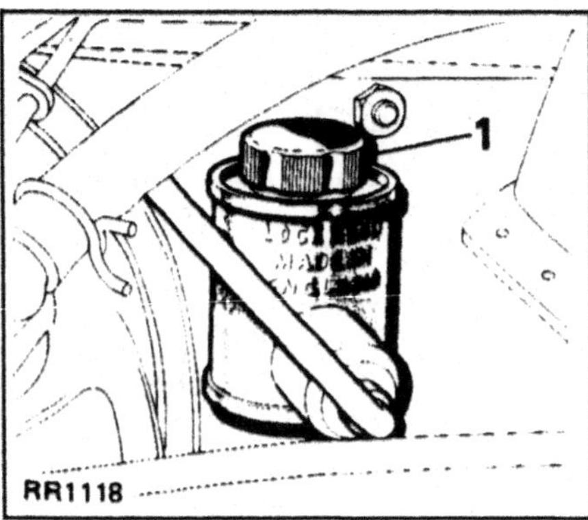

RR1118

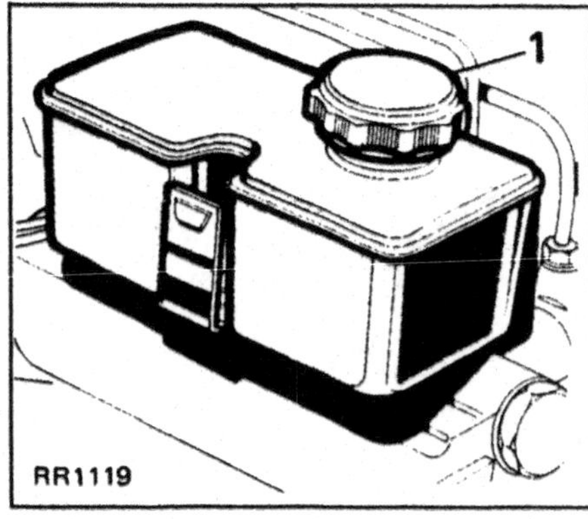

RR1119

Automatic transmission

Automatic gearbox fluid level - Fig. RR1239
The combined filler tube cap/dipstick (1) is marked with maximum and minimum 'Check Cold' levels (2).
Ensure that the vehicle is on level ground with the handbrake applied when checking oil level. Ensure the engine is running at idle and with neutral selected. Withdraw the dipstick from the filler tube and wipe the blade with a piece of clean paper or a non fluffy cloth. Reinsert the dipstick fully and withdraw it immediately and check the fluid level indication. This must be between the two markings on the dipstick.
If necessary, top up via the combined dipstick/filler tube using the correct grade of fluid stated in the 'Data' section.
Do not overfill. After checking fluid level, be sure that the dipstick is reseated correctly to prevent dirt or water from entering the gearbox.

Manual transmission

Check/top up clutch fluid reservoir - Fig. RR1118
Check the fluid level in the reservoir (1), mounted on the bulkhead adjacent to the brake servo.

Remove the cap, top up if necessary to bottom of filler neck. Use the correct fluid specified in Data, Section 6.

If significant topping up is required, check for leaks at master cylinder, slave cylinder and connecting pipes.

Check/top up brake fluid reservoirs - Fig. RR1119
The tandem brake reservoir is integral with the servo unit and master cylinder.

Remove cap (1) to check fluid level; top up if necessary until the fluid reaches the bottom of the filler neck. Use the correct fluid specified in Data, Section 6.

If significant topping up is required check master cylinder, brake disc cylinders and brake pipes and connections for leakage; any leakage must be rectified immediately.

CAUTION: When topping up the reservoir, care should be taken to ensure that brake fluid does not come into contact with any paintwork on the vehicle.

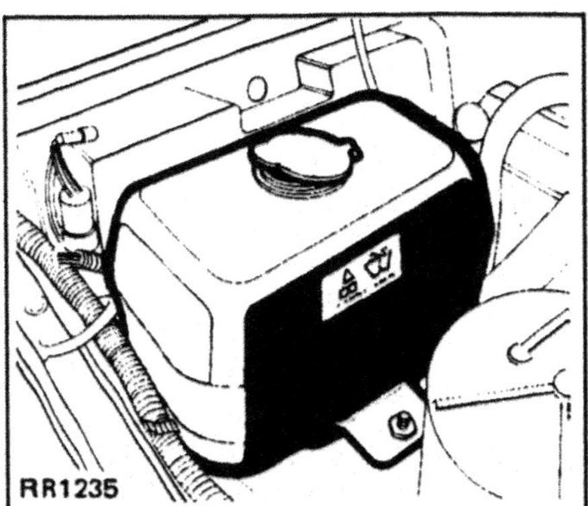

RR1235

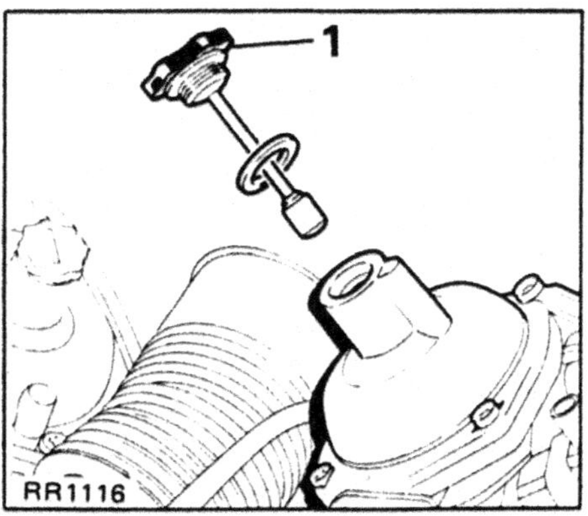

RR1116

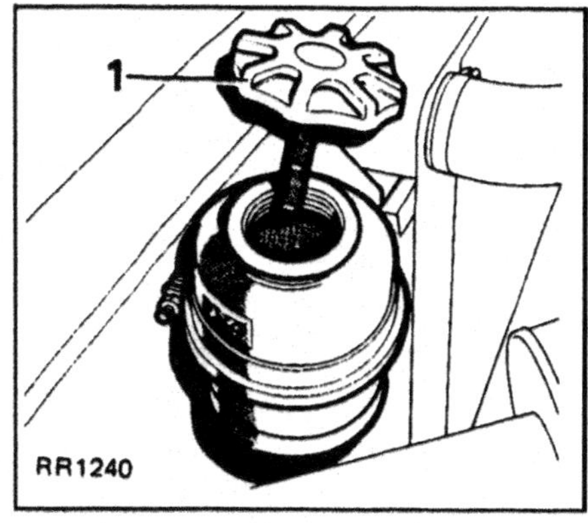

RR1240

Check/adjust operation of both screen washers and top up reservoir - Fig. RR1235

The combined windscreen/rear screen/headlamp washer rservoir is located on the bulkhead on the passenger side of the vehicle.

Unclip the cap and top up reservoir to within approximately 25 mm (1 in) below bottom of filler neck.

Use a screen washer solvent in the reservoir, this will assist in removing mud, flies and road films from screens.

In cold weather, to prevent freezing of water, add 'Isopropyl Alcohol' or methylated spirits.

Operate the washer switches and check that the nozzles are clear and properly directed.

Check/top up carburetter piston dampers — Fig. RR1116

Unscrew the cap (1) on top of each suction chamber; withdraw cap and hydraulic damper. Replenish the damper reservoir as necessary with engine oil to within about 12 mm ($\frac{1}{2}$ in) from the top of the tube.

Replace cap and hydraulic damper.

Check/top up power steering reservoir - Fig. RR1240

The power steering units are lubricated by the operating fluid. The only lubrication attention required is to check the reservoir level as follows:

Unscrew the fluid reservoir cap (1) which is fitted with a dipstick.

Check that the fluid is up to the high mark on the dipstick.

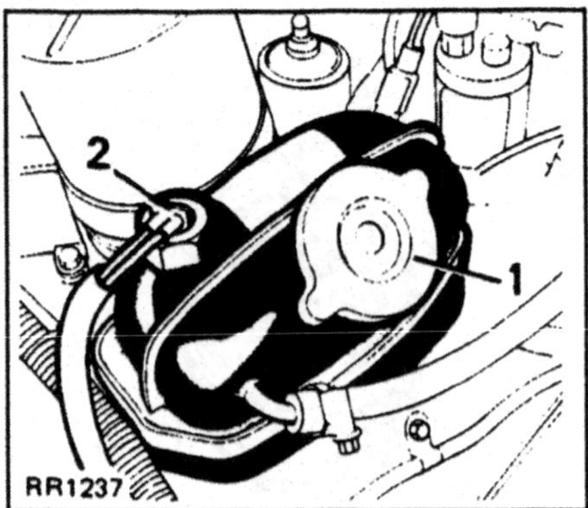

Engine coolant - Fig. RR1237
The level of coolant in the expansion tank should be checked daily or weekly dependant on operating conditions.

The expansion tank is located in the top of the engine compartment and is fitted with a spring loaded filler cap (1) and a low coolant sensor (2).

WARNING: *Do not remove the expansion tank filler cap when the engine is hot, because the colling system is pressurised and personal scalding could result.*

When removing the filler cap, first turn it anti-clockwise a quarter of a turn and allow all pressure to escape, before turning further in the same direction to lift it off.

With a cold engine, the correct coolant level should be up to the 'Water Level' plate situated inside the expansion tank below the filler neck.

When replacing the filler cap, it is important that it is tightened down fully, not just to the first stop. Failure to tighten the filler cap properly may result in water loss, with possible damage to the engine through overheating.

Frost precautions and engine protection
To prevent corrosion of the aluminium alloy engine parts it is imperative that the cooling system is filled with the specified strength solution of clean water and the correct type of anti-freeze, winter and summer, or water and inhibitor if frost precautions are not required. Never fill or top up with water only, always add an inhibitor if anti-freeze is not used. See Data, Section 6 for specified anti-freeze and inhibitor.

CAUTION: *Do not use salt water even with an inbitor otherwise corrosion will occur. In certain territories where the only available water supply has some salt content use only rain or distilled water.*

Inhibitor solution should be drained and flushed out and new inhibitor solution introduced every two years or sooner where the purity of the water is questionable.

Anti-freeze can remain in the cooling system and will provide adequate protection for two years provided that the specific gravity of the coolant is checked before the onset of the second winter and topped up with new anti-freeze as required. The specific gravity of 50% anti-freeze solution at 20°C (68°F) is 1.075.

After the second winter the system should be drained and thoroughly flushed by using a hose inserted in the radiator filler orifice. Before adding new anti-freeze examine all joints and renew defective hoses to make sure that the system is leak-proof.

To change the solution proceed as follows:

Ensure that the cooling system is leak-proof; anti-freeze solutions are far more searching at joints than water alone.

Place a suitable container in position to accomodate the old coolant and remove the radiator filler plug to assist drainage. Release the bottom hose at its junction with the radiator and remove the drain plugs one on each side of the cylinder block.

Note: It is impracticle to drain the coolant reatined in the heater system. After draining, flush through the system with clean water.

Securely refit drain plugs, reconnect the bottom hose and pour in approximately 4,5 litres (one gallon) of water. Add the recommended quantity of anti-freeze (or inhibitor if frost protection is not required).

Top up the radiator with water, refit the radiator filler plug and washer securely.

Add water to the expansion tank, up to the 'Water Level' plate, and replace cap.

Run the engine until normal operating temperature is attained, that is, thermostat open. Allow the engine to cool, then check the coolant level and top up if necessary.

Range Rover models have the cooling system filled with 50% of anti-freeze mixture. This gives protection against frost down to minus 47°C (-53°F). Vehicles so filled can be identified by the green label tied to the radiator.

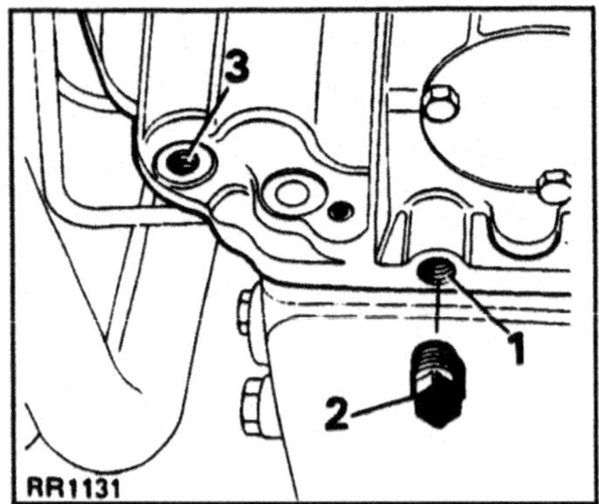

RR1131

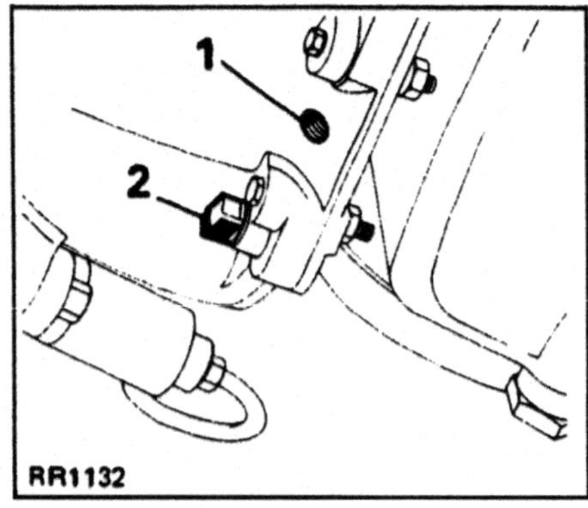

RR1132

Automatic gearbox models

Converter housing drain plug - Fig. RR1131
The drain hole (1) in the bottom of the converter housing must only be plugged to prevent the entry of water or mud while the vehicle is operating in very muddy conditions, or wading.

If the plug (2) is continually used in position (1), it must be frequently removed to allow any water or oil to drain away and the plug replaced before wading or muddy work is resumed.

In normal conditions, the drain hole should be kept clear and the plug securely screwed into its retaining position (3).

Note: If excessive amounts of oil are present during drainage, the cause should be investigated.

Manual gearbox models

Drain flywheel housing if plug has been fitted for wading - Fig. RR1132
The flywheel housing can be completely sealed to exclude mud and water under severe wading conditions, by means of a plug fitted in the bottom of the housing (1).

When not in use, the plug is reatined in position (2), and should only be fitted in position (1) when the vehicle is expected to do wading or very muddy work.

When the plug is in use it must be removed periodically and any water or oil in the housing allowed to drain off before the plug is replaced.

Note: If excessive amounts of oil are present during drainage, the cause should be investigated.

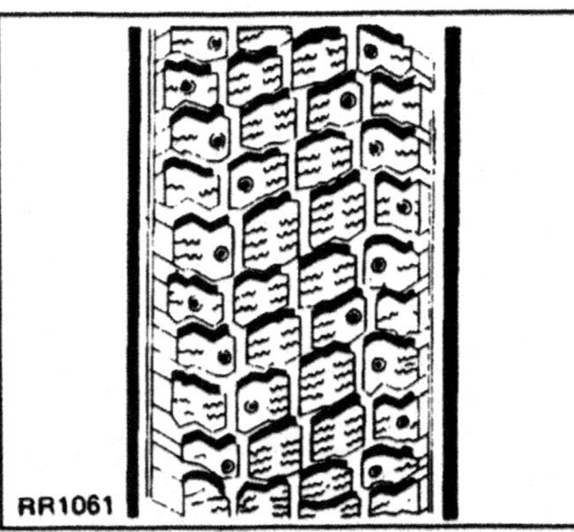

RR1061

Check/adjust tyre pressures including spare.

These should be checked at least every month for normal road use and at least weekly, preferably daily, if the vehicle is used off the road or for high-speed touring. See Data Section for specified pressures.

Whenever possible check with the tyres cold, as the pressure is about 0,21 bar (3 lb/in^2) 0,2 kg/cm^2 higher at running temperature.

Replace the valve caps, as they form a positive seal.

Check that pressures on all tyres, including the spare, are correct. Any unusual pressure loss in excess of 0,21 bar (3 lb/in^2) 0,2 kg/cm^2 per week should be investigated and corrected.

Check tyres for tread depth and visually for external cuts in the fabric, exposure of ply or cord structure.

Most tyres fitted to Range Rovers as original equipment include wear indicators in their tread pattern. When the tread has worn to a remaining depth of 1,6 mm (1/16") the indicators appear at the surface as bars which connect the tread pattern across the full width of the tyre. When the indicators appear in two or more adjacent grooves, at three locations around the tyre, a new tyre should be fitted. If the tyres do not have wear indicators, the tread should be measured at every maintenance inspection and when the tread has worn to a remaining depth of 1,6 mm (1/16"), new tyres should be fitted. Do not continue to use tyres that have worn to the specified limit or the safety of the vehicle could be affected and legal regulations concerning tread depth may be broken.

Check that there are no lumps or bulges in the tyres or exposure of the ply or cord structure.

Clean off any oil or grease, using white spirit sparingly. At the same time remove embedded flints, etc. from the treads with the aid of a penknife or similar tool, and check that tyres have no 'breaks' in the fabric or cuts to sidewalls, etc.

It is advisable to run-in new tyres by driving at reasonable speeds for the first 400 km (250 miles) or so before driving at high speeds.

Wheel and tyre units are accurately balanced on initial assembly with the aid of weights secured to wheel rims.

Check that tyres comply with manufacturers specification.

WARNING: Many off-road types of tyre have a maximum speed capability below that of the Range Rover. Therefore, when tyre replacements are required, radial-ply tyres of the approved type must be used. Under no circumstances should cross-ply tyres be used.

Fuel injection vehicles MUST be fitted with 'S' rated high-speed tyres.

See tyre details given in the 'Data' section.

Always use the same make and type of radial-ply tyre throughout the vehicle.

WARNING: Wheels and tyres. Unless both wheel rim and tyre are marked 'TUBELESS', an inner tube MUST be fitted.

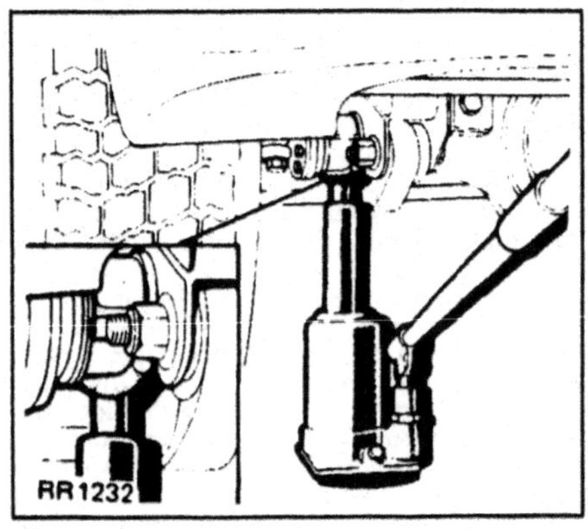

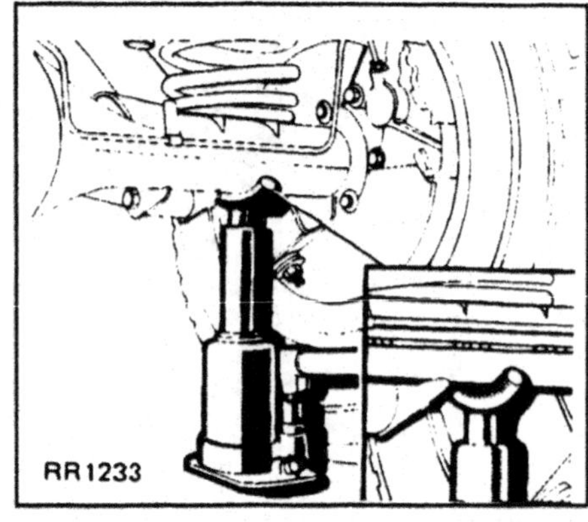

Tools

The jack and chock, together with a tool roll, will be found attached to the inside of the rear right hand body panel and should be secured in this location when not in use. A jack extension handle is also provided.

Jacking the vehicle

The jack should be used on level firm ground wherever possible and no person should remain in a vehicle being jacked.

⚠️ *WARNING: The hand brake acts on the transmission, not on the rear wheels, and may not hold the vehicle when jacking unless the following procedure is used. If one front wheel and one rear wheel are raised no vehicle holding or braking effect is possible. Wheels should be chocked in all circumstances.*

Always engage the differential lock. Note that the differential lock is only engaged if the warning light is illuminated with the engine ignition switched on.

Apply the hand brake, engage position '1' (automatic transmission) or first gear (manual transmission) on the main gearbox and engage low range in the transfer box.

⚠️ *WARNING: It is unsafe to work under the vehicle using only the jack to support it. Always use heavy duty stands or other suitable supports to provide adequate safety.*

To jack up a front wheel - Fig. RR1232

Position the jack so that when raised, it will engage with the front axle casing immediately below the coil spring where it will be located between the flange at the end of the axle casing and a large bracket to which front suspension members are mounted.

To jack up a rear wheel - Fig. RR1233

Position the jack so that when it is raised, it will engage with the rear axle casing immediately below the coil spring and as close as possible to the shock absorber mounting bracket.

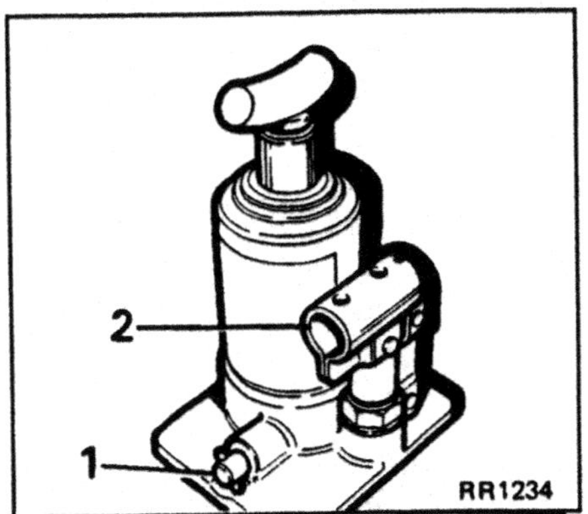

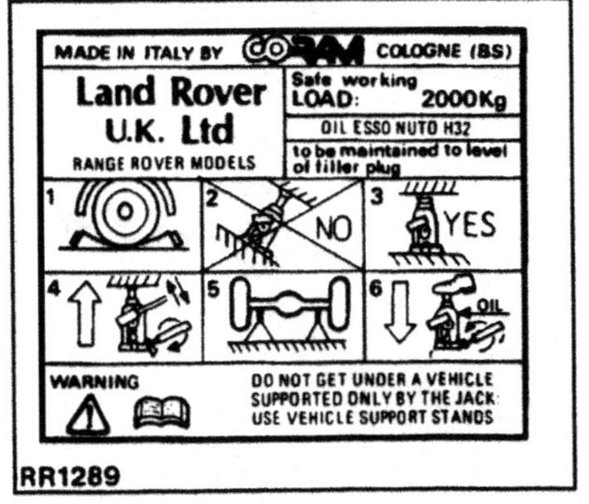

Operating the hydraulic jack - Fig. RR1234
Check that the release valve (1) at the bottom of the jack body is closed (turned fully clockwise). Position the jack under the vehicle, ae previously described. Assemble the two-piece operating handle and insert the handle into the socket (2) on the side of the jack. Pump the handle up and down to raise the jack.

To lower the jack, withdraw the handle from the socket, engage it over the pegs on the release valve (1) and use it to turn the release valve anti-clockwise.

Care of the jack - Fig. RR1289
Neglect of the jack may lead to difficulty in a roadside emergency. Examine the jack occasionally and clean to prevent rust.

The jack oil level should be checked at normal servicing intervals and if necessary topped up with an hydraulic oil with a viscosity to BS4231 grade 32 and ISO proof 32.

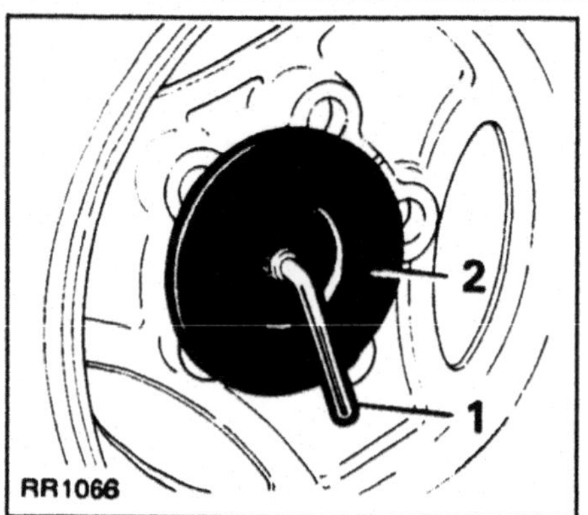

RR1066

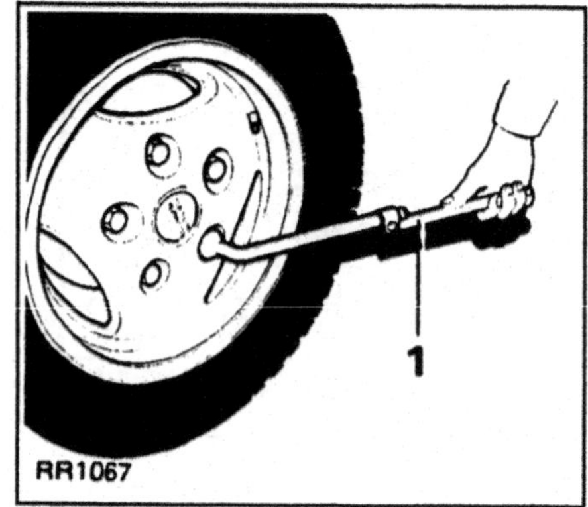

RR1067

Spare wheel

The spare wheel is mounted in the interior of the vehicle, positioned at the left hand rear side. A fabric wheel cover is fitted over the wheel to prevent soiling of articles in the vehicle.

Spare wheel removal - Fig. RR1066

Remove the load space cover and interior side panels (if fitted) and remove the loose cover from the wheel. Unscrew the locking lever (1) to allow removal of the clamping plate (2) and removal of the wheel.

Wheel changing - Fig. RR1067

Slacken the five wheel nuts, using the hinged type wheel nut wrench (1) - from the vehicle tool kit - in the fully extended position. This will provide additional leverage for removal of wheel nuts.

Jack up the corner of the vehicle - see 'Jacking the vehicle' details.

Remove the nuts and gently withdraw the wheel over the studs.

Lightly oil or grease the wheel studs to assist in replacement and if alloy wheels are being fitted, lightly smear the wheel mounting spigot face with oil or an approved anti-seize compound.

Spraying should not be employed as extreme care must be taken to ensure that oil or compound is not allowed to contact any brake components.

This measure is necessary to minimise the tendency of adhesion between wheel and spigot. Where in an emergency situation this is not immediately practicable, the spare wheel should be fitted for the time being but subsequently removed and treated at the earliest possible opportunity under normal conditions.

After carefully locating the wheel on the studs, tighten the wheel nuts as much as possible with the hinged wheel nut wrench. The hinged part will automatically fold to provide normal leverage for refitting. Lower the vehicle to the ground and finally fully tighten the nuts.

After wheel changing, transfer the plastic centre finisher (fitted to certain models) from the previously fitted wheel to the newly fitted wheel.

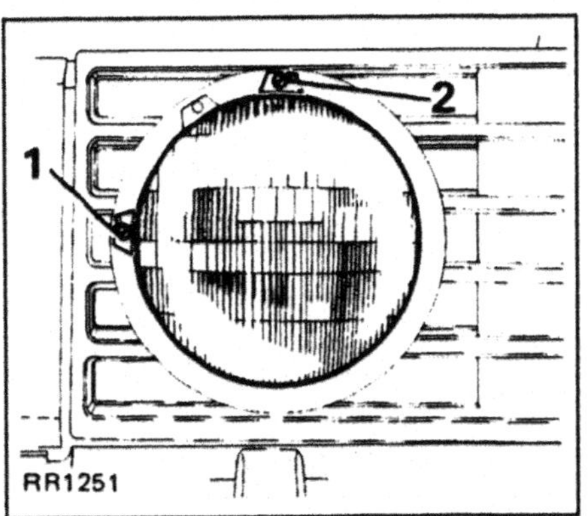

RR1251

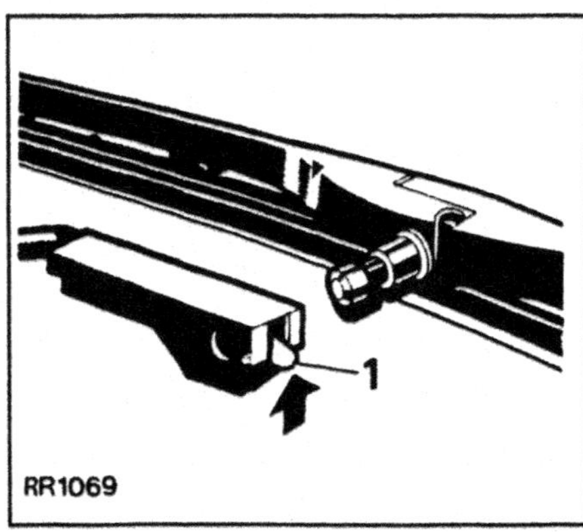

RR1069

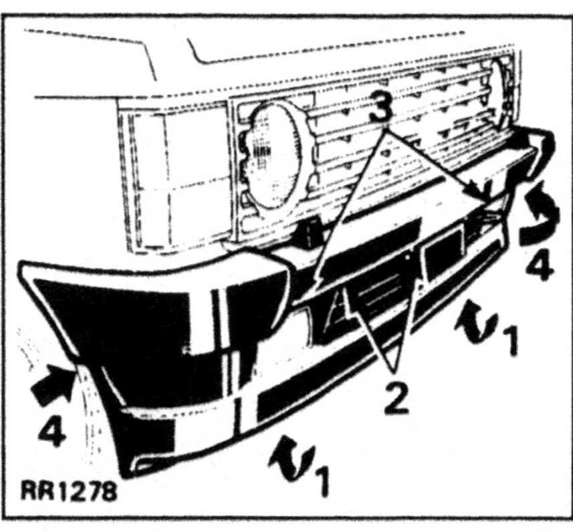

RR1278

Headlamp beam alignment - Fig. RR1251
This operation requires special equipment and should be carried out by your local Distributor or Dealer.

In an emergency each headlamp unit can be adjusted by means of the headlamp horizontal adjusting screw (1) and the headlamp vertical adjusting screw (2).

Check and, if necessary, renew wiper blades - Fig. RR1069
To renew a wiper blade, lift the retaining lever (1) and remove the blade. Locate the new blade spindle into the arm and check that it is retained by the lever (1).

Spoiler removal - Fig. RR1278
Where terrain is encountered which may damage the front spoiler fitted to some models of the Range Rover, removal of the detachable spoiler is recommended and can be done quite easily as follows.

Disconnect the auxiliary driving lamp connections (1) accessible through the front wheel arches and from the front, remove the two screws complete with spring washers (2) securing the centre of the spoiler. Then remove the four nuts and washers (3) located behind the bumper above the lamp housings. After removal of two more screws and washers (4) which secure the spoiler to the corners of the front wings, the spoiler - complete with driving lamps - can be lifted clear. The lamp connectors and wiring on the vehicle should be safely secured before the vehicle is driven.

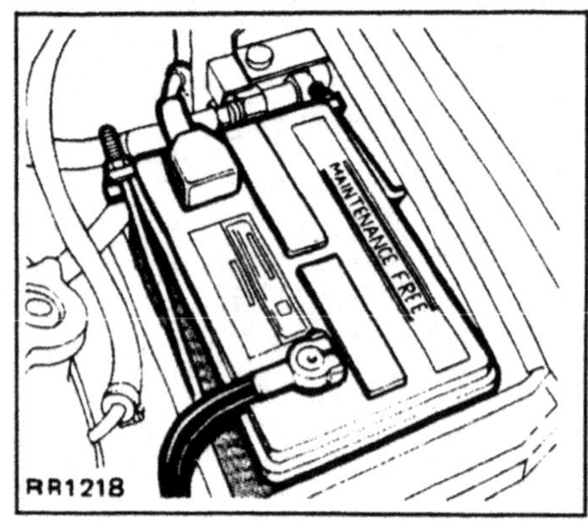

Electronic distributor - Fig. RR1249

The electronic ignition system uses an appropriate distributor.

This has a conventional advance/retard vacuum unit and centrifugal automatic advance mechanism.

A pick-up module, in conjunction with a rotating timing reluctor inside the distributor body, generates timing signals. These are applied to an electronic ignition amplifier unit fitted under the ignition coil mounted on top of the left front wing valance.

Should it become necessary to check any aspect of the system, the work must be done by a qualified Range Rover distributor or dealer who has the specialised equipment necessary.

The only driver maintenance possible is periodic removal of the distributor cap and rotor arm (1) for the application of three drops of oil to the felt pad in the top of the distributor shaft. Use a clean dry nap-free cloth to wipe the inside of the cap and the top of the clear plastic insulating cover (2) which protects the magnetic pick-up module. This cover must not be disturbed.

Battery - Fig. RR1218

A low maintenance battery is installed in the vehicle. Dependant upon climate conditions the electrolyte levels should be checked as follows: temperate climates every 3 years, hot climates every year.

The exterior of the battery should be occasionally wiped clean to remove any dirt or grease.

Periodically remove the battery terminals to clean and coat with petroleum jelly.

To check if maintenance is required, gently prise off the vent covers and inspect the electrolyte level of the centre cell. This should be no lower than 1 mm (0.04 in) above the top of the plates. If necessary, top up (with distilled water only) to a maximum of 3 mm (0.12 in) above the plates.

WARNING: *If a new replacement battery is to be fitted to the vehicle, it should be the same type as the original. Alternative batteries may vary in size and terminal positions and this could be a possible fire hazard if the terminals or leads come into contact with the battery clamp assembly. When fitting a new battery, ensure that the terminals and leads are well clear of the battery clamp assembly.*

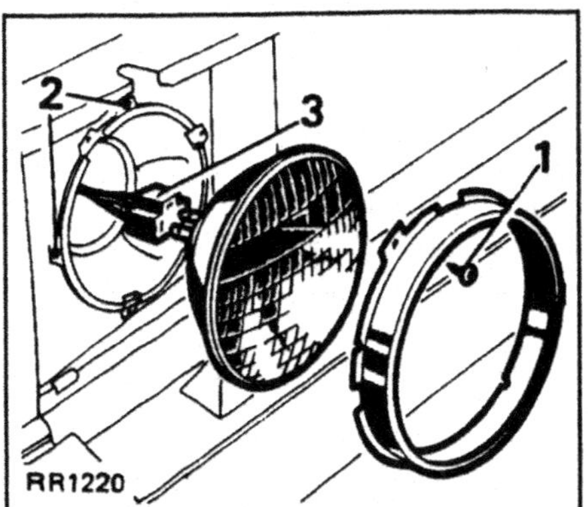

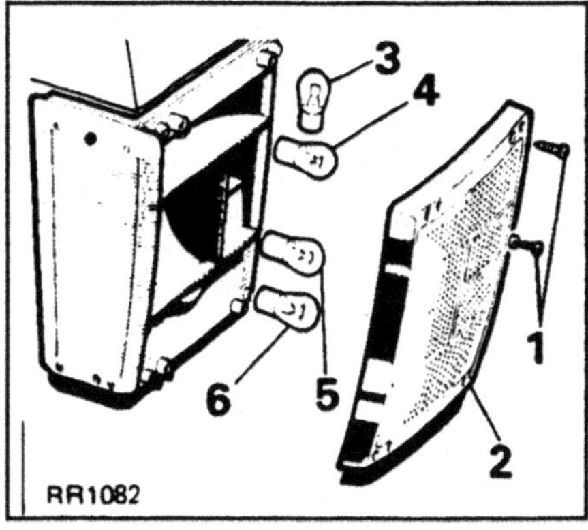

Headlamp sealed beam unit replacement - Fig. RR1220

Prop open the bonnet and remove the grille.

Supporting the headlamp unit to prevent it falling, release the three screws (1) in the retaining rim. Do not disturb the two beam alignment adjusting screws (2).

Draw the unit forward out of the headlamp housing for access to the multi- plug lead (3); disconnect the lead and replace the sealed beam unit.

Front sidelight or indicator bulb replacement - Fig. RR1242

Open the bonnet, remove the two crosshead screws (1) securing the lamp assembly to the vehicle and lift the assembly away just sufficiently to allow access to the rear of the unit. From the rear, remove the cover (2), squeeze the retaining lugs (3) and lift the bulb holder block (4) out of the lens unit for access to the bulbs. The direction indicator flasher bulb (5) is located in the upper part of the block and the sidelight or parking light bulb (6) in the lower section.

Remove the faulty bulb by slight rotation anti-clockwise and withdraw from the block. After renewal of the bulb, refitting of the assembly is simply the reverse of removal.

To replace flasher, tail, reverse and fog guard lamp bulbs - Fig. RR1082

Remove four screws (1) retaining lens.
Remove lens (2).
Replace bulb: tail/stop lamp bulb (3), direction indicator flasher lamp bulb (4), centre inner reverse lamp bulb (5) or bottom fog guard lamp bulb (6).
Refit lens, do not overtighten screws.

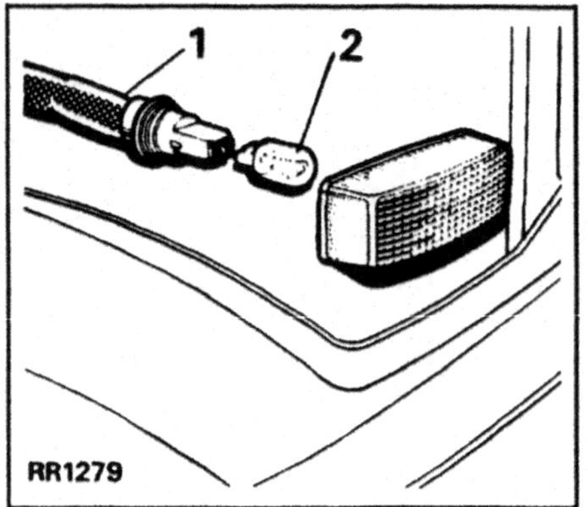

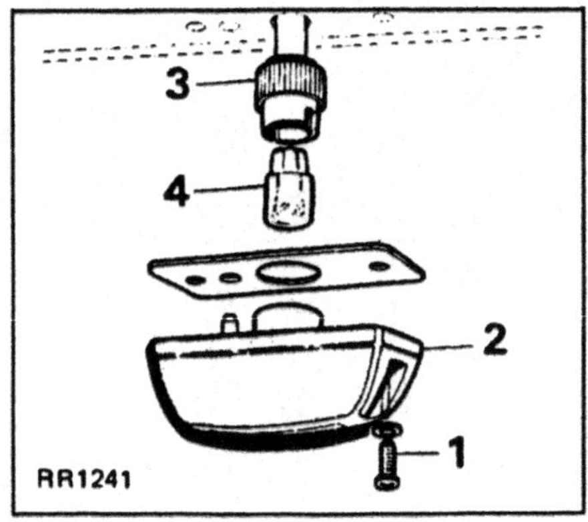

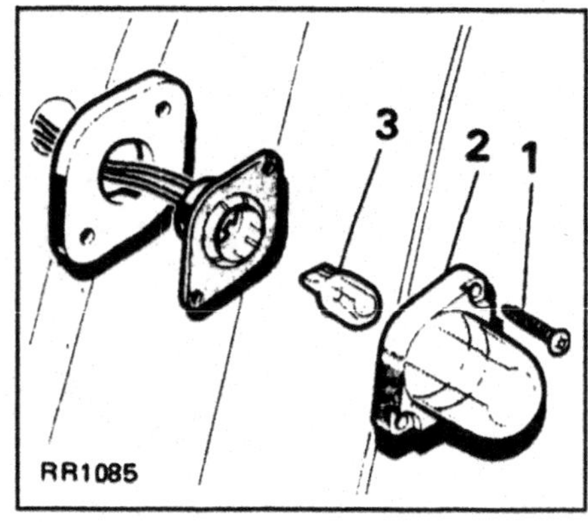

Direction indicator side repeater lamps, on front wings - Fig. RR1279

Note: The amber lens of this unit is not removeable for bulb renewal.

From the underside of the wing, easily accessible through the front wheelarch, a slight anti-clockwise twist of the bulb holder (1) will release it from the assembly so that the capless 12 volt, 5 watt bulb (2) can be pulled out and renewed. Replacement, of course, is simply reversal of the above.

Number plate illumination - Fig. RR1241

For access to the bulb, remove the two screws (1) complete with fibre washers, and draw off the lens assembly (2) complete with its mounting gasket and bulb holder (3). A slight anti-clockwise twist of the holder will release it from the assembly so that it can be withdrawn to reveal the bulb (4). If necessary, remove and renew the 12 volt, 5 watt bulb and refit the assembly ensuring that the gasket is correctly located.

Underbonnet lamp - Fig. RR1085

To renew the underbonnet lamp bulb:

Release the two screws (1) and remove the lens (2). Pull the capless bulb (3) from its holder, insert the new bulb and refit the assembly.

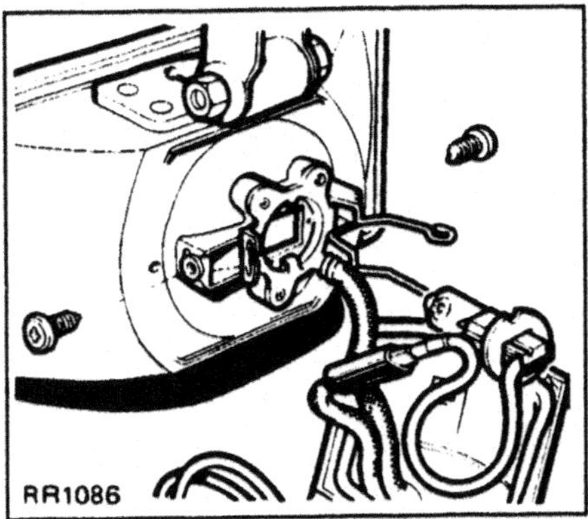

RR1086

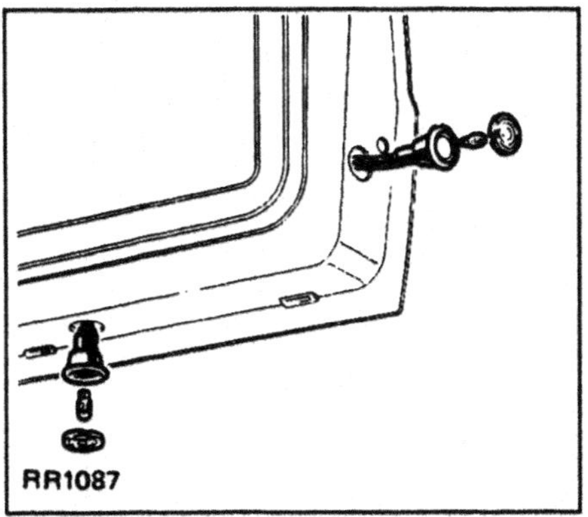

RR1087

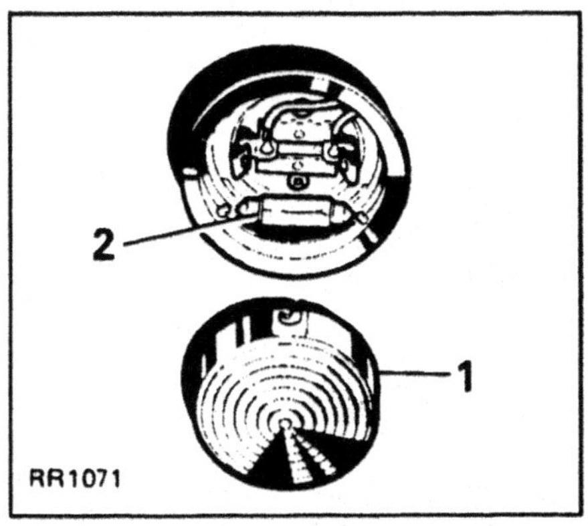

RR1071

Auxiliary driving lamp bulb replacement - Fig. RR1086

Disconnect the negative (-) lead of the battery. Gain access to the rear of the lamp through the front wheel arch.

Withdraw the electrical connector from the rear of the lamp and remove the lamp securing nut and washer located beneath the front wing adjacent to the front body fixing. Then from the front of the vehicle, manoeuvre the lamp out of the spoiler aperture. Remove the two screws retaining the rear cover of the lamp, withdraw the cover, disconnect the 'Lucar' connector and release the spring clip securing the bulb.

Change the 12 volt, 55 watt H3 halogen bulb taking care not to touch the bulb envelope with the fingers. Ensure that the two notches on the bulb body locate properly with registers on the lamp unit and refit the assembly.

Door edge/puddle lamps bulb replacement - Fig. RR1087

Disconnect the negative (-) lead of the battery and carefully prise out the lamp lens. Withdraw the lamp body from the door as far as the electrical leads permit and pull out the bulb. Replace it with the correct 12 volt, 5 watt capless type bulb, refit the lamp lens and return the assembly to its seating in the door edge.

Interior roof lamps - Fig. RR1071

There are two circular lamps in the front and rear of the compartment.
Turn lens (1) anti-clockwise and withdraw.
Replace the 12 volt, 10 watt bulb (2) and refit lens.

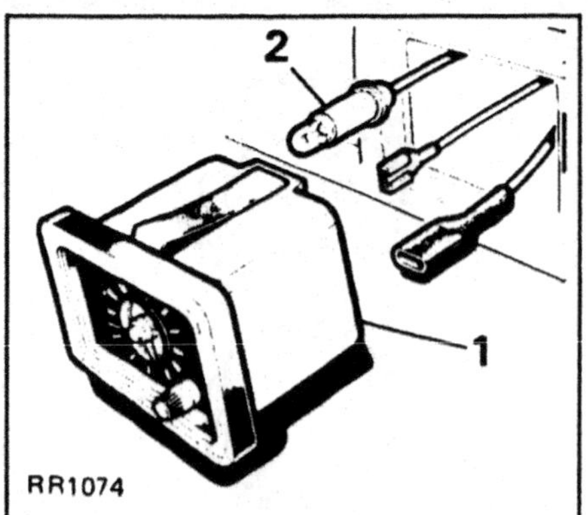

RR1074

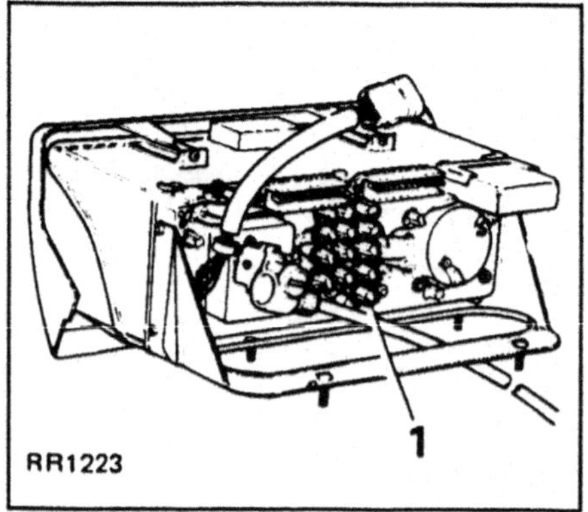

RR1223

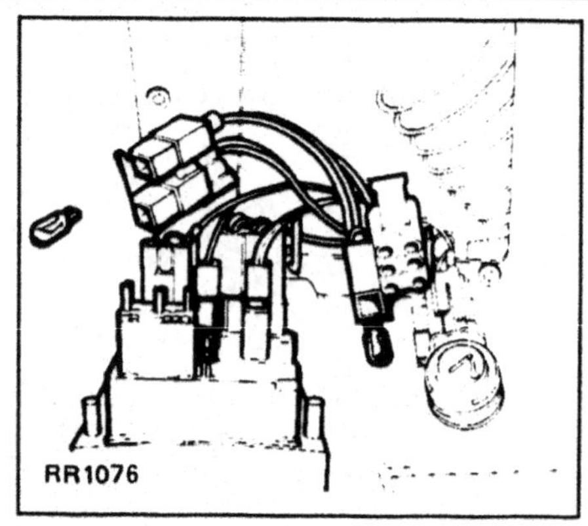

RR1076

Clock bulb replacement - Fig. RR1074

First disconnect the negative (-) lead of the battery.

Carefully prise the clock (1) out of the fascia panel and draw it forward enough to allow removal of the 12 volt, 2 watt bayonet type bulb and holder (2) from the rear of the instrument. After renewal of the bulb, refitting of the unit is simply the reverse of removal. The clock hands can be reset by depressing and rotating the knob (3) on the clock face.

Binnacle centre warning light cluster bulb renewal - Fig. RR1223

Disconnect the negative (-) lead of the battery before unclipping the back cover of the binnacle for access to the rear of the cluster (1). Remove the appropriate bulb holder unit by rotating it anti-clockwise and withdrawing it.

Note: The 'No Charge' ignition warning light bulb, identified by its red holder, is of 12 volt, 2 watt wedge base type and is the only one in the cluster that can be pulled from its holder and replaced independently. The remainder are 12 volt, 1.2 watt bulb holder units which can be released from the back of the binnacle by slight anti-clockwise, rotation, removed and replaced by similar units locked in position by clockwise rotation.

Auxiliary switch panel bulb replacement - Fig. RR1076

This panel incorporates four 12 volt, 1.2 watt wedge base (capless) bulbs: two (amber) for the rear fog lamps switch and the heated rear screen switch plus two (green) panel illumination bulbs each positioned in the centre of a group of four switches.

To replace any of these bulbs, first disconnect the negative (-) lead of the battery and carefully prise the panel surround away from the centre console. From the rear of the panel, unclip the multi-plug holding the relevant bulb which can then be pulled out. Renew the bulb, refit the multi- plug and carefully press the panel and surround back into position.

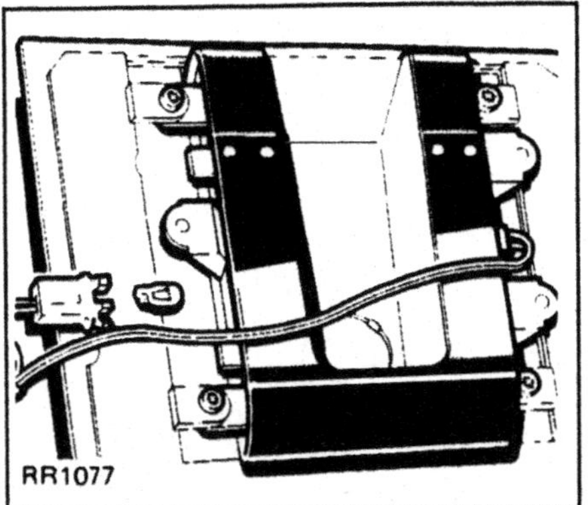

RR1077

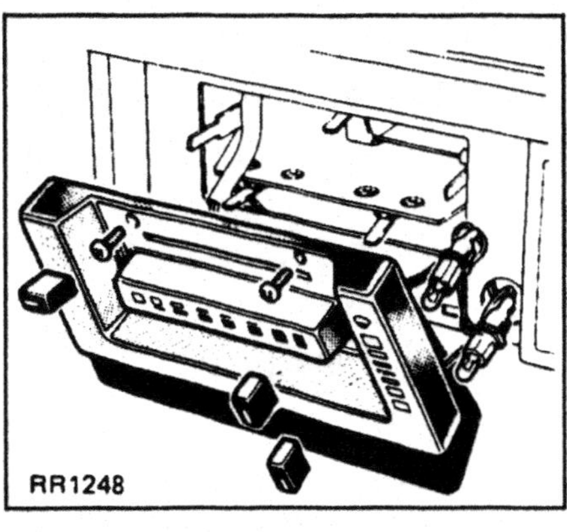

RR1248

Automatic gearbox selector panel bulb replacement - Fig. RR1077
Disconnect the negative (-) lead of the battery, unclip the cover from the top of the gear selector knob, remove the circlip retaining the detent button and withdraw the button. Remove the lower circlip above the knob securing nut, remove the nut and serrated washer and slide the selector knob off the shaft. Carefully prise the inset panel, complete with the illumination panel and ashtray, out of the floor-mounted console and extract the appropriate bulb holder. If necessary, remove the four screws securing the illumination panel to the outer surround. Pull the 24 volt, 5 watt wedge base (capless) bulb from the holder and replace as necessary.

Refitting is the reverse of removal procedure but care must be taken to prevent the trapping of any electrical lead between mating surfaces.

Do not overtighten the selector knob retaining nut.

Interior climate control panel bulb replacement - Fig. RR1248
This panel is illuminated by four 12 volt, 1.2 watt wedge type (capless) bulbs located in the rear of the panel.

To gain access, disconnect the negative (-) lead of the battery, pull off the four finger-tip control knobs from the levers, remove the two screws at the top of the panel and carefully draw the panel away from the centre console only as far as the electrical leads will permit.

Pull the appropriate bulb holder out of the panel and extract the bulb. Insert the new bulb in the holder, push the holder firmly back into its location in the rear of the panel and refit the assembly ensuring that no electrical lead is trapped between panel and console.

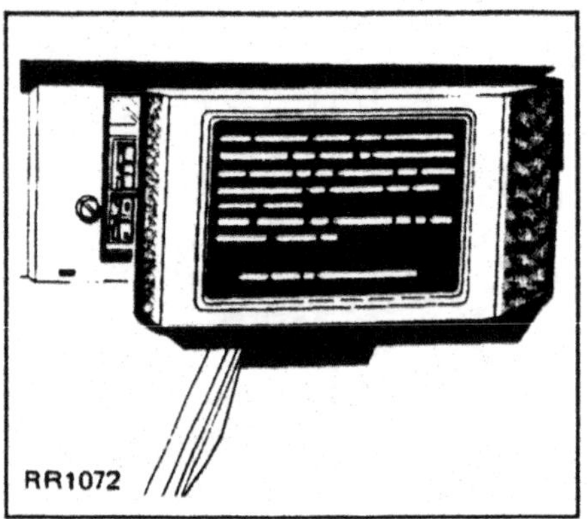

Fuse Box - Figs. RR1072 and RR1280

The fuse box on the lower fascia contains appropriate blade type fuses each of which is colour coded and marked with its continuous current rating.

To gain access, the cover must be slid slightly away from the driving position (to release the 'L' shaped lugs which locate in slots at each corner) before being lifted off.

A fused extractor on the inside of the cover allows easy removal and replacement of any fuse. A label (Fig. RR1280) identifying the position of each fuse is also attached inside the cover.

Key to fuse box circuits

Fuse No.	Colour Code	Fuse Value	Circuit served	Ignition Key Controlled
Main Fuse Panel				
1	Brown	7.5 amp	RH headlamp dipped beam and power wash	·
2	Brown	7.5 amp	LH headlamp dipped beam	·
3	Brown	7.5 amp	RH headlamp main beam	·
4	Brown	7.5 amp	LH headlamp main beam	·
5	Tan	5 amp	RH parking lights and instrument illumination	·
6	Tan	5 amp	LH parking lights and radio illumination*	·
7	Blue	15 amp	Front wash/wiper motors	AUX
8	Yellow	20 amp	Heating/air conditioning motor*	AUX
9	White	25 amp	Heated rear screen	IGN
10	Violet	3 amp	Mirror heaters*	IGN
11	Blue	15 amp	Headlamp flash, door, underbonnet and internal lamps, radio clock and horns	IGN
12	Red	10 amp	R/LH rear fog lamps	·
13	Blue	15 amp	Low coolant monitor, stop and reverse lamps, direction indicators, instruments, low oil monitor and screen wash fluid monitor	IGN
14	Blue	15 amp	Auxiliary feed trailer	·
15	Blue	15 amp	Auxiliary driving lamps*	·
16	Red	10 amp	Rear wash/wiper motor	AUX
17	Yellow	20 amp	Cigar lighters (front and rear)	IGN
18	Red	10 amp	Fuel pump	IGN
19	Red	10 amp	Central locking*	·
20	White	25 amp	Window lifts*	AUX
Auxiliary fuse panel - (A)				
A1	Yellow	20 amp	Air conditioning fan*	IGN
A2	Yellow	20 amp	Air conditioning fan*	IGN
A3	Tan	5 amp	Air conditioning compressor clutch*	IGN
A4	·	·	Spare	·
A5	Violet	3 amp	Electric mirror motors*	IGN

*Note: Radio/cassette combination - An in-line type 7 amp fuse is incorporated in the power input lead of the unit. * Where applicable*

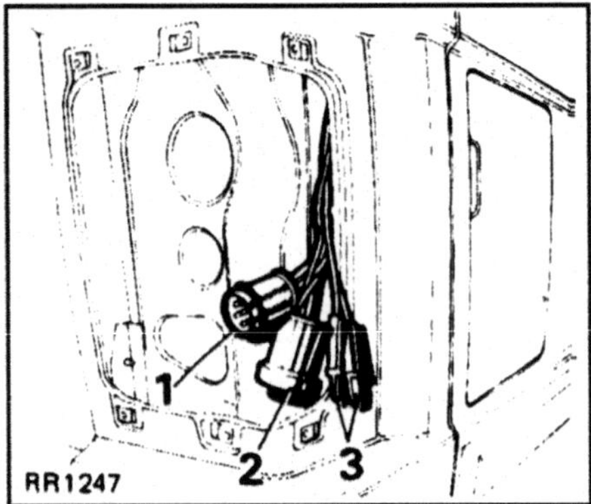

Trailer socket facility - Fig. RR1247
Incorporated in the vehicle electrical circuit is a facility for fitting a multi-pin trailer lighting socket.

The pick-up point is located behind the right hand rear tail light cluster and is accessible by removing the tail light assembly.

The pick-up point consists of a multi-pin pre-wired plug, a separate auxiliary fused line feed and reverse light lead.

Disconnect the battery.

Remove the rear tail light assembly and disconnect the electrical plug (1).

Remove the protective cap (2) from the trailer pick-up point plug. Feed a seven core cable (fitted with a pre-wired plug to one end-suitable for connection to pick-up point) down between the inner and outer body panels through the rear light aperture.

Pull the cable through the aperture between the chassis side member and fuel tank.

Fit two retaining clips to the cable and secure it to the rear end cross member. Connect the electrical leads to the vehicle trailer socket. (Refer to current trailer wiring regulations). Secure trailer socket to the tow bar. If it is necessary to provide a line feed and reverse light feed, provision is made for this by the presence of two extra leads (3) in the rear light aperture. Means of identification are as follows:

Fused auxiliary line feed-Pink lead

Reverse light feed-Green/Brown lead

Refit the rear tail light and reconnect the battery.

Care of the belts

The safety belts fitted to this vehicle represent valuable and possible life-saving equipment which should be regarded with the same importance as steering and brake systems. Frequent inspection is advisable to ensure continued effectiveness in the event of an accident.

Inspect belt webbing periodically for signs of abrasion or wear, paying particular attention to fixing points. Do not attempt to make any alterations or additions to the seat belts or their fixings as this could impair their efficiency.

If belts are correctly worn and stowed, deterioration will be kept to a minimum and protection to a maximum.

Seat belt assemblies must be replaced if the vehicle has been involved in an accident or if, upon inspection, there is evidence of cutting or fraying of the webbing, incorrect buckle or tongue locking function and/or any damage to the buckle.

Seat belt cleaning

Do not attempt to bleach the belt webbing or re-dye it. If the belts become soiled, sponge with warm water using a non-detergent soap and allow them to dry naturally. Do not use caustic soap, chemical cleaners or detergents for cleaning: do not dry with artificial heat or by direct exposure to the sun.

Checking inertia reel mechanism

The following road test must be carried out only under maximum safe road conditions, i.e. on a dry, straight, traffic-free road. With the safety belt fitted, drive the car at 8 km/h (5 m.p.h.) and brake sharply. The safety belt should lock automatically holding the user securely in position. It is important when braking that the body is not thrown forward in anticipation.

Snatch test

Whilst seated, fasten the seat belt and grip the shoulder belt at approximately shoulder level with the opposite hand. Pull the belt sharply in a downwards direction; the belt should lock.

Body care

It is always preferable to clean the bodywork and exterior trim with water and sponge, using plenty of water. Do not wash the vehicle in the direct rays of the sun, or use strong soap or chemical detergents. Any cleaning agents used should be washed of promptly and not allowed to dry on the bodywork. Dry with a chamois leather. After a period of use, the formation of traffic film will cause the paintwork to lose some of its lustre, even though the vehicle has been carefully and regularly washed. Brilliance may be restored after washing by using a non-abrasive cleaner and polish. Being the most durable, wax preparations are preferable, but where these are used regularly the old wax must first be removed with a cleaner before application of new wax. The frequency at which polishing is necessary will depend on local conditions of air polution.

The use of salt on the roads during frosty weather, sometimes in quite strong concentrations, is widely practised. Due to its highly corrosive nature, salt deposited should be washed off as soon as possible by thorough underwashing of the vehicle with a hose. Avoid using wax on the vinyl-covered rear quarter panels.

Door and body sill drain holes

Drain holes in the bottom of the doors and the sills should be kept clear using stiff wire.

Underbody maintenance

Corrosive materials used for ice and snow removal and dust control can collect on underbody parts. If these materials are not removed, accelerated rusting can occur on underbody parts such as frame, floor pan and the exhaust system.

At least every spring, flush these materials from the underbody with plain water. Take care to clean well any areas where mud and other debris can collect.

Cast alloy road wheels

The cast alloy road wheels are covered with a protective coating. To prevent corrosion it is essential that this coating is not damaged. To clean the wheels use a warm soapy liquid, stubborn stains can be removed using a soft brush.

Vinyl covered rear quarter panels

Wash the vinyl surface over with warm soapy water (use soap flakes or mild tablet soap). If dirt is ingrained the use of a soft nail brush will help. Rinse off with clean cold water ensuring that all soap is removed. During normal cleaning of the vehicle the vinyl will not be affected by mild detergents such as are used in automobile car washes. Avoid the use of wax polish, creams, solvents or strong detergents. Under no circumstances should white spirit or motor fuel be used to remove oil or grease marks from the vinyl surface.

Interior

We suggest you brush and clean the inside of the vehicle each time you wash and polish the outside. Use a vacuum cleaner where possible and ensure complete removal of all dust from the interior and trim. Clean the upholstry with a clean cloth or soft brush dampened with a little luke-warm, non-caustic, soapy water. Do not use detergents or household cleaners as these may cause damage. Remove all traces of suds with a clean, damp cloth and thoroughly dry the upholstery with a dry duster or towel. Wipe the fascia and instrument panel with a damp cloth only.

Wax or other polishes should not be used inside the vehicle. Dust in the headlining should be removed with a vacuum cleaner. Stains may be removed by rubbing briskly, without pressure, with a clean lint-free white cloth moistened with methylated spirit.

Carpets

Carpets may be cleaned with a brush or vacuum cleaner. Use a good quality carpet cleaner to remove stains.

Heated rear screen

The following precautions must be taken to avoid irreparable damage being caused to the printed circuit which is 'fired' on to the interior of the screen.

Do not remove labels or stickers from the screen with the aid of sharp instruments or similar equipment likely to scratch the glass.

Care should be taken to avoid inadvertently scratching the glass with a ringed finger etc., when cleaning or wiping the screen.

Do not clean the screen with harsh abrasives.

Paint finish damage

Any stone chips, fractures or deep scratches in the bodywork should be repaired promptly. Bare metal will corrode quickly and can develop into major repair expense. Minor chips and scratches can be repaired with touch-up materials available from your dealer. Larger areas of damage must be corrected to professional standards immediately.

Sheet metal damage

If your vehicle is damaged and requires sheet metal replacement, be sure the body repair shop restores rust protection by applying anti-corrosion material to the parts repaired or replaced.

SERVICE AND MAINTENANCE

5

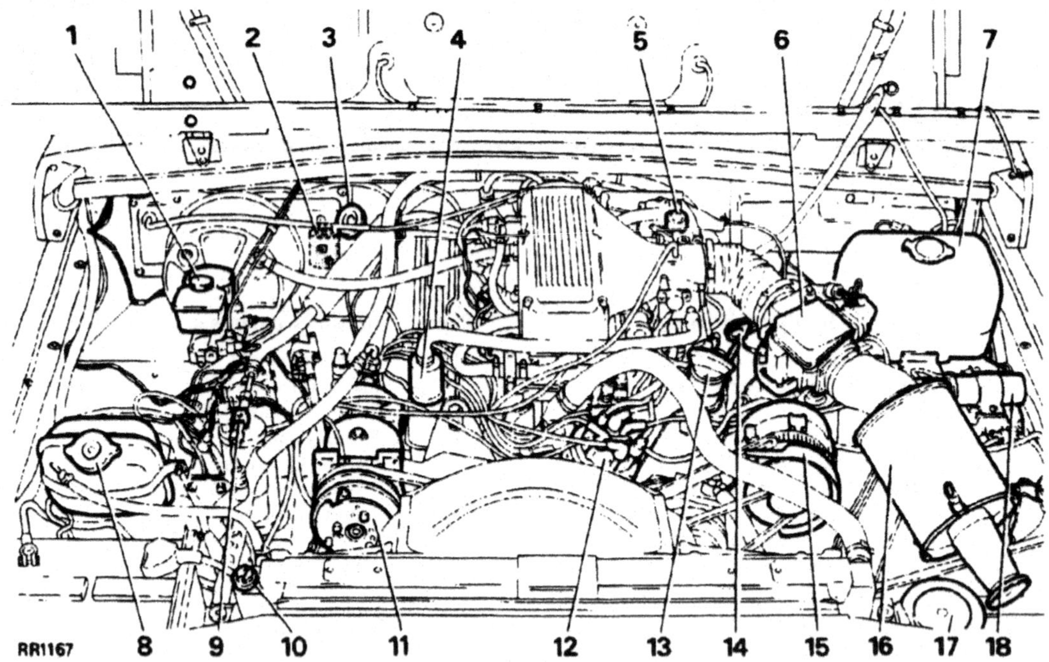

Fig. RR1167 - Under bonnet components of the electronic fuel injection, automatic transmission Range Rover with air conditioning.

1. Brake fluid reservoir
2. Clutch fluid reservoir (manual model only)
3. Automatic transmission fluid dipstick
4. Breather flame trap
5. Engine crankcase breather
6. Airflow meter
7. Front and rear screen wash and headlamp wash reservoir
8. Engine coolant expansion tank
9. Air conditioning receiver dryer sightglass
10. Radiator filler plug
11. Air compressor
12. Electronic distributor
13. Engine oil filler cap
14. Engine oil dipstick
15. Alternator
16. Air cleaner
17. Power steering fluid reservoir
18. Constant energy unit

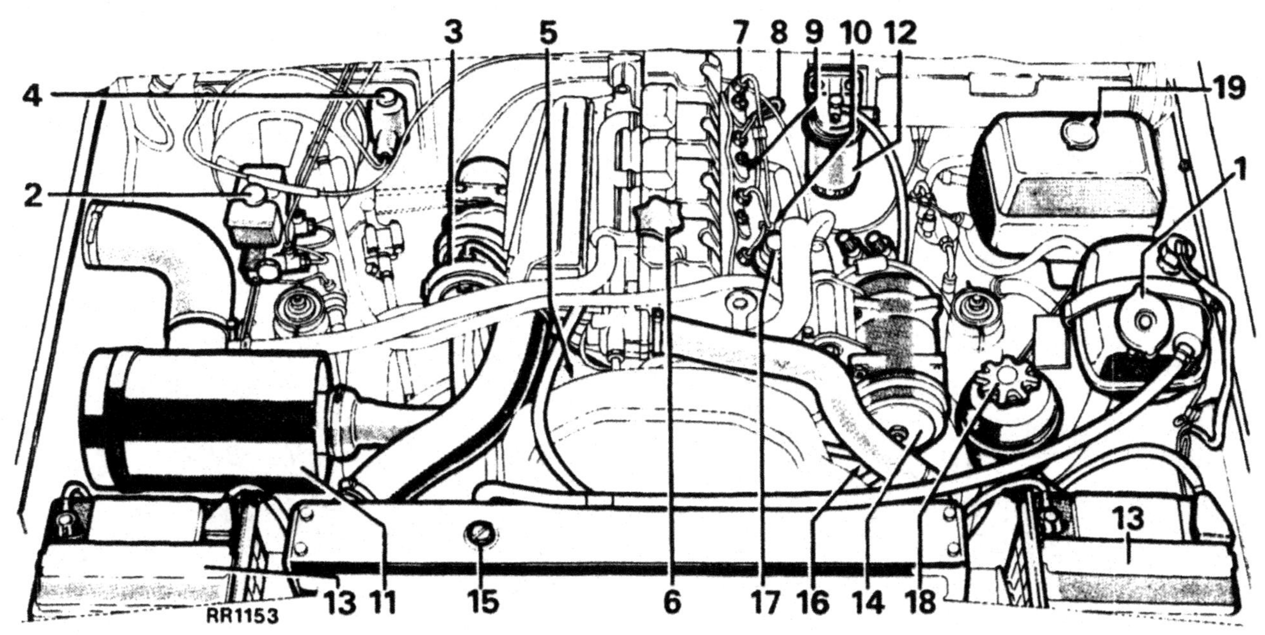

Engine Compartment
1. Coolant filler cap
2. Brake fluid reservoir
3. Turbo-charger
4. Clutch fluid reservoir
5. Oil filter cartridge
6. Engine oil filler cap
7. Injector
8. Engine oil dipstick
9. Glow plug

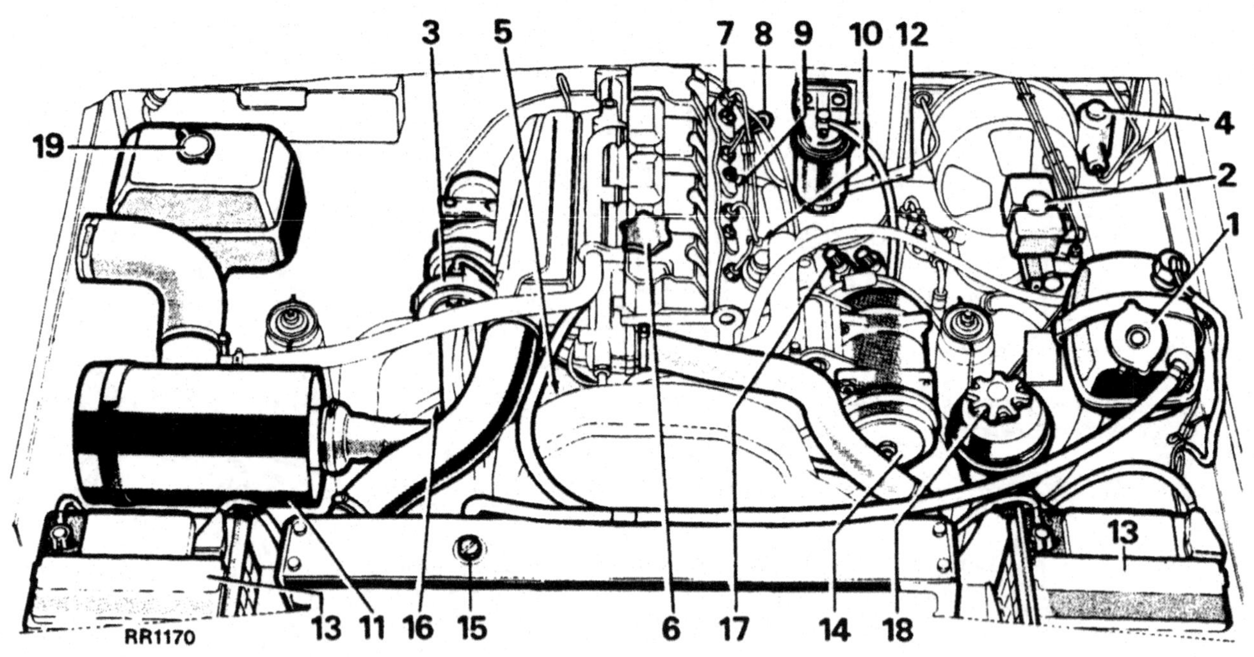

10. Fuel lift pump
11. Air cleaner
12. Fuel filter
13. Battery
14. Air conditioning compressor (option)

15. Coolant filler plug
16. Alternator
17. Fuel injection pump
18. Power steering fluid reservoir
19. Screen washer reservoir

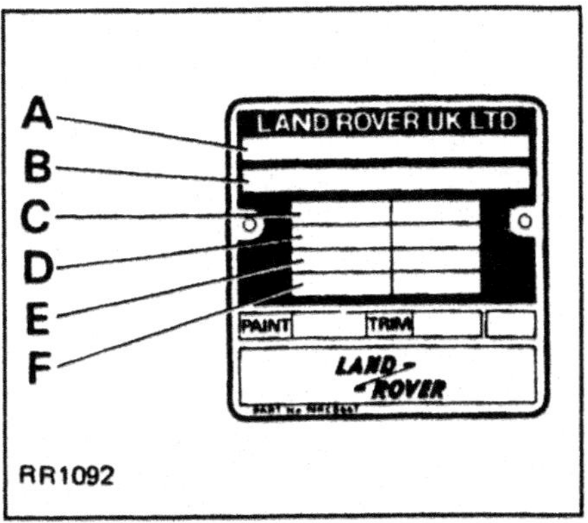

RR1092

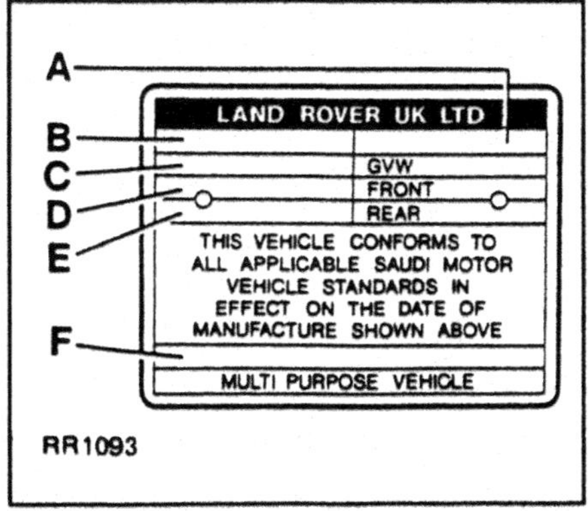

RR1093

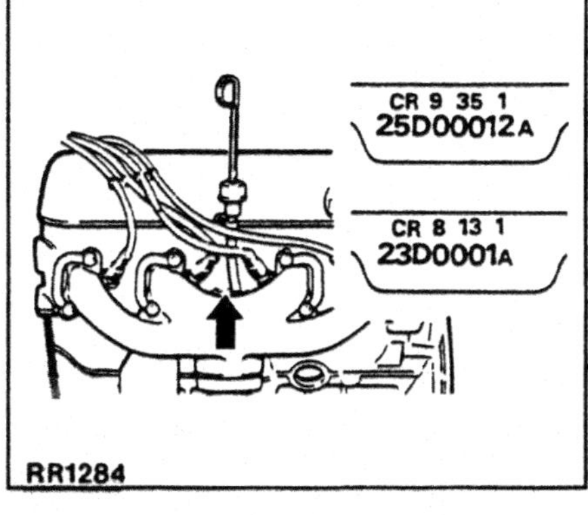

RR1284

Vehicle identification number (VIN)

The plate carrying the VIN together with the recommended maximum vehicle weights will be found under the bonnet riveted to the top of the front grille at the front of the engine compartment.

The VIN is also stamped on the right side of the chassis adjacent to the front shock absorber. Always quote the complete number when writing to the Company or your Distributor or Dealer on any matter concerning your Range Rover.

Key to vehicle identification number plate - (U.K. Europe and Australia) - Fig. RR1092
A   Type approval
B   VIN (minimum of 17 digits)
C   Maximum permitted laden weight
D   Maximum vehicle and trailer weight
E   Maximum road weight - front axle
F   Maximum road weight - rear axle

Key to vehicle identification number plate - (Saudi Arabia) - Fig. RR1093
A   Year of manufacture
B   Month of manufacture
C   Maximum vehicle weight
D   Maximum road weight - front axle
E   Maximum road weight - rear axle
F   VIN (minimum of 17 digits)

Engine serial number - Fig. RR1284 (example number only illustrated)

The engine serial number is stamped on a cast pad on the cylinder block between numbers 3 and 5 cylinders, i.e. on the left hand cylinder bank.

Note: *The appropriate engine compression ratio is stamped above the serial number and should be recorded, as the recommended fuel octane rating and some of the maintenance procedures vary according to the engine compression ratio, see other pages in this section and the 'Data' Section 6.*

Spare parts and accessories
When new parts or accessories are required, obtain genuine Land Rover parts, or parts supplied through sources approved by the Company.

Land Rover Distributors and Dealers are obligated to supply only such parts.

Through other sources, parts are often sold as being suitable for Range Rovers but frequently these are not made to the same standard or specification as the Company parts and are therefore less likely to give the requisite performance.

Genuine Land Rover parts and accessories are designed and tested for your vehicle and have the full backing of the Land Rover Limited Vehicle Service Statement. ONLY WHEN GENUINE LAND ROVER PARTS ARE USED CAN RESPONSIBILITY BE CONSIDERED UNDER THE TERMS OF THE STATEMENT.
In accordance with Company policy, the Genuine Parts range is one of continued improvement and should always be used when servicing or replacing parts on your Range Rover. For further information on the Genuine Parts range and Accessories see your Land Rover Distributor or Dealer.

Safety features embodied in the vehicle may be impaired if other than genuine parts are fitted. In certain territories, legislation prohibits the fitting of parts not to the vehicle manufacturer's specification. Owners purchasing accessories while travelling abroad should ensure that the accessory and its fitted location on the vehicle conform to mandatory requirements existing in their country of origin.

Vehicle Service Statement (Warranty)
Land Rover Limited issue (under the heading of Vehicle Service Statement) an undertaking regarding its Service Policy. Home market: The Vehicle Service Statement is supplied in the Literature Pack. Export market: The Warranty, Vehicle Service Statement, should be obtained from the Distributor or Dealer at the time of purchase.

The following notes are given for guidance in the event of a claim being put forward.
1. The vehicle or the part in respect of which a claim is made must be taken immediately to a Land Rover Distributor or Dealer. This should, wherever possible, be the Distributor or Dealer responsible for the sale of the vehicle to the owner.
2. The Distributor or Dealer will examine the parts or vehicle and will without charge advise on the action to be taken in respect of the claim. It will be noted that the Company must reserve the right to examine any alleged defective parts or material prior to the settlement of any claim.
3. It must be understood that the factors of wear and tear and any possible lack of maintenance or unapproved alteration will be taken into consideration in respect of any claim submitted.
4. It will be noted that tyres and glass are expressly excluded. The manufacturers of those tyres which the Company fits as standard to its vehicles will always be prepared to consider any genuine claim.
5. It is recommended that owners should arrange with their Insurance Company to provide separate cover for glass at the small extra cost involved.

Emission control
As air pollution from all sources is increasing, new and more stringent regulations are continually being introduced to limit the amount of harmful emissions from the internal combustion engine.

This requirement therefore determines the specification and type of equipment fitted to the vehicle and the calibration requirements for such equipment.

Owners should ensure that whenever new parts are fitted to their vehicles they obtain from the Distributor or Dealer who carried out the repairs assurance in writing that the parts concerned conform to the safety and emission control regulations currently in force.

Range Rover models supplied to European countries where emission control regulations apply are specially equipped to control the emissions of hydrocarbons, oxides of nitrogen and carbon monoxide from the exhaust system.

Crankcase emission control is achieved by venting the crankcase fumes to the carburetter intake to be burnt in the combustion chambers.

Electronic Fuel Injection (E.F.I.)
All engines with E.F.I., meet the emission regulations applicable in the territory to which they are supplied.

Notes on routine and general maintenance

This section has been prepared to give clear and simple information necessary for the efficient care and maintenance of your vehicle.

Lubrication and regular service maintenance are necessary to keep any vehicle in good mechanical condition and to minimise engine emissions during normal driving.

On the following pages will be found instructions on how to carry out many of the maintenance adjustments required.

Absolute cleanliness is essential when carrying out the work.

Climatic and operating conditions affect maintenance intervals to a large extent; in many cases, therefore the determination of such intervals must be left to the good judgement of the owner or to advice from a Range Rover Distributor or Dealer, but the recommendations will serve as a firm basis for maintenance work.

Note: The fuel system is pressurised and is controlled by electronic components. Any adjustment, maintenance or servicing requires absolute cleanliness, specialist knowledge and equipment which the average Range Rover driver will not possess. Therefore attention to any part of the system should only be entrusted to your local Dealer or Distributor to ensure safety and opptimum vehicle performance is obtained.

Planned maintenance

As efficient maintenance is one of the most prominent factors in ensuring the continued reliability and efficiency of your Range Rover, a detailed schedule has been prepared and is reproduced in the following pages to advise you of the planned maintenance requirements of your vehicle at specific mileages.

Some of the operations may require the use of specialised knowledge and equipment and are best left to your Range Rover Dealer or Distributor. The operations are shown numerically in the sequence recommended for maximum efficiency and the list gives the mileage intervals at which the work should be done. Unless otherwise state:

Column 'A' - indicates operations that should be done initially at 10,000 km (6,000 miles) or 6 months whichever occurs the sooner and at every 20,000 km (12,000 miles) or every 12 months whichever occurs the sooner, thereafter.

Column 'B' - indicates operations required at every 20,000 km (12,000 mile) intervals or every 12 months whichever occurs the sooner.

Note: In addition to the maintenance listed, it is recommended that:

At 30,000 km (18,000 mile) intervals or every 18 months, whichever is the sooner, the hydraulic brake fluid should be completely renewed.

At 60,000 km (36,000 mile) intervals or every 3 years, whichever is the sooner, all hydraulic brake fluid, seals and flexible hoses should be renewed, all working surfaces of the master cylinder, wheel cylinders and caliper cylinders should be examined and renewed where necessary.

At 60,000 km (36,000 mile) intervals remove all suspension dampers, test for correct operation, refit or renew as necessary.

 *WARNING: The levelling unit contains pressurised gas and must not be dismantled nor the casing screws removed. Repair is by replacement of the complete unit only.*

Boge Hydromat self levelling unit.

The Boge Hydromat levelling unit is totally self-contained and cannot be serviced. A slight oil seepage is permissible as this takes place due to the designed self lubrication, however should the level of seepage give rise for concern please take the vehicle to your nearest Land Rover dealer for investigation and correction if necessary.

Vehicles operating under arduous conditions will require more frequent servicing.

 *WARNING: Two wheel roller tests must be restricted to 5 km/hour (3 miles/hour) because the Range Rover is in constant four wheel drive.*

	A	B	
1		☐	Check conditions and security of seats, seat belt mounting, seat belts and buckles
2		☐	Check operation of foot brake and clutch* with engine running; stop engine
3		☐	Check operation of all lamps, horns, warning indicators
4		☐	Check operation of front/rear screen wipers and washers and condition of wiper blades
5	☐	☐	Check security and operation of hand brake; release fully after checking
6		☐	Check rear view mirrors for security, cracks and crazing
7	☐	☐	Remove road wheels
8	☐	☐	Check tyres for: compliance with manufacturers specification; visually for cuts, lumps, bulges, uneven tread wear and depth; tyre pressures (including spare) adjust if required - see 'Data' Section
9	☐	☐	Inspect brake pads for wear, calipers for leaks and discs for condition
10	☐	☐	Check for oil/fluid leaks from steering and suspension systems
11		☐	Check condition and security of steering unit, joints and gaiters
12	☐	☐	Refit road wheels to original position

	A	B	
13		☐	Drain flywheel/converter housing if drain plug is fitted for wading (refit)
14	☐		Check/top up engine oil
15		☐	Renew engine oil and filter
16	☐	☐	Check/top up automatic transmission fluid*) Automatic
17	24,000 ml / 40,000 km		Renew automatic) Transmission transmission fluid* and filter)
18	☐		Check/top up gearbox oil) Manual
19		☐	Renew gearbox oil) Gearbox
20	☐	☐	Check/top up transfer box oil) Automatic
21	24,000 ml / 40,000 km		Renew transfer box oil) Transmission)
22	☐		Check/top up transfer box oil) Manual
23		☐	Renew transfer box oil) Gearbox
24	☐	☐	Check/top up front axle oil
25	24,000 ml / 40,000 km		Renew front axle oil
26	☐	☐	Check/top up swivel pin housing oil
27	24,000 ml / 40,000 km		Renew swivel pin housing oil
28	☐	☐	Check/top up rear axle oil
29	24,000 ml / 40,000 km		Renew rear axle oil
30		☐	Check visually brake, fuel, clutch pipes/unions for chafing, leaks and corrosion

* Where applicable

	A	B	
31	☐	☐	Check exhaust system for leakage and security
32		☐	Lubricate hand brake mechanical linkage and adjust to manufacturers instructions if required
33	☐	☐	Lubricate propeller shaft universal joints
34	24,000 40,000	ml km	Lubricate propeller shaft sliding joints
35		☐	Check tightness of propeller shaft coupling bolts
36		☐	Ensure front and rear axle breathers are free from obstruction
37		☐	Check security and condition of suspension fixings
38		☐	Check for oil leaks from engine and transmission
39	48,000 80,000	ml km	Clean fuel pump filter
40		☐	Check suspension self levelling unit for leaks
41	48,000 80,000	ml km	Renew fuel filter (E.F.I. engines)
42		☐	Renew fuel filter element (carburetter engines)
43		☐	Renew air cleaner element(s)
44		☐	Check air cleaner dump valve, clean or renew
45	24,000 40,000	ml km	Renew engine breather filter
46		☐	Clean or renew engine flame trap(s)
47	☐	☐	Check condition of driving belts - adjust if required
48	48,000 80,000	ml km	Renew charcoal canister
49		☐	Check crankcase breathing system for leaks, hoses for security and condition
50	☐		Clean/adjust spark plugs
51		☐	Renew spark plugs
52	☐	☐	Top up carburetter piston dampers*
53	☐	☐	Check/top up cooling system
54		☐	Check brake servo hose for security and condition
55		☐	Check ignition wiring and HT leads for fraying, chafing and deterioration.
56		☐	Clean distributor cap, check for cracks and tracking.
57	☐	☐	Check/adjust ignition timing (refer to the relevant repair operation manual for details)
58		☐	Lubricate accelerator control linkages and pedal pivot
59		☐	Check throttle operation
60	☐	☐	Lubricate all locks (not steering lock), hinges and doors - check mechanisms
61		☐	Check operation of all doors, bonnet and tailgate locks

* Where applicable

	A	B	
62	☐	☐	Check/adjust carburetter mixture setting, fuel injection idle air mixture and engine idle speed with engine at normal running temperature
63	☐	☐	Check operation of air intake temperature control system
64		☐	Check/adjust steering box
65	☐	☐	Check power steering system for leaks, hydraulic pipes and unions for chafing and corrosion
66	☐	☐	Check/top up fluid in power steering reservoir
67	☐	☐	Check/top up clutch fluid reservoir
68	☐	☐	Check/top up brake fluid reservoir
69	☐	☐	Check/top up windscreen, rear screen and headlamp washer reservoirs.
70		☐	Check cooling and heating system for leaks, hoses for security and condition
71		☐	Check/top up battery electrolyte
72		☐	Remove battery connections; clean and grease - refit
73		☐	Check/adjust headlamp alignment
74		☐	Check front wheel alignment

	A	B	
75	☐	☐	**Road test - Check:**
	☐	☐	And ensure automatic gearbox starter/isolator switch will only operate in 'P' and 'N'*
	☐	☐	For excessive engine noise
	☐	☐	Clutch for slipping/judder/spinning*
	☐	☐	Gear selection/noise - high and low range
	☐	☐	Automatic gear selection/shift speeds*
	☐	☐	Steering for noise/abnormal effort required
	☐	☐	All instruments, pressure, fuel and temperature gauges, warning indicators
		☐	Heater and air conditioning systems*
	☐	☐	Heated rear screen
	☐	☐	Shock absorbers (irregularities in ride)
	☐	☐	Foot brake, on emergency stop, pulling to one side, binding, pedal effort
	☐	☐	Handbrake efficiency
		☐	Fully extend seat belt, check for correct operation of retraction and latching. Inertia belts lock when snatched and when vehicle is on slope
	☐	☐	Road wheel balance
	☐	☐	Transmission for vibrations
	☐	☐	For body noises (squeaks and rattles)

* Where applicable

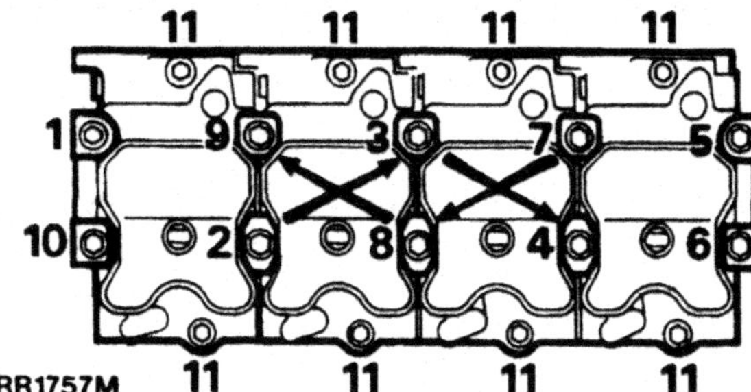

The following supplementary schedule should be used together with the schedule in the preceding pages for the complete maintenance of Range Rover Diesel models.

Every 500 km (250 miles)
- Check engine oil level

After first 1,500 km (1,000 miles)
- Tighten inlet manifold, exhaust manifold and turbo-charger bolts
- Change engine oil and oil filter
- Check drive belt tension
- General check for fluid leaks
- Check tappet clearance

Every 10,000 km (6,000 miles)*
- Change engine oil and oil filter
- Drain sedimenter
- Change fuel filter
- Check for fluid leaks
- Check drive belt tension

Every 20,000 km (12,000 miles)**
- Clean lift pump filter
- Clean fuel sedimenter
- Clean fuel tank breather pipe
- Change air filter element
- Check engine cold idle speed

Every 40,000 km (24,000 miles)
- Check tappet clearance
- Check glow plug operation (continuity)
- Remove diesel injectors, spray test and refit

Every 80,000 km (48,000 miles)
- Remove intercooler element and flush out

Every 96,000 km (60,000 miles)
- Check turbo-charger impeller shaft axial and radial clearance
- Check wastegate operation

Special Maintenance Instruction -Fig. RR1757M
Tighten in the sequence shown above, the centre six cylinder head bolts a further 10° at the first 40,000 km (24,000 miles) only and similarly at the first 40,000 km (24,000 miles) after the cylinder heads have been removed and refitted.
The maintenance intervals in this schedule are for European highway driving conditions. For change intervals of engine oil and all filters, under severe abnormal operating conditions, consult your nearest Range Rover Dealer.

* Or every 6 months whichever is sooner.
** Or every 12 months whichever is sooner.

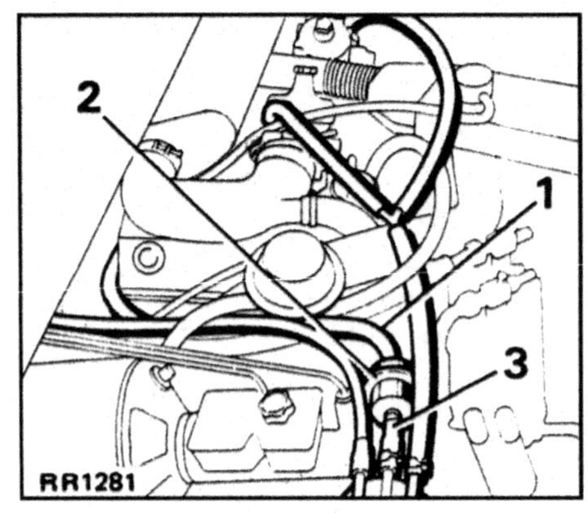

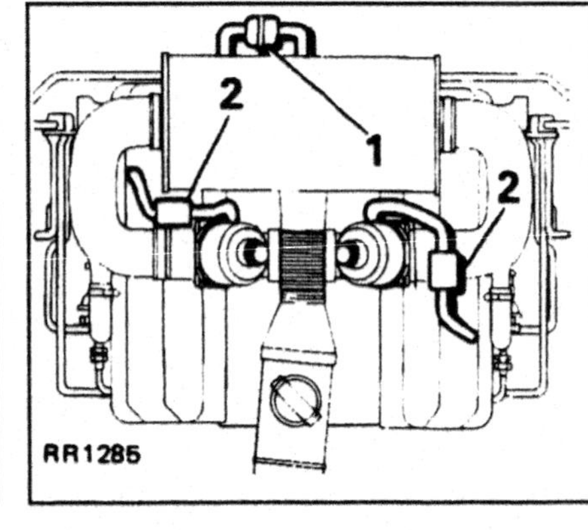

Carburetter fuel systems

Exhaust emissions are controlled by 'Pulsair' self-induced air injection into exhaust ports via one-way pulse air valves, alterations to carburation characteristics and ignition settings. Carburetter adjustments and ignition timing are accurately set at the factory and under normal circumstances do not require attention except at the specified maintenance periods as detailed on the following pages.

However, should it become necessary to check any aspect of carburetter adjustment or ignition timing, the work must be carried out by a qualified Range Rover Distributor or Dealer who has the specialised equipment needed to carry out adjustments to the close limits necessary to ensure that the engine conforms to legal requirements in respect of exhaust emission.

Evaporative loss control system (where fitted) - Fig. RR1281

Fitted on vehicles for certain territories, this system reduces the amount of fuel vapour vented to atmosphere.

An adsorption canister, located in the engine compartment collects vapour from the engine fuel system and is purged by engine depression which causes the vapour to be burnt in the combustion chamber.

The illustration shows the system on a carburetter model: the system on fuel injection models uses only two hoses and vapour is vented into the plenum chamber.

Renewal of the canister is described later in this section (Fig. RR1283) but if further assistance is required consult your nearest Distributor or Dealer.

Crankcase emission control - Fig. RR1285

To comply with current regulations concerning engine emission control, crankcase emissions from the Range Rover V8 engine are vented into the carburetter to be burnt with the fuel/air mixture.

The breathing cycle is performed by tapping clean air from the rear of the air cleaner, then to the crankcase via a hose and filter (1).

The crankcase fumes rise via the pushrod tubes to the rocker covers where they are then transferred to the carburetter via hoses and flame traps (2).

Finally the fumes are drawn into the engine to be burnt with the fuel/air mixture.

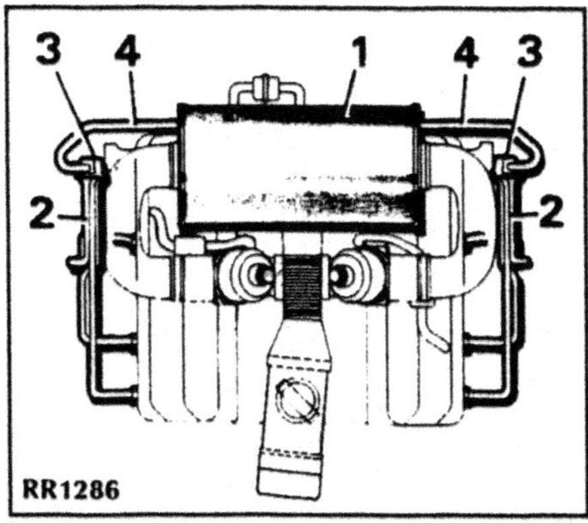

Carburetter models with emission engines 'Pulsair' system

'Pulsair' is a system of self-induced air injection into the exhaust ports through one-way valves and a configuration of pipes from the air cleaner. The system is used to reduce further the carbon monoxide (CO) emission to the atmosphere in compliance with territorial regulations.

'Pulsair' air injection system - Fig. RR1286
1. Air cleaner
2. Pulsair manifold
3. Check valve housing
4. Connecting hoses

Ignition timing

The correct setting of ignition timing is of extreme importance, and the satisfactory functioning of the emission control system relies to a large extent on its accuracy. It is necessary to set the ignition timing dynamically with the engine at idling speed. This requires the use of a suitable tachometer, for determining the engine speed, and a stroboscopic lamp for determining the points in the engine cycle at which the ignition sparks occur. It is obvious therefore that this work should be carried out by a Range Rover Distributor or Dealer.

However where, in an emergency, the equipment and expertise are not available, the following may prove useful.

See Data Section 6 engine details for ignition timing for the various engine version.

If distributor has been disturbed:

Prior to engine being started, set the ignition timing statically (to the specification given in the 'General Data' Section 6) by the basic timing lamp method. (This sequence is to give only an approximation in order that the engine may be run. The engine must not be started after distributor disturbance until this check has been carried out.)

Couple stroboscopic timing lamp and tachometer to engine following the manufacturers instructions.

Disconnect the vacuum pipe from the distributor.

Start engine; with no load and not exceeding 3,000 rpm, run engine until normal operating temperature is reached. Check that the normal idling speed falls within the tolerance specified in Data section.

Idle speed for timing purposes must not exceed 750 rpm, and this speed should be achieved by removing a breather hose, **NOT BY ADJUSTING CARBURETTER IDLE SETTING SCREWS.**
With the distributor clamping bolt slackened, turn distributor until the timing flash coincides with the timing pointer and the correct timing mark on the rim of the torsional vibration damper as shown in the table.

Retighten the distributor clamping bolt to 19 to 21,7 Nm (14 to 16 lbf/ft).

Recheck timing to ensure that retightening has not disturbed the distributor position.

Refit vacuum pipe.

Disconnect stroboscopic timing lamp and tachometer from engine.

Ignition timing - Diesel

Due to the special skills and equipment required for this work, it should only be carried out by a Range Rover Distributor or Dealer.

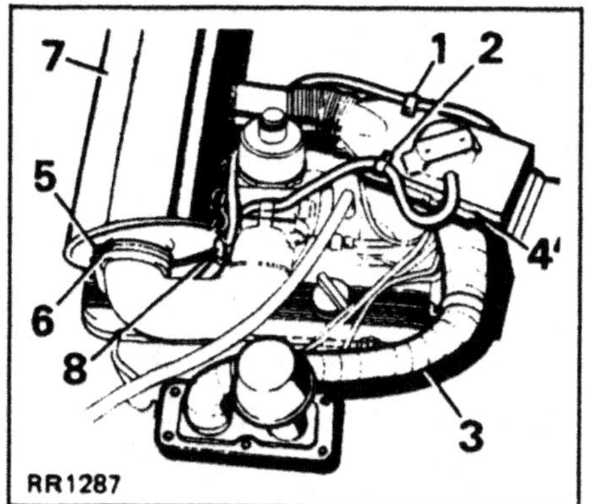

Renew air intake cleaner elements

Attention to the air cleaner is extremely important. Replace elements and clean or renew dump valve every 20,000 km (12,000 miles) or 12 months. Under severe dusty conditions this must be done more frequently as performance will be seriously affected if the engine is run with an excessive amount of dust or industrial deposits in the elements.

For air cleaner removal proceed as follows, following the instructions applicable to the type of air cleaner fitted:

Carburetter models

Air cleaner removal - Fig. RR1287

Slacken the clip (1) retaining the advance/retard vacuum pipes from the air intake and release pipes from intake.

Slacken the clip (2) retaining hose air cleaner to temperature sensing device from air intake and remove pipe from flap valve on intake.

Slacken the hose clip attaching warm air intake hose (3) to air intake.

Withdraw air intake (4) from steady post and hoses.

Slacken the clips (5) and remove the air cleaner elbows.

Emission engines - Slacken the clips (6) and withdraw 'Pulsair' hoses if necessary.

Remove the air cleaner (7) from the retaining posts by lifting and easing forward.

At the same time disconnect the hose engine breather filter to air cleaner. Place air cleaner to one side.

Remove hose (8) with the non-return valve from the manifold.

The air cleaner can now be completely removed.

Note: When removing the elbows from air cleaner and intake adaptor, care must be taken not to damage the 'O' ring seals and rubber sealing rings as this may affect conformity to emission regulations.

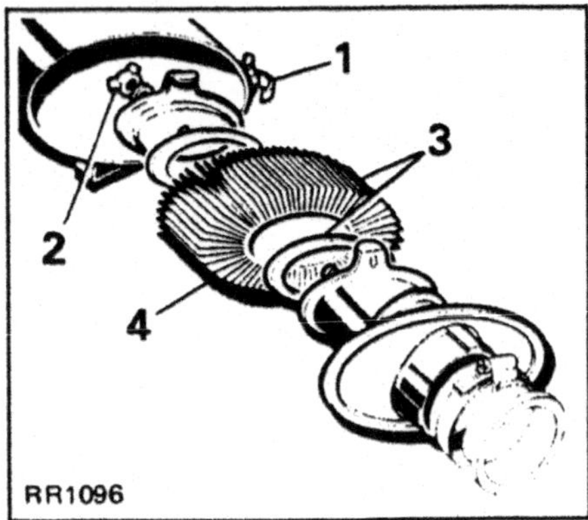

RR1096

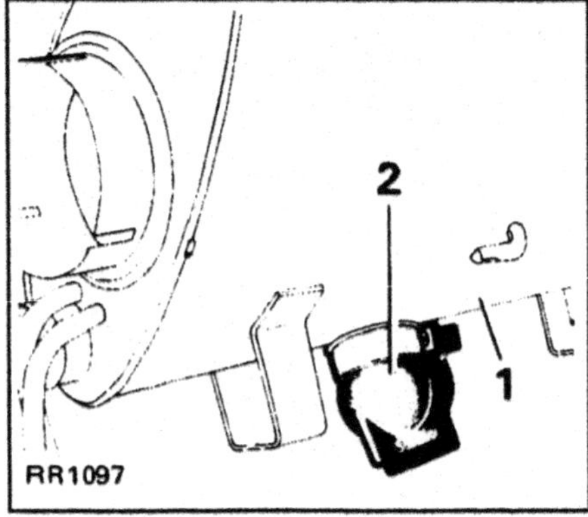

RR1097

Air cleaner elements - Fig. RR1096
Release the two clips (1) at each side of air cleaner casing and withdraw the frames and elements.

Release wing nuts and withdraw plate and sealing washers (2) and discard old elements.

Discard any faulty rubber seals (3).

Assemble new elements (4) to air cleaner frames and secure with seals, end plate and wing nuts.

Fit the carrier frames and elements into the air cleaner body and secure with clips.

Check, clean or renew dump valve as follows:

Check air cleaner/dump valve, clean or renew - Fig. RR1097
A flexible dump valve is fitted to the underside of the air cleaner casing to collect debris or water that enters the air cleaner body.

Remove the air cleaner (1).

Squeeze open the dump valve (2) and check that the interior is clean. Also check that the rubber is flexible and in a good condition.

If necessary, remove the dump valve to clean the interior. Fit a new valve if the original is in a poor condition.

Refitting the air cleaner
Reconnect hose with non-return valve to the manifold connection.

Place air cleaner on to the retaining posts.

At the same time reconnect the breather filter hose to the base of the air cleaner.

Emission engines - Reconnect and secure 'Pulsair' hoses.

Replace air intake on to steady post and reconnect air cleaner and warm air intake hoses. Tighten clip.

Reconnect pipe, air cleaner to temperature sensor and vacuum advance/retard pipe to air intake. Position pipes in retaining clips on air intake and tighten clips.

Apply a smear of petroleum jelly (not engine oil) to the 'O' rings and sealing rings to aid fitment. Refit the air cleaner elbows and tighten the clips.

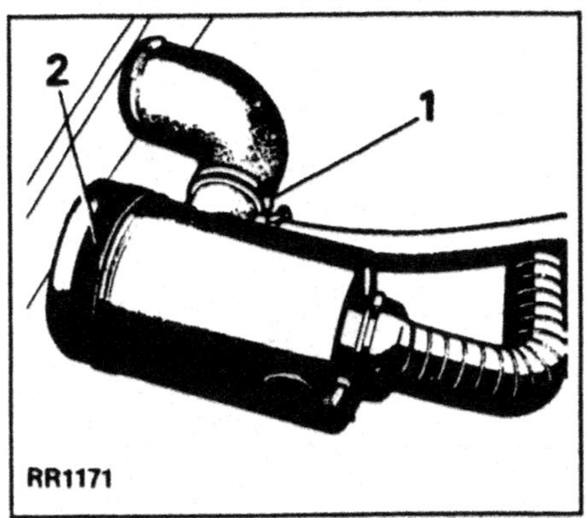

RR1171

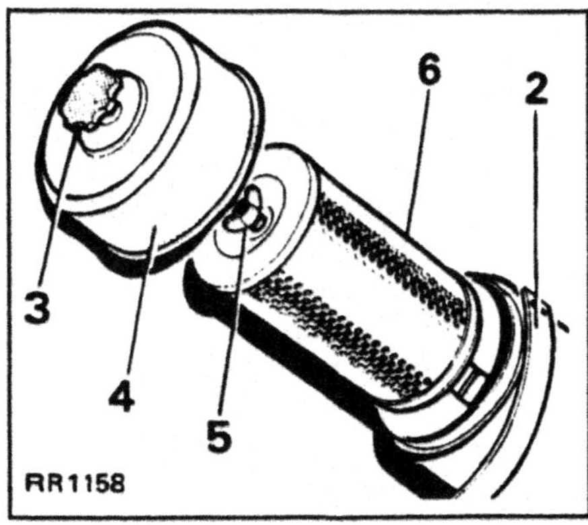

RR1158

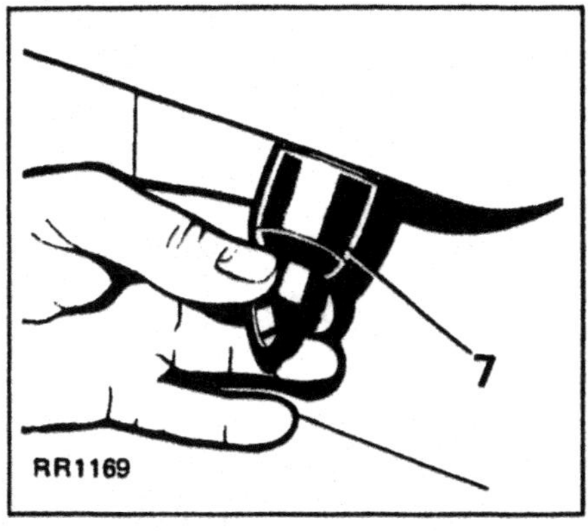

RR1169

Diesel model

Renew air cleaner element - Fig RR1171 and Fig RR1158

Disconnect the hose (1) from the air cleaner. Release the retaining strap (2) and lift up the air cleaner assembly.

Unscrew the knob (3) and remove the end cover (4) from the air cleaner casing. Unscrew the wing nut (5), discard the element (6) and wipe clean the casing and cover.

Check air cleaner dump valve - Fig. RR1169

Squeeze open the dump valve (7) and check that the interior is clean. Also, check that the rubber is flexible and in good condition. If necessary, remove the dump valve to clean the interior. Fit a new valve if the original is in poor condition.

Fit a new element, rubber seal end first, and reassemble the air cleaner.

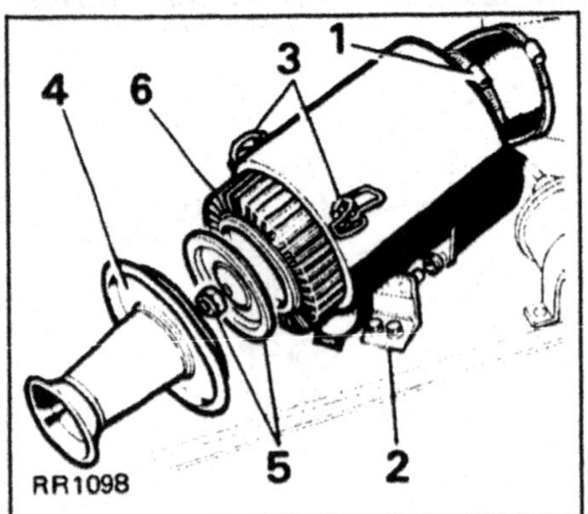

RR1098

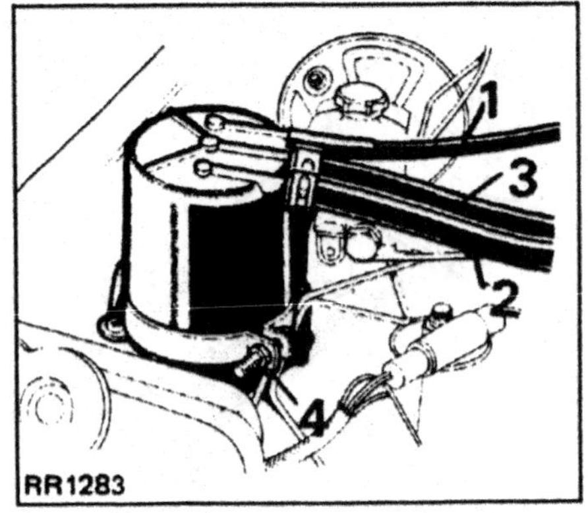

RR1283

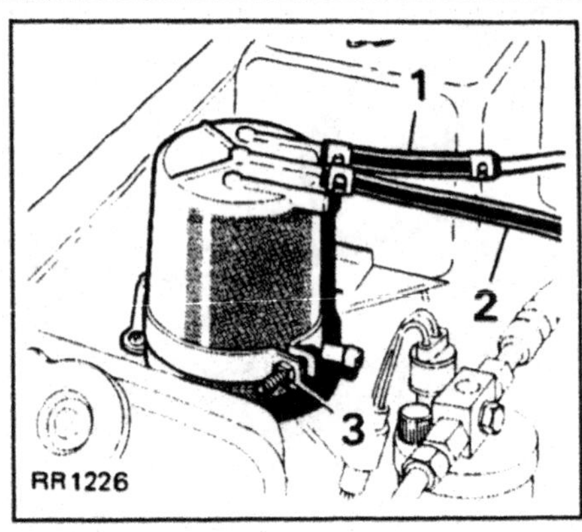

RR1226

Fuel injection models

Air cleaner element renewal - Fig. RR1098
Release the clip (1) securing the hose to the rear of the air cleaner body. Remove the two nuts and bolts (2) on the retaining bracket and remove the complete air cleaner assembly from the vehicle.

Release the three clips (3) and detach the front inlet tube (4). Remove the nut and end plate (5), withdraw and discard the old element (6).

Insert the new element, reassemble the unit and refit in the vehicle.

Evaporative loss control system (Gulf States carburetter models only)

Adsorption canister renewal - Fig. RR1283
Disconnect the three hoses (1, 2 and 3) from the top of the canister, slacken the canister clamp screw (4) and remove and discard the canister.

Fit the new canister, reversing the above instructions.

⚠️ *WARNING: The use of compressed air to clean an adsorption canister or clear a blockage in the evaporative system is very dangerous and should not be practised. An explosive gas present in a fully saturated canister may be ignited by the heat generated when compressed air passes throught the canister.*

Evaporative loss control system (Gulf States and Australian fuel injection models only)

Adsorption canister renewal - Fig. RR1226
Disconnect the two hoses, (1 and 2) from the top of the canister, slacken the canister clamp screw (3) and remove and discard the canister.

Fit the new canister, reversing the above instruction.

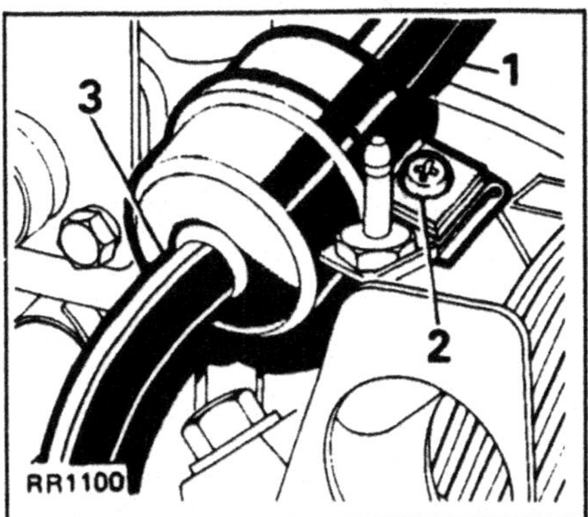

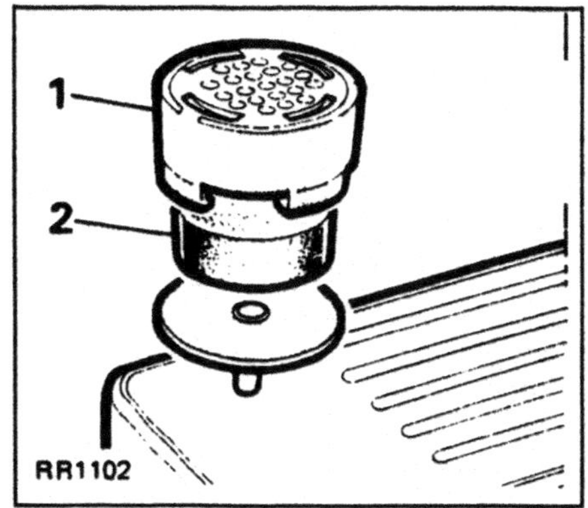

Carburetter models

Renew engine breather filter - Fig. RR1100

Remove the air cleaner.

Withdraw the rear hose from the filter (1) and slacken the filter clip (2). Withdraw the filter from the clip and front hose (3). Fit new filter with the end marked 'IN' facing the air cleaner.

Alternatively, if the filter is marked with arrows, they must point rearwards. Refit hoses and tighten clips.

Fuel injection models

Crankcase air intake filter renewal - Fig. RR1102

Carefully prise the filter outer cover (1) upwards to release it from the rocker cover (2). Remove and discard the sponge filter element and insert the new element. Replace the filter holder by clipping it firmly into place on the rocker cover.

CAUTION: On no account use any spurious sponge foam for this application as this could create difficulties with the engine breathing system.

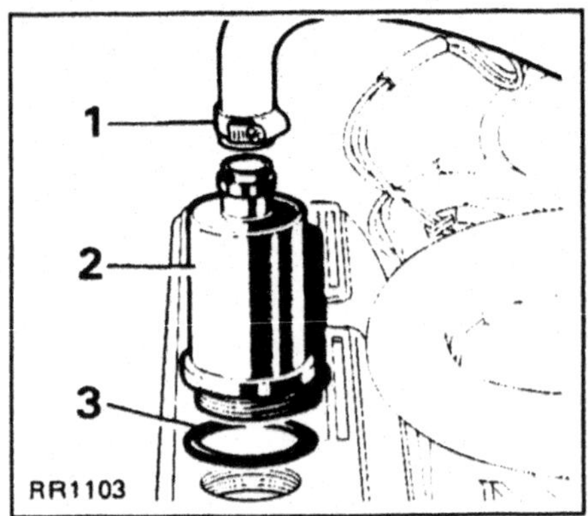

RR1103

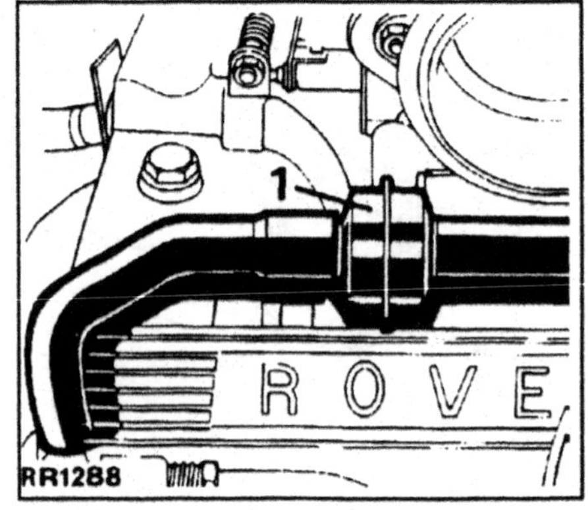

RR1288

Fuel injection models

Crankcase flame trap/breather filter cleaning or renewal - Fig. RR1103 Release the clip (1) and draw the hose off the canister (2), then unscrew the canister and remove it from the rocker cover.

Remove the large 'O' ring (3) from the screwed end of the canister and visually inspect the condition of the wire gauze inside. If it is in poor condition, the complete assembly should be renewed but if the condition of the gauze is acceptable the canister and gauze can be immersed in a petrol bath for a short time to clear any debris within. On removal from the bath the canister and gauze should be allowed to dry out in still air.

When dry, fit a new rubber 'O' ring and screw the canister into the rocker cover to hand tightness only. Refit the hose and its clip securely.

WARNING: Do not use compressed air to dry off traces of petrol or remove debris as this could cause fire or personal injury.

Carburetter models

Engine flame trap cleaning or removal - Fig. RR1288
Pull the flame trap hoses (1) out of the retaining clips and pull the hoses from the flame trap (2). Withdraw the flame trap and inspect the internal gauze. If it is in poor condition renew the unit but if it is in acceptable condition, clean it in a petrol bath and allow it to dry in still air.

Refit the hoses securely to the renewed or cleaned flame trap and return the hoses to their respective retaining clips.

Note: The hose from flame trap to plenum chamber should be inspected for cracks, general deterioration and blockage caused by debris. Any hose which may be suspected is to be replaced.

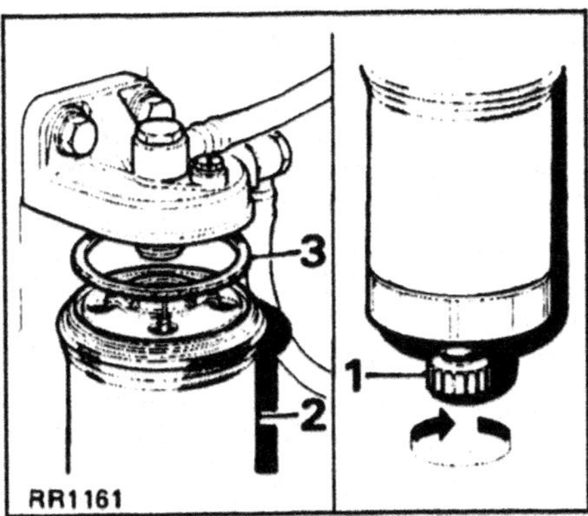

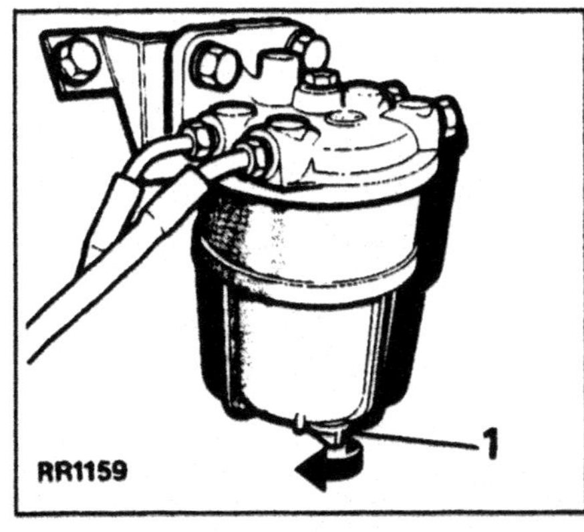

Main fuel filter - Fig. RR1161

Draining off water and sediment

It is essential that any water and sediment in the fuel filter is drained off, as water in the fuel can result in damage to the injection pump.

Hold a small receptacle beneath the drain cock.

Unscrew the drain cock (1) at the bottom of the filter half a turn.

Drain off water and sediment.

Immediately fuel starts to flow from the drain cock tighten the drain cock.

Note: Any delay in tightening the drain cock when fuel starts to flow could possibly mean bleeding the fuel system.

Renewing the fuel filter element

Clean the area around the filter head, and place a container beneath the filter.

Unscrew the filter (2) - a quantity of fuel will be released - and discard the filter. A hexagon is formed on the base of the filter for unscrewing it with a filter wrench.

Wet the seal (3) of the new filter with fuel.

Screw the new filter into position and tighten with a filter wrench.

Ensure that the drain cock at the bottom of the filter is screwed up tight.

Fuel sedimenter

The sedimenter is attached to the left-hand side of the chassis frame near the fuel tank, and increases the working life of the fuel filter by removing the larger droplets of water and larger particles of foreign matter from the fuel.

Drain off the water as follows:

Drain off water - Fig. RR1159

Slacken off drain plug (1) and allow water to run out. When pure diesel fuel is emitted, tighten the drain plug.

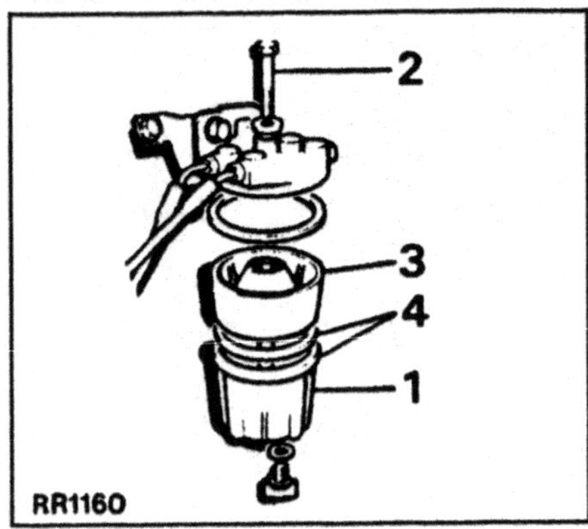

RR1160

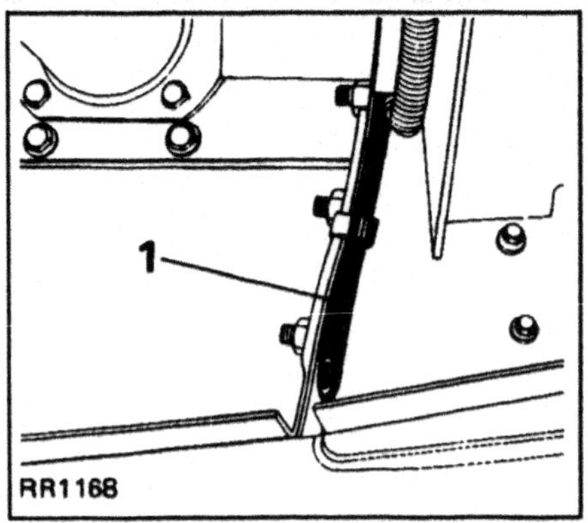

RR1168

Clean element - Fig. RR1160
If fuel is used from dubious storage facilities, the sedimenter should be removed and cleaned as circumstances require or as specified in the maintenance schedule.

Disconnect the fuel inlet pipe from the sedimenter and raise pipe above the level of the fuel tank and support in this position to prevent fuel draining from the tank.

Support the sedimenter bowl (1), unscrew the bolt (2) on the top of the unit and remove the bowl.

Remove the sedimenter element (3) and clean all parts in kerosene. Fit new seals (4) and reassemble the sedimenter.

Slacken off the drain plug; when pure diesel fuel runs out, tighten plug. Start the engine and check the sedimenter for leaks.

Cleaning fuel tank breather pipe - Fig. RR1168
The fuel tank breather pipe must be cleaned regularly to prevent diesel oil residue and road dust causing blockage. The pipe is located underneath the vehicle and runs down the body panel joint, to the rear of the fuel tank filler neck.

Clean the pipe at the intervals specified in the maintenance schedule, or more frequently if operating in dusty or muddy conditions.

Wipe clean the end of the breather pipe (1) and use a short piece of wire to clear the inside.

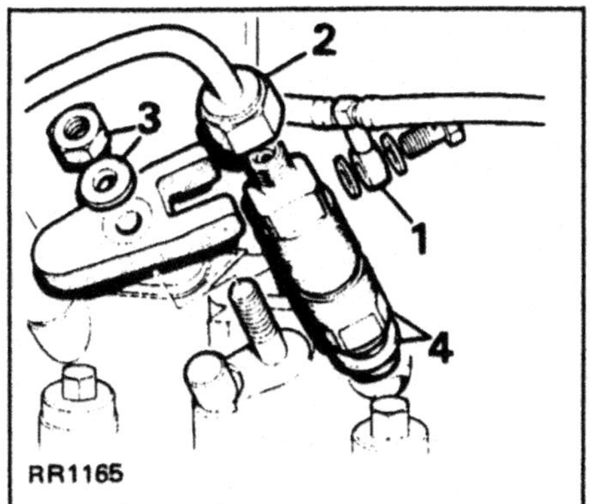

Injectors - Fig. RR1165
To locate a faulty injector, slacken the feed pipe union nut on the suspected injector and run the engine slowly. If there is no change in the engine performance or if a faulty condition, such as a smoky exhaust, has disappeared, it can be assumed that the injector is faulty and a replacement injector should be fitted.

Unscrew the retaining nut and remove the rocker cover adjacent to the injector to be removed.

Disconnect the fuel leak-off pipe (1) and the high pressure pipe (2) from the injector.

Unscrew the mounting nut (3), and remove the mounting clamp, injector (4) and sealing washer.

Before fitting an injector fit a new sealing washer.

Fit the injector, its mounting clamp and tighten the injector retaining nut to a torque tightness of 1,7 kgf m (12 lbf ft).

Refit the high pressure feed pipe and leak-off pipe.

Refit the rocker cover; renew the gasket if it is damaged; check that the collars and seals are located on the top of the rocker cover before fitting and tightening the rocker cover.

Note: Fit the rocker cover with the oil filler cap on No. 1 cylinder and the rocker cover with the breather pipe to No. 2 and 3 cylinders.

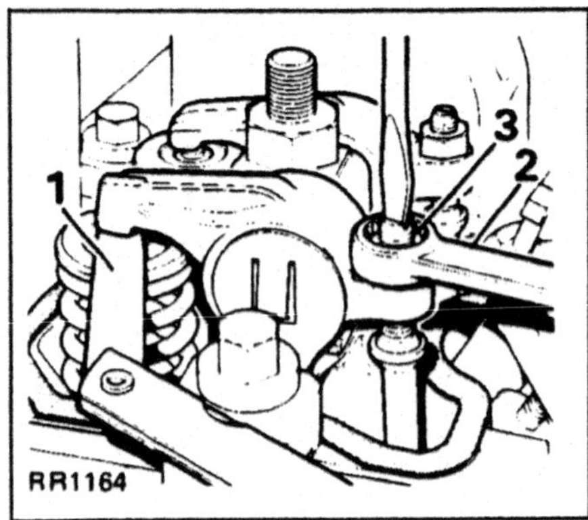

RR1164

Tappet adjustment - Fig. RR1164
The correct clearance is: inlet and exhaust, 0,30 mm (0.012 in) engine cold.

Remove rocker cover
Unscrew the centre retaining bolts and remove the rocker covers for each cylinder, taking care not to lose the seals from the top of the rocker covers.

Check and adjust tappets.
Turn the engine over until number one valve (counting from front of engine) is fully open.

Using a 0,30 mm (0.012 in) feeler gauge (1) check the clearance between the valve tip and rocker pad of number seven valve.

Adjust the clearance by slackening the lock nut (2) and turning the tappet adjusting screw (3) clockwise to reduce clearance and anti-clockwise to increase clearance. Recheck the clearance after tightening the lock nut.

Continue to check and adjust the remaining tappets ion the follwoing sequence:

Set No. 1 tappet with No. 7 valve fully open
Set No. 8 tappet with No. 2 valve fully open
Set No. 5 tappet with No. 3 valve fully open
Set No. 4 tappet with No. 6 valve fully open
Set No. 7 tappet with No. 1 valve fully open
Set No. 2 tappet with No. 8 valve fully open
Set No. 3 tappet with No. 5 valve fully open
Set No. 6 tappet with No. 4 valve fully open

Alternative method
Rotate the crankshaft until the valves of number four cylinder are rocking then adjust the clearance of number one valves. Adjust the remaining valve clearances in the following order:-

Adjust:-
Valves of No. 3 cyl with No. 2 valves rocking
Valves of No. 4 cyl with No. 1 valves rocking
Valves of No. 2 cyl with No. 3 valves rocking

Refitting the rocker covers
Clean the rocker cover gasket sealing face.

Inspect the rocker cover gaskets; renew if damaged.

Position the rocker cover with the oil filler cap on No. 1 cylinder, and the rocker cover with the breather pipe to No. 3 cylinder.

Check that the collars and seals are located on the top of the rocker covers, then fit the rocker covers and tighten the retaining nuts.

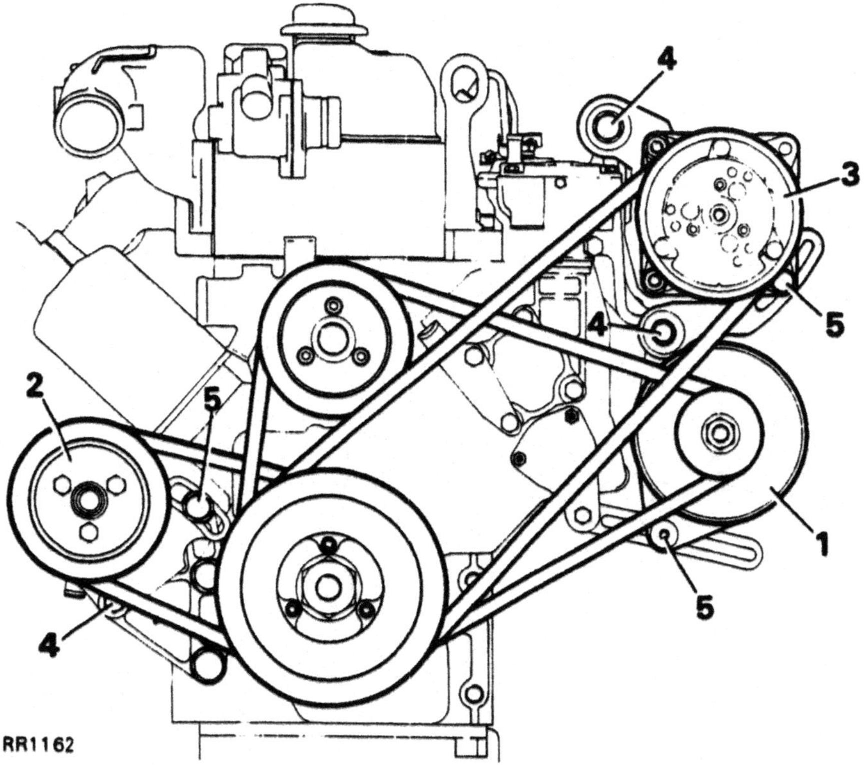

Check and adjust drive belts

WARNING: Disconnect the battery to prevent any possibility of the starter motor being operated.

The procedure for checking and adjusting the drive belts for the alternator (1), power steering pump (2) and the optional, air conditioning compressor (3) is similar.

Note: Any marks on the outside of the air conditioning drive belt, caused by the belt slipper bracket, can be ignored.

Right-hand steering - Fig. RR1162

5 DIESEL MODEL DRIVE BELTS - LEFT HAND STEERING

Check the tension of each drive belt, the belts should deflect within the following dimensions, when checked at the mid-point between the pulleys with moderate hand pressure.

Alternator drive belt, 7 to 12 mm (1/4 to 1/2 inch).

Power steering pump drive belt 3 to 7 (1/8 to 1/4 inch).

Air conditioning compressor drive belt (option) 7 to 12 mm (1/4 to 1/2 inch).

If any of the drive belts require adjustment, slacken the applicable pivot bolt (4) and the adjusting bracket nut and screw (5), pull the driven unit away from the engine until the belt is tight. Tighten the adjusting bracket then tighten the pivot bolt. Check the belt tension and readjust if necessary.

Left-hand steering - Fig. RR1163

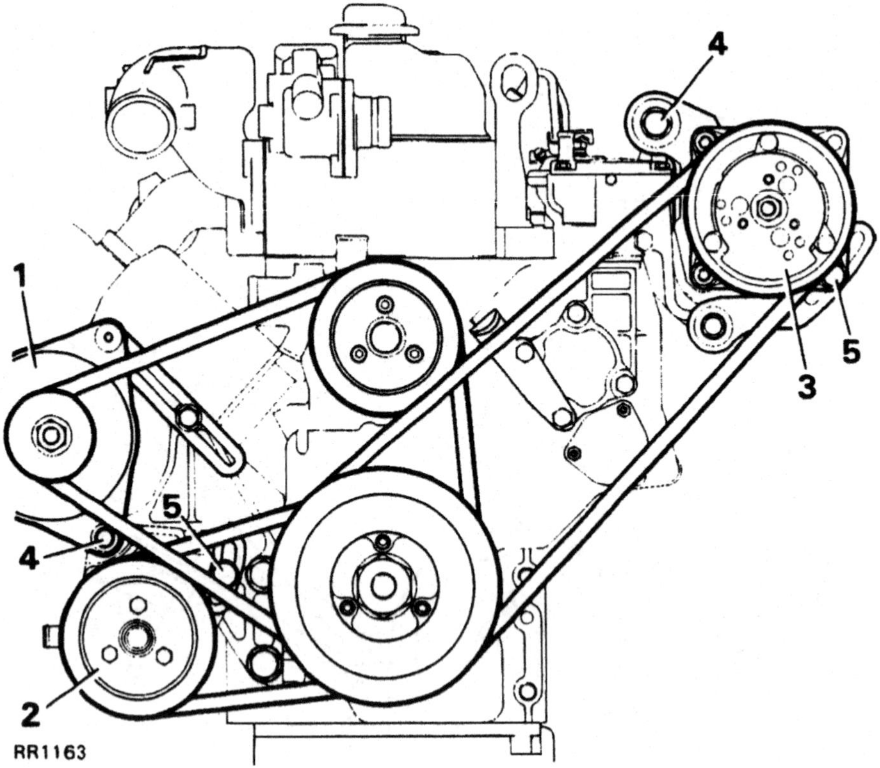

RR1163

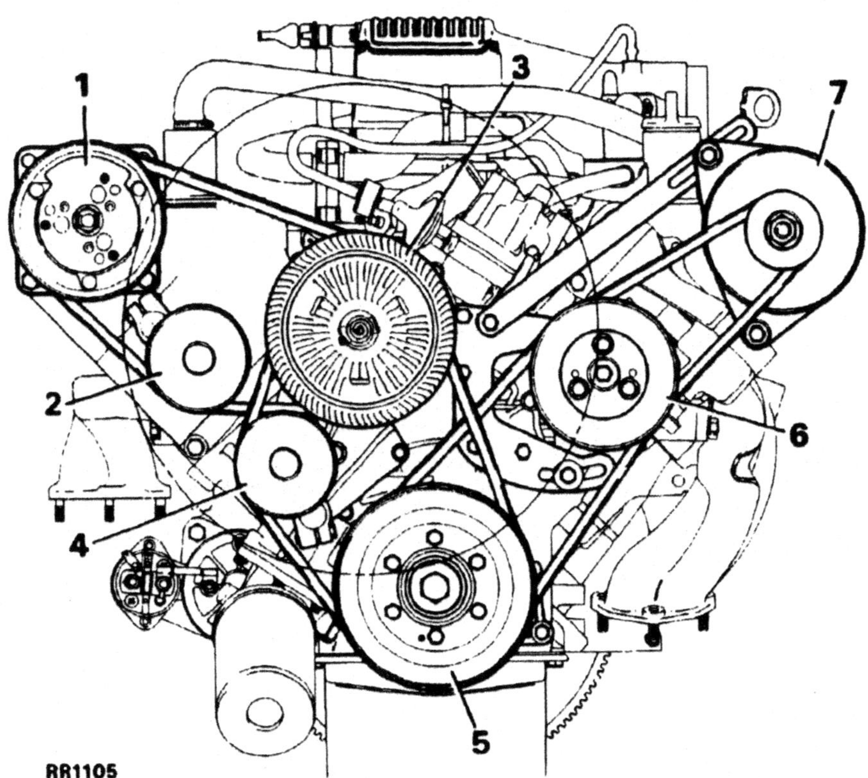

Driving belt arrangement - Fig. RR1105 (Air conditioned model illustrated)

1. Air conditioning compressor
2. Jockey wheel
3. Viscous fan/water pump unit
4. Jockey wheel
5. Crankshaft
6. Power steering pump
7. Alternator

RR1105

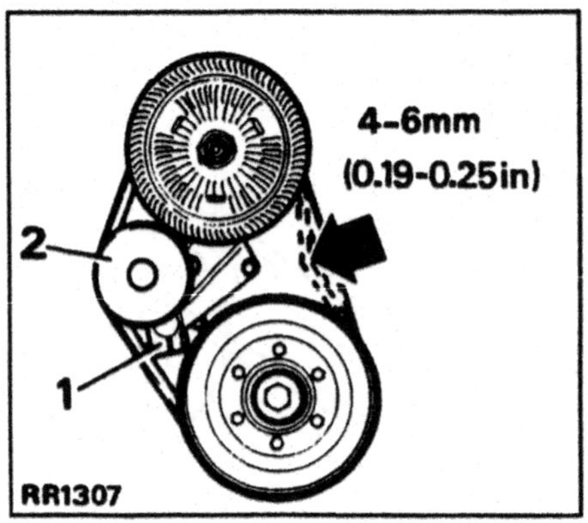

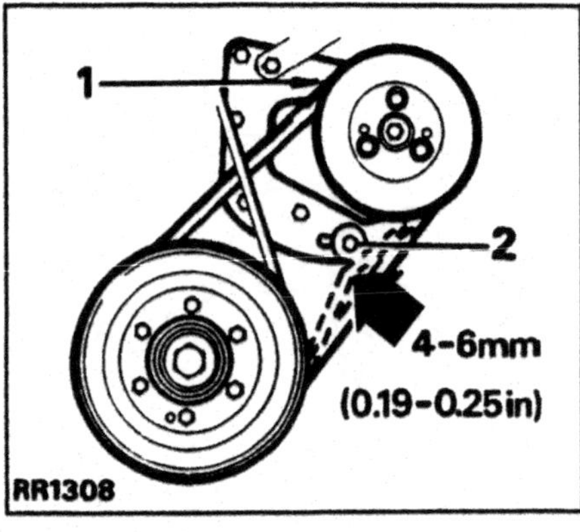

Driving belt tension

Each belt should be tight enough to drive without undue strain on bearings. Using moderate finger pressure at the points indicated in the illustrations, each belt should not deflect more than 11 to 14 mm (7/16 to 9/16 in). Deflection beyond this limit indicates belt slackness which may cause a loud whining or knocking noise in operation and intermittent drive.

Fan belt adjustment - Fig. RR1307

Slacken the jockey wheel securing bolt (1) and adjust the wheel (2) position until the correct tension is obtained. Tighten the securing bolt and re-check the deflection.

Steering pump belt adjustment - Fig. RR1308

Slacken the pivot bolt (1) and the adjustment bolt (2) and adjust the position of the unit until the correct tension is obtained. Then re-tighten the two bolts and re-check the deflection.

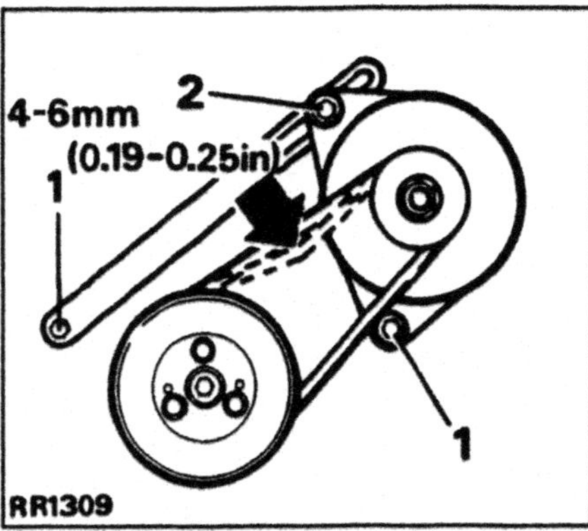

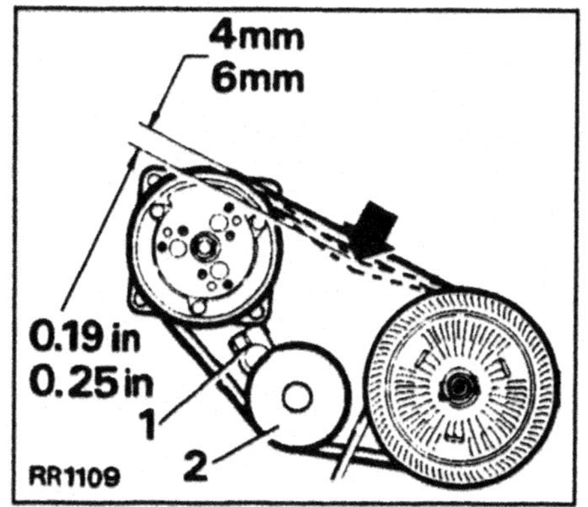

Alternator belt adjustment - Fig. RR1309
Slacken the pivot bolts (1) securing the alternator and pivot bracket, then slacken the adjustment bolt (2). Adjust the position of the unit until the correct tension is obtained then retighten the pivot bolts on the alternator and adjustment bolt, finally tighten the pivot bracket bolt. Recheck the deflection.

Compressor drive-belt - Fig. RR1109
The belt must be tight with not more than 4 to 6 (0.19 to 0.25 in.) total deflection when checked by hand mid-way between the pulleys on the longest run.

Where belt has stretched beyond the limits, a noisy whine or knock will often be evident during operation.

If necessary, adjust as follows:

Slacken the jockey wheel securing bolt (1) and adjust the wheel (2) position until the correct tension is obtained. Tighten the securing bolt and re-check the deflection.

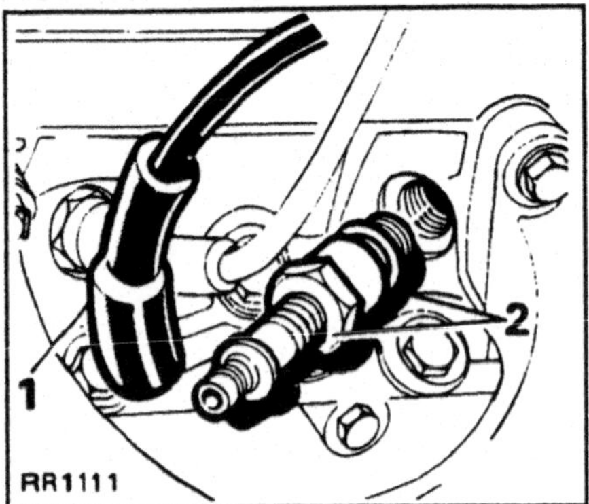

RR1111

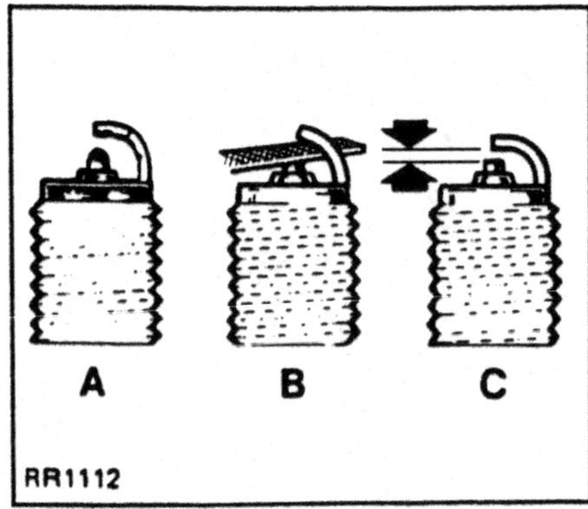

RR1112

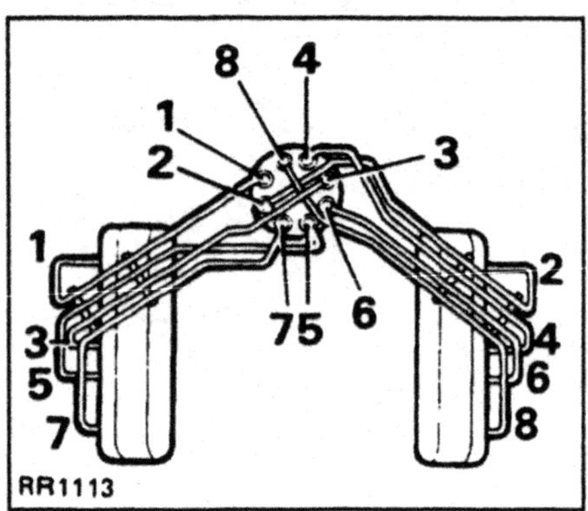

RR1113

Removing spark plugs - Fig. RR1111
To remove spark plugs proceed as follows:

Remove the leads (1) from the spark plugs.

When removing spark plug leads hold the rubber shroud and NOT the H.T. leads. This will ensure no damage will occur to the H.T. lead connector during removal.

Using the special spark plug spanner and tommy bar supplied in the vehicle tool kit, remove the plugs and washers (2).

Before removing spark plugs ensure that the recesses are free from debris to avoid foreign matter entering the cylinder head.

Clean/adjust spark plugs - Fig. RR1112
Check to replace the spark plugs as applicable. If the plugs are in good condition but require resetting wire-brush the plug threads, open the gap slightly (A) and carefully file the electrode sparking surfaces flat using a point file (B). Squaring of the electrode sparking surfaces is important for correct plug operation.

Set the electrode gap to the recommended clearance (C) of 0,76 to 0,86 mm (0.030 to 0.034 in).

Refit spark plugs
If satisfactory the plugs and washers may be refitted to the engine and tightened to a torque of 13,5 to 16,2 Nm (10 to 12 lbf.ft).

It is important that only spark plugs specified in Data, Section 6 are used for replacements.

Incorrect grades of plug may lead to piston over-heating, engine failure and serious damage to components.

Take great care when fitting spark plugs not to cross-thread the plug tappings, otherwise costly damage to the cylinder head will result.

Refit high tension leads - Fig. RR1113
When pushing the leads on to the plugs, ensure that the shrouds are firmly seated on the plugs.

High tension leads must be replaced in the correct relationship to each other, as well as ensuring correct firing order 1, 8, 4, 3, 6, 5, 7, 2. Failure to do this will result in cross firing. The correct plug lead positions are illustrated.

General brake maintenance

The hydraulic system comprises two completely independent sections. The rear calipers and the upper pistons in the front calipers form the secondary section, while the lower pistons in the front calipers form the primary section.

Note: References to 'primary' and 'secondary' are not intended to imply main and emergency systems but to denote hydraulic line identification.

Bleeding the brake system - Figs. RR1125, RR1126 and RR1127

If the brakes feel spongy, this may be caused by air in the hydraulic system. This air must be removed by bleeding the hydraulic system at the calipers; one bleed point at each side on the rear, and three at each side on the front. The following additional points should be noted when bleeding the dual system. Varying brake pedal travel will be experienced depending upon the degree of bleeding required. Bleeding the secondary system, with the primary system fully operational, almost full brake pedal travel can be used. When bleeding the primary system, with the secondary system fully operational, approximately half the total brake pedal travel can be used.

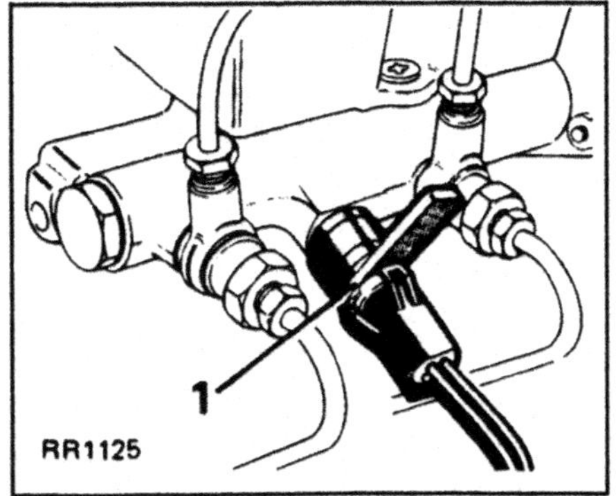

Important: When bleeding the systems commence with the caliper furthest from the master cylinder, and bleed from the screw on the same side as the fluid inlet pipes, then close the screw, and bleed from the screw on the opposite side on the same caliper.

One advantage with the dual system is the possibility of changing certain brake components without the necessity of bleeding both systems. If the rear brake line is disturbed only the secondary system requires bleeding. If the front calipers or master cylinder are disconnected then both primary and secondary systems will require bleeding.

Care must always be taken to observe the following points:

At all times use the recommended brake fluid.

Never leave fluid in unsealed containers. It absorbs moisture quickly and can be dangerous if used in your braking system in this condition.

Fluid drained from the system or used for bleeding is best discarded.

The necessity for absolute cleanliness throughout cannot be over-emphasised.

Bleeding the system requires two people and should be carried out as follows:

Disconnect the leads from the brake pressure warning switch (1) and unscrew the switch four full turns.

(continued)

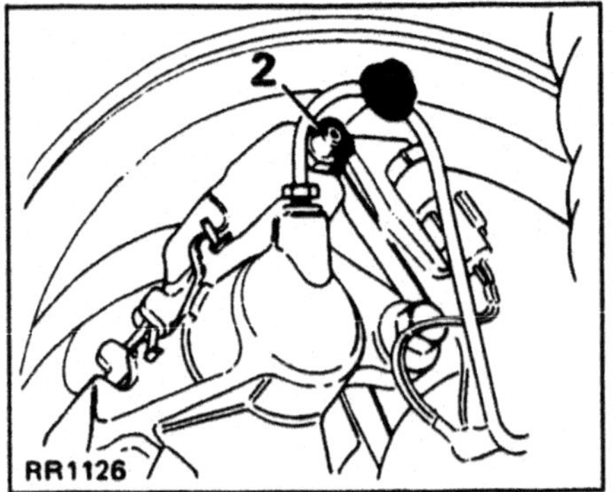

Attach a length of rubber tubing to the bleed screw (2) on the rear left- hand caliper and place the lower end of the tube under the surface of brake fluid contained in a glass jar.
Slacken the bleed screw.
When the fluid appears in the jar, commence pumping the brake pedal slowly; pause at least five seconds at each end of the return stroke to allow the master cylinder piston to recuperate. Continue pumping until the fluid issuing from the the tube is held below the surface of the fluid in the jar.
Hold the tube under the fluid surface, and with the foot brake fully depressed, tighten the bleed screw and replace the dust cap.
Repeat this procedure for the rear right-hand caliper.
Attach a bleed tube to the primary bleed screw on the front caliper **furthest away** from the master cylinder (Fig. RR1127).

Attach a second bleed tube to the secondary bleed screw on the same side of the caliper as the primary bleed screw, using two separate bleed jars.
Slacken both bleed screws.
When the fluid appears in the bleed jars, commence pumping the brake pedal slowly, pausing at each end of the return stroke, to allow the piston to recuperate, until fluid being expelled is free of air in both jars.
Hold the tubes under the fluid surface and with the brake pedal fully depressed, tighten both bleed screws and replace both dust caps.
Attach bleed tube to the remaining secondary bleed screw on the same caliper.
Slacken the bleed screw.
When the fluid appears in the jar commence pumping the brake pedal slowly, pausing at each end of the return stroke, to allow the piston to recuperate, until all air is expelled.
Hold the tube under the fluid surface and with the brake pedal fully depressed, tighten the bleed screw and replace dust cap.

Repeat this procedure for the front caliper **nearest** to the master cylinder.
The fluid in the reservoir should be replenished throughout the operation to prevent another air lock being formed, using only new fluid of the recommended type, from sealed tins.
On completion of bleeding, the brake pressure warning switch must be screwed in and tightened to a torque of 1,7 Nm (15 lbf.in).

Renew hydraulic brake fluid
If the following procedure is adhered to, air will not enter the system and the time taken to change the fluid will be kept to a minimum:
Proceed in the same manner and order as for bleeding the system in General Brake Maintenance and connect a bleed tube (incorporating a glass tube to allow obsdervation of the condition of fluid being bled) between a bleed screw and a suitable bottle.
Pump out most, but not all, of the fluid in the reservoir.

Note: Do not allow the reservoir to empty.

Top up the reservoir with new unused fluid of the correct grade.
Ensure the reservoir is kept topped up and bleed until the old and discoloured fluid is ejected and the new fluid is seen in the glass tube; continue to bleed for two full strokes of the pedal and close the bleed-screw.
Repeat procedure at each bleed-screw in turn.
Top up reservoir and road test vehicle.

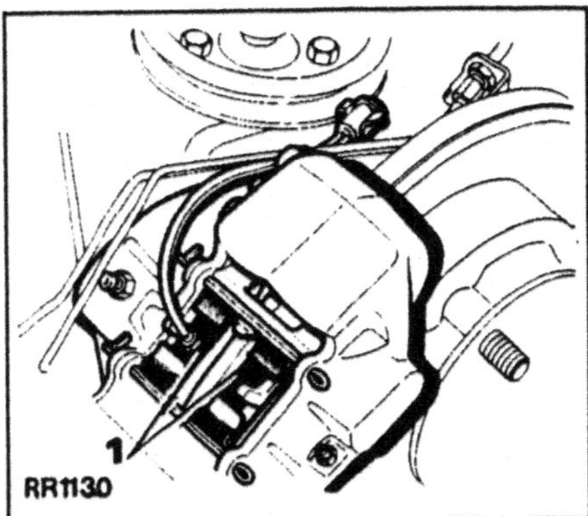

Inspect brake pads for wear and discs for condition - Fig. RR1130

Hydraulic disc brakes are fitted and the correct brake adjustment is automatically maintained, therefore no provision is made for adjustment.

Check for oil contamination on brake pads (1) and discs, also check condition of brakes discs for wear and/or corrosion.

The brake pad wear warning light in the binnacle will be illuminated on application of the footbrake (with ignition on) whenever the right-hand front or rear inboard pads are worn to approximately 3 mm (0.118 in.) thickness and should be renewed.

Brake pads must be renewed in axle sets. On each axle, one of the brake pads fitted has a built in electrical sensor to activate the instrument cluster warning light when the pads are worn.

When purchasing replacement disc pad kits, it is important to ensure that the sensor is located in the correct position and that the new pads have the same friction characteristics as the pads being renewed.

If replacement or rectification is necessary, this should be carried out by your local Range Rover Distributor or Dealer.

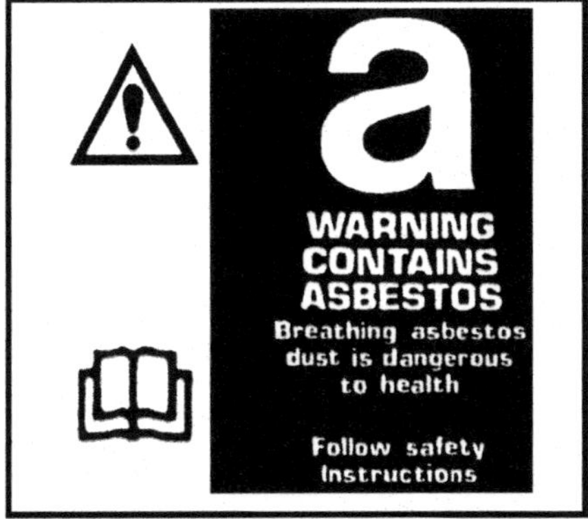

WARNING: Some components on your vehicle, such as gaskets and friction surfaces (brake pads, or automatic transmission brake bands), may contain asbestos. Breathing asbestos dust is dangerous to your health. You are therefore advised to have any maintenance or repair operations on such components carried out be a recognised Range Rover Distributor or Dealer. If, however, service operations are to be undertaken on parts containing asbestos, the following essential precautions must be observed.

- *Work out of doors or in a well ventilated area.*

- *Dust found on the vehicle or produced during work on the vehicle should be removed by extraction not by blowing.*

- *Dust waste should be dampened with water, placed in a sealed container and marked to ensure safe disposal.*

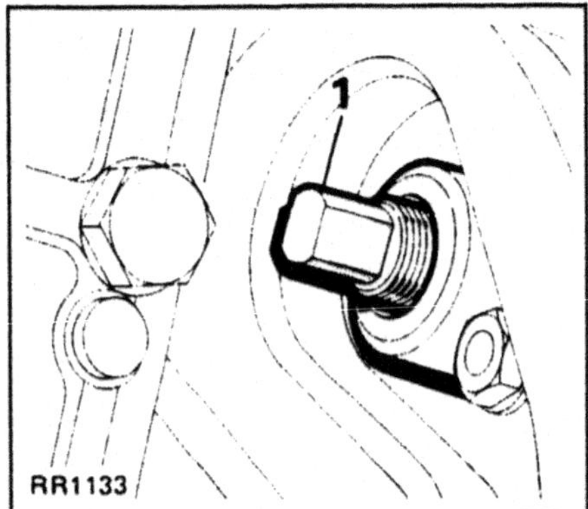

- **If any cutting, drilling etc, is attempted on materials containing asbestos the item should be dampened with water and only hand tools or low speed power tools used.**

For your further guidance, Range Rover replacement parts which contain asbestos are progressively being identified by the above symbol. If you are in any doubt, please consult our dealer.

Check/adjust transmission handbrake - Fig. RR1133

If handbrake movement is excessive, adjust as follows:

Release the handbrake. The adjuster (1) protrudes through backplate.

During rotation of the adjuster a click will be felt and heard at each quarter revolution. Rotate adjuster in a clockwise direction until the brake shoes contact the drum. Then unscrew the adjuster two clicks and give the handbrake a firm application to centralise the shoes.

After centralising the shoes, rotate the drum to ensure that no binding is evident.

If, after adjusting the brake shoes, the hand brake still has excessive movement, the linkage will require adjustment. In this event consult your Dealer.

Lubricants

Land Rover Limited attaches very great importance to the nature of the lubricants used in its products and therefore gives specific recommendations. See Data section.

The recommended lubricants for the Range Rover should be used whenever possible in the grades specified. When ordering oil, the correct grade, as well as the make, should be clearly stated.

The oils recommended by Land Rover Limited are complete in themselves and additives should not be used. Should any of the recommended lubricants not be available in certain territories, the Range Rover Distributor or Dealer for that territory will obtain specific guidance from Land Rover Limited, or owners may communicate with the Company where they so wish.

Multigrade oils, produced by the makers of the lubricants are also approved for the range of SAE grades that they cover.

Engine oil

Maintain oil specified to correct level.

Under severe conditions of mud or dust, the oil changes must be more frequent, even to the extent of a daily change. Under deep wading conditions through water carrying mud and grit, a daily oil change is essential.

Gearbox, transfer box, differentials and swivel pin housings

It is essential to change oil much more frequently than indicated if the vehicle is operated under severe conditions, especially if deep wading is carried out.

Check for oil - fuel - fluid leaks

Open the bonnet and examine the engine for oil leaks. Check for leaks underneath the engine.

Check the fuel pipes, carburetters and hydraulic fluid pipes and hoses within the engine compartment for leaks.

If any leakage is discovered remedial action must be taken immediately.

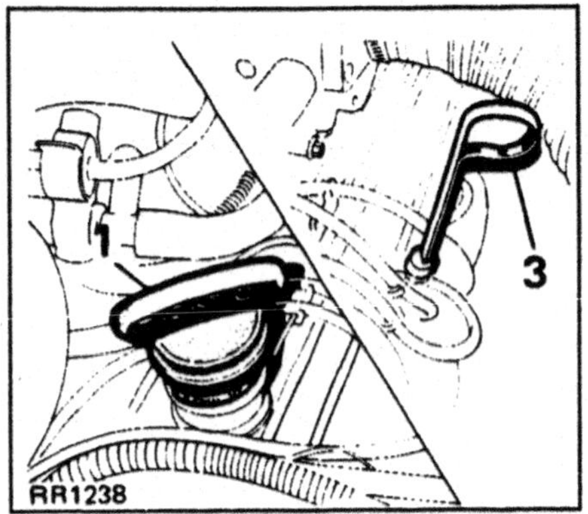
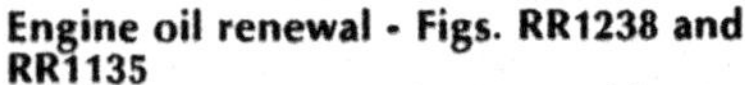

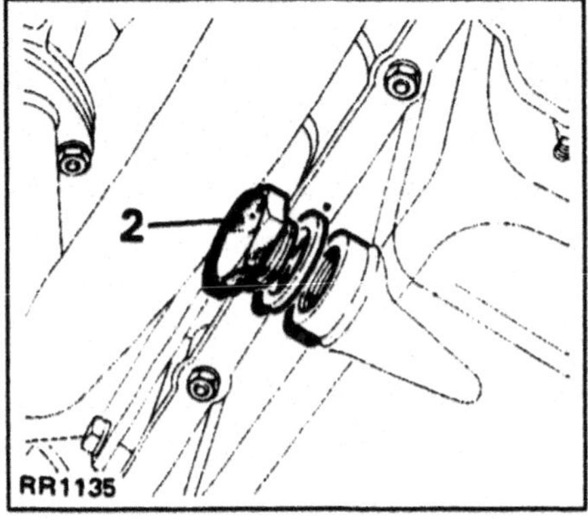

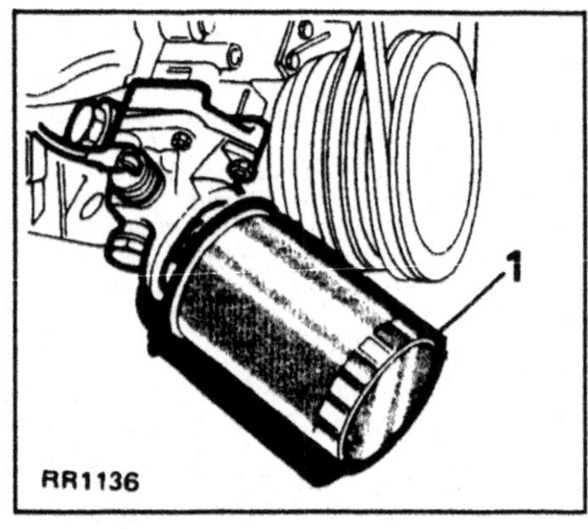

Engine oil renewal - Figs. RR1238 and RR1135

With the engine oil thoroughly warm to assist drainage and with the vehicle safely parked on level ground, remove the oil filler cap (1) and position a suitable receptacle for the old oil under the drain plug (2) in the bottom left side of the sump.

Remove the drain plug and its copper washer and allow the old oil to drain completely.

WARNING: Observe due care when removing the plug and when draining as the oil can be very hot.

On completion of draining, clean the plug and its mating surface on the sump before securely refitting the plug complete with a new copper washer.

Replenish the engine with fresh oil of the correct grade and quantity (as specified in the 'Data' section of the book) through the filler tube, allowing time to obtain a true reading on the dipstick (3). When the correct level of oil is shown on the dipstick, replace the filler cap.

Engine oil filter renewal - Fig. RR1136

To avoid draining the oil pump, it is essential that the engine is filled with oil to the correct level before the filter is removed. It is therefore recommended that the renewal of engine oil is completed before work on the filter commences.

Clean the area around the filter head, and place a container beneath the engine. Using a strap spanner or similar tool, unscrew the filter (1) anti-clockwise and discard it. Smear the seal of the new filter with clean engine oil and screw on the filter clockwise until it is securely in position. Use hand force only and avoid overtightening.

Start and run the engine to fill the oil filter with oil. Check for leaks.

Stop the engine, wait a few minutes, then check the oil level and top up if necessary.

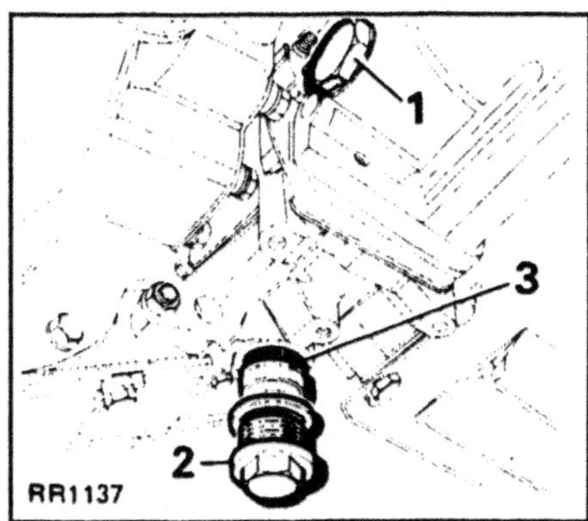
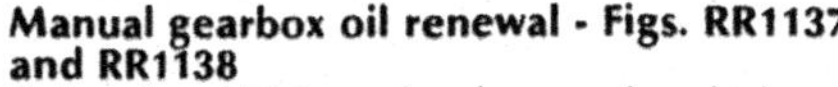

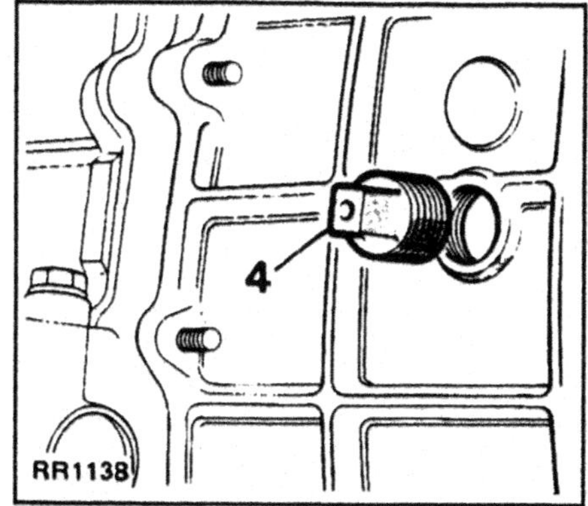

Manual gearbox oil renewal - Figs. RR1137 and RR1138

Drive the vehicle to level ground and place a suitable container under the gearbox to catch the old oil.

Remove the gearbox and extension case drain plugs (1 and 2) and allow the oil to drain completely. Wash the extension case filter (3) in kerosene, refit it and the plugs using new washers if necessary, and tighten securely.

Remove the oil filler level plug (4) and refill with the appropriate quantity of new oil of the correct make and grade until it begins to run out of the filler level hole. Fit the plug and tighten securely.

Since the plug has a tapered thread it must not be overtightened. Wipe away any surplus oil.

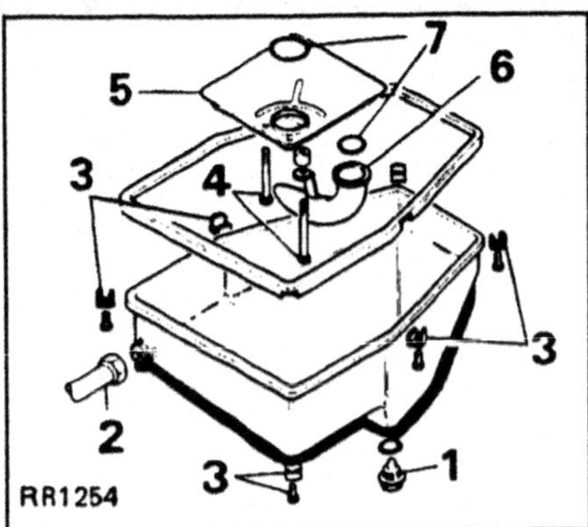

Renewal of gearbox fluid and filter/screen - Fig. RR1254

Where the vehicle is used in arduous conditions, this operation may be required more frequently than in less exacting conditions.

Safely park the vehicle on level ground or over a suitable pit and position a suitable receptacle for the fluid under the gearbox drain plug (1).

Remove the plug and sealing washer from the gearbox sump and allow the fluid to drain out.
Lift the bonnet and remove the gearbox dipstick to aid drainage.

From underneath the vehicle, release the large nut (2) securing the filler tube to the front of the gearbox sump and detach the tube.

Release the six bolts, washers and clamps (3) retaining the gearbox sump and remove it.
Remove the three screws and washers (4) securing the oil screen (5) to the valve body and remove the screen. Seperate the screen from the suction tube (6) and discard the screen and 'O' rings (7). Fit two new 'O' rings to the new oil screen, using a light grease to ensure correct positioning, and fit the suction tube to the oil screen.
Fit the new screen tightening the three screws to a torque of 8 Nm (6 lbf.ft).
Fit a new 'U' gasket to the sump face and refit the sump using all retaining screws and clamps.
Tighten the four corner clamps first followed by the two centre clamps all to a torque of 8 Nm (6 lbf. ft). Reconnect the filks tube to the front of the geabox sump tightening the large nut to a torque of 35 to 42 Nm (25 to 30 lbf.ft).
Clean and refit the plug with a new sealing washer and tighten to 10 Nm (7 lbf.ft).
Replenish the gearbox fluid to the correct level as previously described.

Transfer gearbox oil maintenance - Fig. RR1140

Check oil level daily or weekly if operating under severe wading conditions.

To check oil level: with the vehicle safely parked on level ground, remove the oil level plug (1) located on the rear of the transfer box casing; oil should be level with the bottom of the hole.

If necessary, top up through the oil level plug hole using a pump type oil can. If significant topping up is required, check for oil leaks at drain and filler plugs.

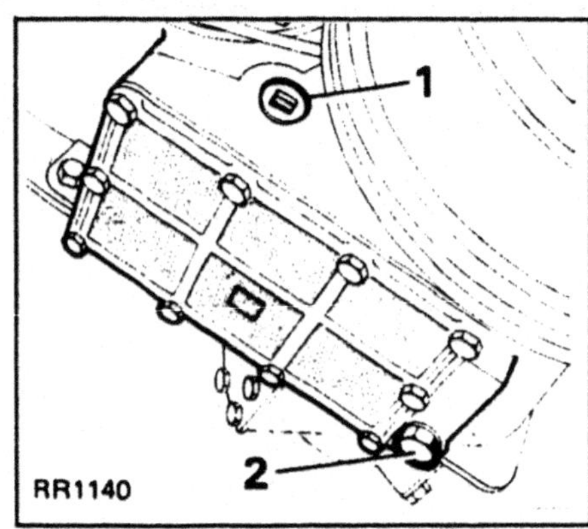

Drain and refill monthly if operating under severe wading conditions.

Immediately after a run when the oil is warm, drain off the oil into a container by removing the drain plug (2) and washer from the bottom of the transfer box.

Allow time for thorough draining of the oil then, using a new washer, refit the drain plug to a torque of 25 to 35 Nm (19 to 26 lbf. ft). Refill the transfer box through the oil level plug hole with the correct grade of oil, to the bottom of the oil level plug hole. For capacity see Data Section.

CAUTION: *Do not overfill, otherwise leakage may occur.*

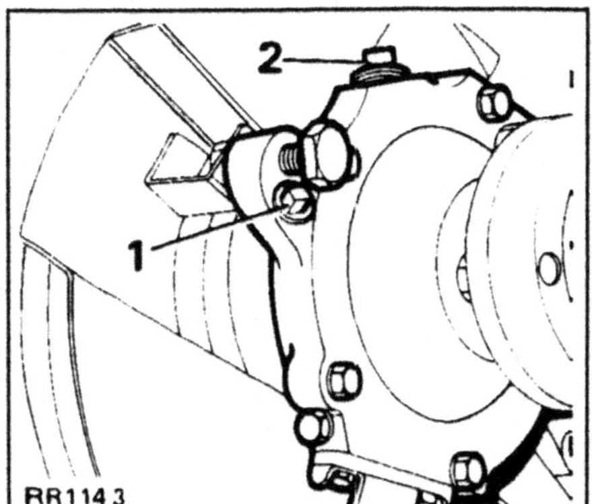

RR1143

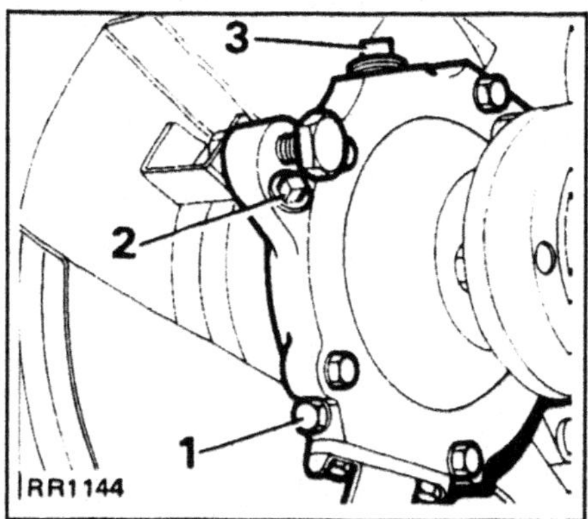

RR1144

Swivel pin housing oil level - Fig. RR1143
The front wheel drive constant velocity joints and swivel pins receive their lubrication from the swivel pin housing.

Check oil level by removing the 1/4 in AF square-headed plug (1) at the front of the swivel pin housing; oil should be level with the bottom of the hole.

Top up if necessary through the filler plug hole (2) using a pump type oil can.

If significant topping up is required, check for oil leaks at plugs, joint faces, and oil seals.

Swivel pin housing oil renewal - Fig. RR1144
Drain and refill monthly if operating under severe wading conditions.

To change the swivel pin housing oil, proceed as follows, immediately after a run, when the oil is warm.

Place a container under each drain plug (1) to prevent oil contaminating the tyres.

Remove the drain plug from the bottom of each housing.

Note: *Remove the filler plug to assist in drainage of oil from swivel pin housing.*

Allow the oil to drain away completely and replace drain plugs.

Refill with oil of the correct grade through the oil filler plug hole (3). For capacity see Data Section 6.

Check the oil level at the plug (2) and allow any surplus oil to drain away.

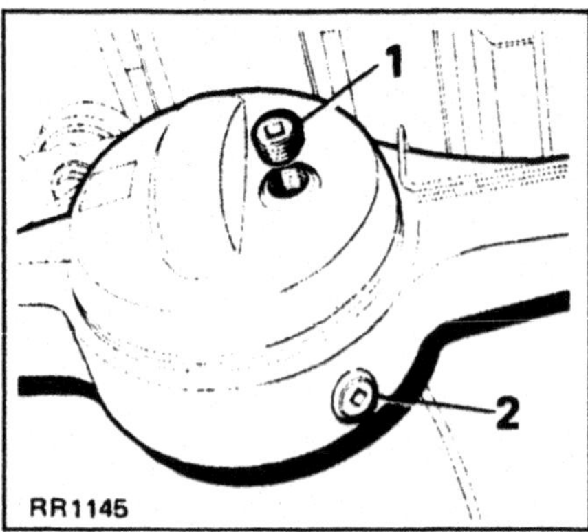

RR1145

Front and rear differential oil level check and renewal - Fig. RR1145
Remove filler/level plug **(1)** check oil level and top up, if necessary, to the bottom of the filler/level plug hole.

If significant topping up is required, check for oil leaks at plugs, joint faces, and oil seals adjacent to axle shaft flanges and propeller shaft driving flange.

Drain and refill monthly under severe wading conditions.

To change the differential oil, proceed as follows:

Immediately after a run, when the oil is warm, place a container under the axle, remove the filler plug to aid drainage and drain off the oil, removing the drain plug **(2)** by using the reverse ends of the plug spanner and tommy bar.

Replace the drain plug and refill with oil of the correct grade. For capacity see Data, Section 6.

IMPORTANT: Do not overfill, otherwise damage to the seals may occur.

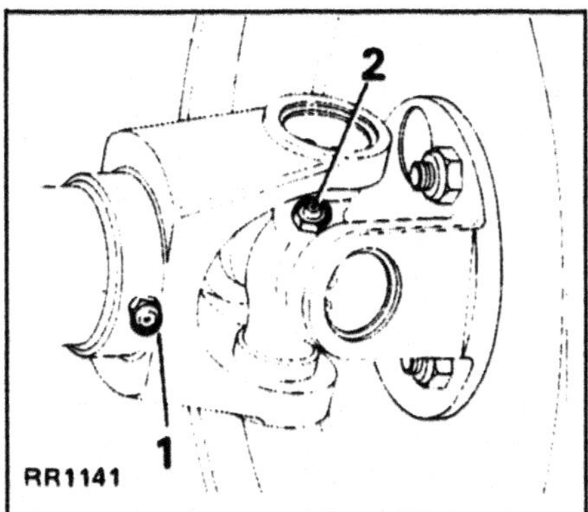

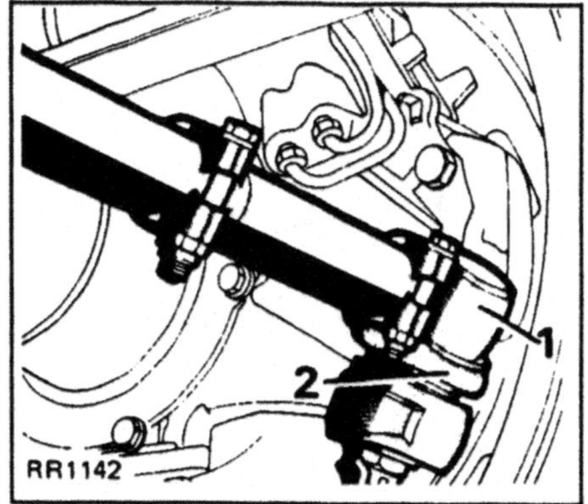

Lubricate propeller shafts - Fig. RR1141
Apply one of the recommended greases to the lubrication nipple (1) on the sliding portion of both propeller shafts.

Apply grease to nipples (2) fitted to the universal joints at each end of both front and rear shafts.

Note: Due to the type of sliding joint used in these propeller shafts, only light greasing is required.

Steering joints - Fig. RR1142
Check rubber boots daily when operating under arduous conditions.

The steering joints (1) have been designed to retain the initial filling of grease for the normal life of the ball joints; however, this applies only if the rubber boot remains in the correct position.

Check to ensure that the rubber boots (2) have not become dislodged or damaged, and check for wear in the joint.

This can be done by moving the ball joint vigorously up and down. Should there be any appreciable free movement the complete joint must be replaced.

Lubricate handbrake mechanical linkage and lever pivot
The handbrake operates a mechanical brake unit mounted on the output shaft from the transfer box. Lubricate the handbrake linkage with grease (see Recommended Lubricants).

Air conditioning system - Fig. RR1051
The air conditioning system operates independantly of the heater to provide cooled and dried recirculated air.

WARNING: The air conditioning system is filled at high pressure with a potentially toxic material. Follow service instructions when dismantling or applying excessive heat, e.g. steam cleaning, painting, etc. Servicing adjustments or rectification procedures must only be carried out by your Range Rover Distributor or Dealer or by a qualified engineer in accordance with instructions in the Repair Operation Manual.

Under no circumstances should non-qualified personnel attempt repair or servicing of air conditioning equipment.

The system is made up of four separate units:

An engine-mounted compressor (A).
A condenser (B) mounted in front of the radiator
A receiver/drier unit (C) located in the engine compartment.
An evaporator unit (D) mounted behind the fascia.

The four units are interconnected by hoses carrying refrigerant. The refrigerant circuit cools the evaporator which is connected to the ventilation system, and thus cools the air inside the vehicle.

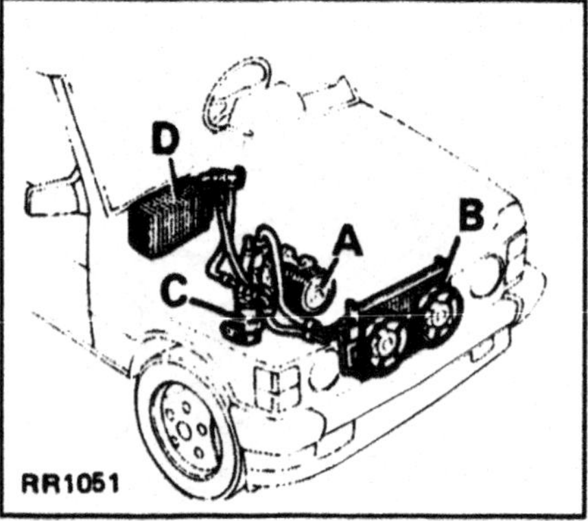

Routine maintenance - Every 20,000 km (12,000 miles)
Check the following items as indicated.

Adjust the compressor drive belt if required.

For specified compressor oils and refrigerant see Lubrication chart, Section 6.

Condenser
Using a water hose or air-line, clean the exterior of the condenser matrix.

Check the pipe connections for signs of fluid leakage.

Evaporator
Examine the pipe connections for signs of fluid leakage.

Receiver/drier sight-glass
After running the engine for five minutes, with the air conditioning system in operation, examine the sight-glass, there should be no sign of bubbles.

If bubbles are present, check the pipe connections for signs of fluid leakage, rectify if necessary and recharge the system.

Compressor
Check the pipe connections for fluid leakage and the hoses for swellings.

Fuses - air conditioning electrical circuit
The air conditioning electrical circuit is protected by a block of four push-in fuses in the fuse box on the lower fascia. (See Section 4).

DATA

6

Petrol Engines

Type V8	Cylinder capacity .... 3528 cm^3 (215 in^3)	Ignition coil .... Lucas 2CE 12 volt electronic
Bore .... 88.9 mm (3.5 in)	Sparking plug type .... Champion N9YC	Distributor type .... Lucas 35 DLM8
Stroke .... 71.12 mm (2.8 in)	Sparking plug gap .... 0.84 to 0.96 mm (0.033 to 0.038 in)	Distributor air gap .... 0.20 to 0.35 mm
Number of cylinders .... Eight	Firing order 1,8,4,3,6,5,7,2	(0.008 to 0.014 in)

000

Electronic fuel injection (EFI) models - emission controlled

Compression ratio 9.35:1		8.13:1
Maximum power .... 123 kW (165 bhp) at 4750 rev/min		112 kW (150 bhp) at 4750 rev/min
Maximum torque .... 280 Nm (207 lbf.ft) at 3200 rev/min		258 Nm (190 lbf.ft) at 2500 rev/min
Idle speed. rev/min .... 700 to 800		750 to 850
Ignition timing (dynamic) .... TDC±1° at 750 rev/min		TDC±1° at 750 rev/min
Exhaust gas CO content at idle .... 0.5 to 1.0%		0.5 to 1.0%
Fuel required .... 97 octane		90 octane
Fuel injection system .... Lucas 'L'		Lucas 'L'
Fuel pump. electrical .... A.C. Delco high pressure (in fuel tank)		A.C. Delco high pressure (in fuel tank)
Fuel pump delivery pressure .... 1.83 to 2.5 kgf/cm^2 (26 to 36 lbf/in^2)		1.83 to 2.5 kgf/cm^2 (26 to 36 lbf/in^2)
Fuel filter .... Bosch in-line canister type		Bosch in-line canister type

Carburetter models

	Emission controlled	Emission controlled
Compression ratio	9.35:1	8.13:1
Maximum power	94 kW (127 bhp) at 4000 rev/min	98 kW (132 bhp) at 5000 rev/min
Maximum torque	263 Nm (194 lbf.ft) at 2500 rev/min	251 Nm (185 lbf.ft) at 2500 rev/min
Idle speed rev/min	700 to 800	700 to 800
Fast idle speed, rev/min	1050 to 1150	1050 to 1150
Exhaust CO content at idle (Pulsair connected)	0.5 to 2.5%	0.5 to 2.5% (No Pulsair on non-emission controlled models)

NOTE: Maximum power and torque figures are derived from bench tests and do not allow for installation losses in the vehicle.

Carburetter models - continued

Ignition timing dynamic or static		TDC ±1° at 750 rev/min
		0.5 to 1.0%
(vacuum pipe disconnected)	6° ±1° BTDC at 750 rev/min	6° ±1° BTDC at 750 rev/min
Fuel required	97 octane	90 to 93 octane
Carburetters (2)	SU HIF44 (Spec. No. 2006)	SU HIF44 (Spec. No. 2005)
Fuel pump, electrical	A.C. Delco low pressure (in fuel tank)	
Fuel pump delivery pressure	0.28 to 0.42 kgf/cm^2 (4 to 6 lbf/in^2)	
Fuel filter	A.C. Delco CD600, element A.C. D.60	

Note: Maximum power and torque figures are derived from bench tests and do not allow for installation losses in the vehicle

All petrol engined models

Lubrication

System	Wet sump, pressure fed
Oil pressure	2.11 to 2.81 kgf/cm^2 (30 to 40 lbf/in^2) at 80 kph (50 mph) in top gear with engine warm (2400 rev/min)
Oil filter - internal	Gauze pump intake filter in sump
Oil filter - external	Full-flow, self-contained cartridge

Cooling system

Type	Pressurised spill return system with thermostat control, fan assisted and pump
Thermostat	88°C
Pump type	Centrifugal

Clutch (Manual transmission models only)

Type	Borg and Beck diaphragm spring
Centre plate diameter	267 mm (10.5 in)
Hydraulic fluid	See 'Recommended fluids' later in this section

Tappets

Type	Hydraulic, non adjustable

Diesel engined models

Engine	Engine type	VM-HR 492 HI	
	Bore	92 mm	3.622 in
	Stroke	90 mm	3.543 in
	No. of cylinders	4	
	Capacity	2393 cm^3	146.03 in^3
	Compression ratio	22:1	
	Maximum power	84 kW (112 bhp) at 4200 rev/min	
	Maximum torque	248 Nm (183 lbf ft) at 2400 rev/min	
	Injection order	1, 3, 4, 2,	
	Valve clearance (cold): Inlet	0,30 mm	0.012 in
	Valve clearance (cold): Exhaust	0,30 mm	0.012 in
	Static injection timing	3° B.T.D.C.	
	Idle speed	750 to 800 rev/min	
	Engine speed at maximum power	4200 rev/min	
	Maximum light running speed	4700 rev/min	
Fuel system	Fuel injection pump	Bosch	
	Type	VE4/10F 2100L 168/1	
	Fuel lift pump	'BCD' mechanical type driven from camshaft	
	Fuel injectors	Bosch KBE 58S 4/4	
	Nozzle type	DN OSD 263	
	Main fuel filter	Bosch	
	Glow plugs	Bosch	
	Injector nut tightness	24 to 28 Nm 2,5 to 3 kgf m	18 to 21 lbf ft
Lubrication	System pressure at 2,000 rev/min (oil at 90-100°C)	3,5 to 4,0 kgf/cm^2	50 to 57 lbf/in^2
Cooling system	Thermostat	88°C $\pm$ 2°C	
	Pressure cap	0,7 kgf/cm^2	15 lbf/in^2
Clutch	Make and type	Borg and Beck diaphragm	
	Diameter	241 mm	9.5 in

Main Gearbox

	Manual

Type .... Five speed and reverse, single helical constant mesh with synchromesh on all forward gears

Main gearbox ratios

5th	0.770:1
4th	1.000:1
3rd	1.397:1
2nd	2.132:1
1st	3.321:1
Reverse	3.429:1

Automatic

Four speed and reverse epicyclic with fluid torque converter and lock up

4th	0.728:1
3rd	1.000:1
2nd	1.480:1
1st	2.480:1
Reverse	2.806:1

Transfer gearbox - LT230T

Type .... Two speed reduction on main gearbox output. Front and rear drive permanently engaged via a lockable differential.

Transfer gearbox ratios

High	1.222:1
Low	3.320:1

Overall ratio (final drive):

	Manual			Automatic	
	high transfer	low transfer		high transfer	low transfer
5th	3.33:1	9.05:1	4th	3.15:1	8.55:1
4th	4.33:1	11.75:1	3rd	4.33:1	11.75:1
3rd	6.05:1	16.41:1	2nd	6.41:1	17.38:1
2nd	9.23:1	25.04:1	1st	10.74:1	29.13:1
1st	14.38:1	39.02:1	Reverse	9.03:1	24.50:1
Reverse	14.85:1	40.27:1			

Rear axle

Type .... Spiral bevel, fully floating shafts

Ratio 3.54:1

Front axle

Type .... Spiral bevel, enclosed constant velocity joints, fully floating shafts

Angularity of universal joint on full lock .... 32°C

Ratio 3.54:1

Propeller shafts

Type .... Front-open type, 28,6 mm (1.125 in) diameter bar.

.... 03EHD type universal joints

.... Rear-open type, 51 mm (2 in) diameter tube.

.... 03EHD type universal joints

Suspension

Front .... Coil springs, radius arms and panhard rod.

Rear .... Coil springs, lower links, 'A' frame location arms with 'Boge' hydromat self-energising levelling device

Hydraulic dampers .... Telescopic double acting non-adjustable 35 mm (1.375 in) bore

Brakes

Foot brake .... Front: Outboard disc brakes with four pistons per caliper

      Disc diameter 298 mm (11.75 in)

      Hydraulic, servo-assisted, self-adjusting

    Rear: Outboard disc brakes with two pistons per caliper

      Disc diameter 290 mm (11.42 in)

      Hydraulic, servo-assisted, self-adjusting

Approx. pad area - front calipers .... $98cm^2$ ($15.2 in^2$) each

  - Rear calipers .... $66cm^2$ ($10.2 in^2$) each

  - Total .... $328cm^2$ ($50.8 in^2$)

Total swept area .... $3199.2 cm^2$ (496 sq.in.)

Handbrake ('park' brake) .... Mechanical 254 mm (10 in) diameter, 70 mm (2.75 in) width duo-servo drum brake on rear of transfer box output shaft.

Steering

Power assisted Type .... Adwest recirculating ball
Turns lock to lock 3.375
Front wheel alignment .... 1,2 to 2,44 mm (0,046 to 0,093 in) toe-out
Camber angle .... 0° Check with vehicle in static unladen condition. That is,
Castor angle .... 3° vehicle with water, oil and 5 gallons of fuel. Rock the vehicle
Swivel pin inclination .... 7° up and down at the front to allow it to take up a static position
Steering wheel .... Four-spoke: 432 mm (17 in) diameter

Tyres

Sizes .... 205R16 or 215/75R16 *Note: Fuel injection vehicles must be fitted with 'S' rated high speed tyres.*

WARNING: Wheels and tyres. Unless both wheel rim and tyre are marked 'TUBELESS', an inner tube MUST be fitted.

See your Range Rover Distributor or Dealer for the type of tyre currently recommended.

Pressures: Check with tyres cold ....

Normal on- and off-road use. All speeds and loads			Off-road 'emergency' soft use maximum speed of 40 kph (25 mph)		
	Front	Rear		Front	Rear
bar	1,9	2,4	bar	1,1	1,6
lbf/in^2	28	35	lbf/in^2	16	23
kgf/cm^2	2,0	2,5	kgf/cm^2	1,1	1,6

For extra ride comfort rear tyre pressures may be reduced to 2,1 bars (31 lbf/in^2) 2,2 kgf/cm^2 when the rear axle weight does not exceed 1250 kg (2755 lb).

Normal pressures may be increased for rough off-road usage where the risk of tyre cutting or penetration is more likely.

Pressures may also be increased for sustained high speed motoring near the vehicles maximum speed. Any such increase in pressures may be up to an absolute maximum pressure of 2,9 bars (42 lbf/in^2) 3,0 kgf/cm^2.

Normal operating pressures should be restored as soon as reasonable road conditions or hard ground is reached.

After usage off the road, tyres and wheels should be inspected for damage particularly if high cruising speeds are subsequently to be used.

Towing: When the vehicle is used for towing, the reduced rear tyre pressures for extra ride comfort are not applicable.

Dimensions

Overall length .... 4,45 m (175 in.)
Overall width .... 1,82 m (71,6 in.)
Overall height .... 1,90 m (74.8 in.)
Wheelbase .... 2,54 m (100 in.)
Track: front and rear .... 1,48 m (58.5 in.)
Ground clearance: under differential .... 190 mm (7.5 in.)
Turning circle .... 11,89 m (39 ft.)
Loading height .... 686 mm (27 in.)
Maximum cargo height .... 1,01 m (40 in.)
Rear opening height .... 1,01 m (40 in.)
Usable luggage capacity, rear seat folded .... $2,00 \text{ m}^3$ (70.6 ft^3)
Usable luggage capacity, rear set in use:
- four door vehicles .... $1,03 \text{ m}^3$ (36.2 ft^3)
- two door vehicles .... $1,17 \text{ m}^3$ (41.48 ft^3)
Maximum roof rack load .... 75 kg (165 lb)

Maximum permissible towed weights

	On-road	Off-road
Trailers without brakes	750 kg 1650 lb	750 kg 1650 lb
Trailers with overrun brakes	3500 kg 7700 lb	1000 kg 2200 lb
4-wheel trailers with continuous or semi-continuous brakes, i.e. coupled brakes	4000 kg 8800 lb	1000 kg 2200 lb

Note: It is the Owner's responsibility to ensure that all regulations with regard to towing are complied with. This applies also when towing abroad. All relevant information should be obtained from the appropriate motoring organisation.

Vehicle weights

Petrol-engined models	Manual			Automatic		
	Front Axle kg (lb)	Rear Axle kg (lb)	Total kg (lb)	Front kg (lb)	Rear kg (lb)	Total kg (lb)
2 DOOR Unladen weight	893 (1969)	867 (1910)	1760 (3880)	920 (2028)	871 (1920)	1791 (3948)
EEC kerb weight	912 (2011)	983 (2167)	1895 (4178)	939 (2070)	987 (2070)	1926 (4246)
Gross vehicle weight *	1100 (2425)	1510 (3329)	2510 (5534)	1100 (2425)	1510 (3329)	2510 (5534)
4 DOOR Unladen weight	909 (2004)	883 (1947)	1792 (3951)	925 (2039)	911 (2008)	1836 (4048)
EEC kerb weight	928 (2046)	999 (2202)	1927 (4248)	944 (2081)	1027 (2264)	1971 (4345)
Gross vehicle weight *	1100 (2425)	1510 (3329)	2510 (5534)	1100 (2425)	1510 (3329)	2510 (5534)

Diesel-engined models	Manual		
	Front Axle kg (lb)	Rear Axle kg (lb)	Total kg (lb)
2 DOOR Unladen weight	981 (2163)	861 (1898)	1842 (4061)
EEC kerb weight	998 (2200)	986 (2174)	1984 (4374)
Gross vehicle weight *	1200 (2645)	1510 (3329)	2510 (5533)
4 DOOR Unladen weight	997 (2198)	877 (1933)	1874 (4131)
EEC kerb weight	1014 (2235)	1002 (2209)	2016 (4444)
Gross vehicle weight *	1200 (2645)	1510 (3329)	2510 (5533)

Note: UNLADEN WEIGHT is the minimum vehicle specification, excluding fuel and driver.
EEC KERB WEIGHT is the minimum vehicle specification, plus full fuel tank and 75 kg (165 lb) driver.
GROSS VEHICLE WEIGHT is the minimum all-up weight of the vehicle including driver, passengers, payload and equipment. This figure is liable to vary according to legal requirements in certain countries.

When air condition is fitted 42 kg (93 lb) must be added to the above front axle weight and total weight and total weight figures (unladen and EEC kerb weights).

Vehicle weights and payloads

When loading a vehicle to its maximum (Gross Vehicle Weight), consideration must be taken of the unladen vehicle weight, the distribution of the payload and two hitch loading (where applicable) to ensure that axle loadings do not exceed the permitted maximum values.

* Note: To accommodate different loading conditions (e.g. due to fitment of optional equipment such as winches) the sum of the maximum allowable front and rear axle loads exceeds the Gross vehicle weight. It is the customer's responsibility to limit the vehicle's payload in an appropriate manner such that neither maximum axle loads nor Gross Vehicle Weight are exceeded.

Approximate capacities

Component		Litres	Imperial unit
Engine sump oil	· petrol engines	5,1	9 pints
	· diesel engines	7	12 pints
Extra when refilling after fitting new filter	· petrol engines	0,56	1 pint
	· diesel engines	0,8	1.4 pints
Main gearbox oil	· manual model	2,27	4 pints
	· automatic model	9,1	16 pints
Transfer gearbox oil		2,5	4.4 pints
Rear differential oil		1,7	3 pints
Front differential oil		1,7	3 pints
Swivel housing oil (each)		0,35	0.6 pints
Power steering box and reservoir fluid		2,9	5 pints
Cooling system		11,3	20 pints
Fuel tank		79,5	17.5 gallons

Note: All levels must be checked by dipstick or level plugs as applicable. When draining the automatic gearbox, oil will remain in the torque converter therefore fill to level on dipstick.

Anti-freeze solutions

	Litres	Pints
Cooling system capacity	11,3	20
Anti-freeze required for 50% solution	5,7	10

Note: Coolant solution must not fall below proportions of one part anti-freeze to three parts water, i.e. minimum 25% anti-freeze in coolant, otherwise engine damage will occur.

Corrosion inhibitor

When anti-freeze is not required, the cooling system must be flushed out with clean water and filled with a solution of one part Marstons SQ36 inhibitor to nine parts water to provide a 10% mixture concentration.

Recommended lubricants, fuel and fluids

Use only the recommended grades of oil as set out below.

The oil level dipstick will be found on the left-hand side of the engine and the oil filler cap is screwed into the right-hand rocker cover at the front of the engine.

Oil consumption is likely to improve during the first 6,000 km (4,000 miles) of the vehicle's life as the piston rings, etc. bed in.

These recomendations apply to temperate climates where operational temperatures may vary between -10°C (14°F) and 35°C (95°F)

COMPONENTS	BP	CASTROL	DUCKHAMS	ESSO	MOBIL	PETROFINA	SHELL	TEXACO
Petrol engine sump and carburetter dashpots	BP Visco 2000 (15W/40) or BP Visco Nova (10W/30)	Castrol GTX (15W/50) or Castrolite 10W/40	Duckhams (15W/50) Hypergrade Motor Oil	Esso Superlube (15W/40)	Mobil Super 10W/40 or Mobil 1 Rally Formula 5W/50	Fina Supergrade Motor Oil 15W/40 or 10W/40	Shell Super Motor Oil 15W/40 or 10W/40	Havoline Motor Oil 15W/40 or Eurotex HD (10W/30)
Diesel engine sump	BP Vanellus C3 Extra (15W/40)	Castrol Deusol Turbomax (15W/40)			Mobil Delvac 1400 Super (15W/40)		Shell Myrina (15W/40)	

The following list of oils is for emergency use only if the above oils are not available. They can be used for topping-up without detriment, but if used for engine oil changing, they are limited to a maximum of 5,000 km (3,000 miles) between oil and filter changes.

Use only oils to MIL-L-2104D or CCMC D2 or API Service levels CD or SE/CD - 15W/40

	BP	CASTROL	DUCKHAMS	ESSO	MOBIL	PETROFINA	SHELL	TEXACO
	BP Vanellus Multigrade (15W/40)	Castrol Deusol RX Super (15W/40)	Duckhams Hypergrade (15W/50)	Esso Essolube XD-3 (15W/40)	Mobil Delvac Super (15W/40)	Fina Dilano HPD (15W/40)	Shell Rimula X (15W/40)	Texaco URSA Super Plus (15W/40)
Automatic gearbox	BP Autran DX2D	Castrol TQ Dexron IID	Duckhams Fleetmatic CD or Duckhams D-Matic	Esso ATF Dexron IID	Mobil ATF 220D	Fina Dexron IID	Shell ATF Dexron IID	Texamatic Fluid 9226
Manual gearbox	BP Autran G	Castrol TQF	Duckhams Q-Matic	Esso ATF Type G	Mobil ATF 210	Fina Purfimatic 33G	Shell Donax TF	Texmatic Type G

Recommended lubricants, fuel and fluids (temperate climates) - continued

COMPONENTS	BP	CASTROL	DUCKHAMS	ESSO	MOBIL	PETROFINA	SHELL	TEXACO
Front differential, Rear differential, Swivel pin housings	BP Gear Oil SAE 90EP	Castrol Hypoy SAE 90EP	Duckhams Hypoid 90	Esso Gear Oil GX 85W/90	Mobil Mobilube HD90	Fina Pontonic MP SAE 80W/90	Shell Spirax 90EP	Texaco Multigear Lubricant EP 85W/90
Prop. shaft, front and rear	BP Energrease L2	Castrol LM Grease	Duckhams LB 10	Esso Multi-purpose Grease H	Mobil- grease MP	Fina Marson HTL2	Shell Retinax A	Marfak All purpose Grease
Power steering box and fluid reservoir Transfer box	BP Autran DX2D *	Castrol TQ Dexron IID *	Duckhams Fleetmatic CD or Duckhams D-Matic *	Esso ATF Dexron IID *	Mobil ATF 220D *	Fina Dexron II *	Shell ATF Dexron IID *	Texamatic Fluid 9226 *
Brake and clutch reservoirs	Brake fluids having a minimum boiling point of 260°C (500°F) and complying with FMVSS 116 DOT3 or DOT4							
Lubrication nipples (hubs, ball joints, etc.)	BP Energrease L2	Castrol LM Grease	Duckhams LB 10	Esso Multi-purpose Grease H	Mobil- grease MP	Fina Marson HTL2	Shell Retinax A	Marfak All purpose Grease
Ball joint assembly Top link	Dextagrease Super GP							
Seat slides, Door lock striker	BP Energrease L2	Castrol LM Grease	Duckhams LB 10	Esso Multi-purpose Grease H	Mobil- grease MP	Fina Marson HTL2	Shell Retinax A	Marfak All purpose Grease
	NLGI-2 Multi-purpose Lithium-based Grease							

* Or fluids listed for manual gearbox

Recommended lubricants, fuels and fluids (temperate climates) - continued

Bonnet pintle	Graphite Lock Grease Type 'R'
Door locks (anti-burst) Inertia reels	**DO NOT LUBRICATE.** These components are 'life' lubricated at the manufacturing stage
Battery lugs Earthing surfaces Where paint has been removed	Petroleum jelly *Note: Do not use Silicone Grease*
Fuel	Petrol engines - 9.35:1 compression ratio - 97 octane fuel (4 star rating in UK) 8.13:1 compression ratio - 90 octane fuel (2 star rating in UK) Diesel engines - 22:1 compression ratio - Diesel fuel oil, distillate, diesel fuel, automotive gas oil or Derv fuel to British Standard 2869, 1967 Class A1
Windscreen washers	Screen Washer Fluid
Engine cooling system	FOR ALL PETROL AND DIESEL MODELS Use an ethylene glycol based anti-freeze (containing no methanol) with non-phosphate corrosion inbibitors suitable for use in aluminim engines to ensure the protection of the cooling system against frost and corrosion in all seasons. Use one part anti-freeze to one part water for protection down to -36°C (-33°F) *IMPORTANT: Coolant solution must not fall below proportions of one part anti-freeze to three parts water, i.e. minimum 25% anti-freeze in coolant otherwise damage to engine is liable to occur.* When anti-freeze is not required, the cooling system must be flushed out with clean water and refilled with a solution of one part Marstons SQ36 inhibitor to nine parts water, i.e. minimum 10% inhibitor in coolant
Air conditioning system Refrigerant	METHYLCHLORIDE REFRIGERANTS MUST NOT BE USED Use only with refrigerant 12. This includes 'Freon 12' and 'Arcton 12'
Compressor Oil	Shell Clavus 68 BP Energol LPT68 Sunisco 4GS Texaco Capella E Wax Free 68

6 LUBRICANTS AND FLUIDS

Recommended lubricants, fluids and anti-freeze solutions - All climates and conditions

COMPONENTS	SERVICE CLASSIFICATION: Specification	SERVICE CLASSIFICATION: SAE Classification	AMBIENT TEMPERATURE °C
			-30 -20 -10 0 10 20 30 40 50
Petrol models Engine sump Dash pots (carburetter models only) Oil can	Oils must meet BLS.22.OL.07 or CCMC G3 or API service levels SF	5W/30 5W/40) 5W/50) 10W/30 10W/40) 10W/50)	
	Oils must meet BLS.22.OL.02 or CCMC G1 or G2 or API service levels SE or SF	15W/40) 15W/50) 20W/40) 20W/50) 25W/40) 25W/50)	
Diesel models engine sump	SHPD oils meeting CCMC D3	10W/30 15W/40	
	* **Emergency only:** Oils meeting MIL-L-2104D or CCMCD2 or API CD		
Main gearbox, automatic	ATF Dexron IID		
Main Gearbox manual	ATF M2C33 (F or G)		
Transfer gearbox Final drive units Swivel pin housings	API GL4 or GL5 MIL-L-2105 or MIL-L-2105B	90 EP 80W EP	
Power steering	ATF M2C 33 (F or G) or LATF Dexron II D		

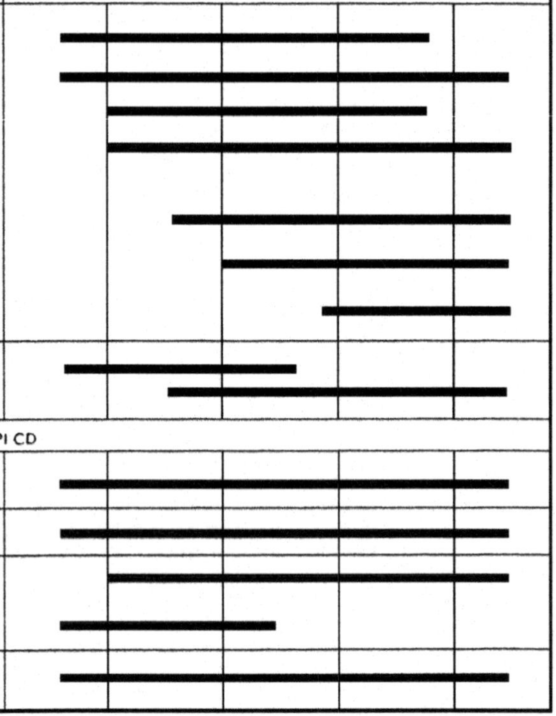

* Oils for emergency use only if the above oils are not available. They can be used for topping up without detriment, but if used for engine oil changing, they are limited to a maximum of 5,000 km (3,000 miles) between oil and filter changes.

Recommended lubricants, fluids and anti-freeze solutions - All climates and conditions - (continued)

Lubrication nipples (hubs, ball joints, prop. shafts, etc.)	NLGI-2 Multipurpose Lithium based grease
Brake and clutch reservoirs	Universal Brake Fluids or other Brake Fluids having a minimum boiling point of 260°C (500°F) and complying with FMVSS 116 DOT4
Windscreen washers	Screen Washer Fluid
Engine cooling system	FOR ALL PETROL AND DIESEL MODELS Use an ethylene glycol based anti-freeze (containing no methanol) with non-phosphate corrosion inbibitors suitable for use in aluminim engines to ensure the protection of the cooling system against frost and corrosion in all seasons. Use one part anti-freeze to one part water for protection down to -36°C (-33°F) *IMPORTANT: Coolant solution must not fall below proportions of one part anti-freeze to three parts water, i.e. minimum 25% anti-freeze in coolant otherwise damage to engine is liable to occur.* When anti-freeze is not required, the cooling system must be flushed out with clean water and refilled with a solution of one part Marstons SQ36 inhibitor to nine parts water, i.e. minimum 10% inhibitor in coolant
Air conditioning system Refrigerant	METHYLCHLORIDE REFRIGERANTS MUST NOT BE USED Use only with refrigerant 12. This includes 'Freon 12' and 'Arcton 12'
Compressor Oil	Shell Clavus 68 BP Energol LPT68 Sunisco 4GS Texaco Capella E Wax Free 68

Electrical equipment

System	12 volt negative earth
Distributor	Lucas 35 DLM8
Battery	Chloride maintenance-free 9-plate 210/85/90
Alternator	Lucas A133/65
Starter motor	Lucas M78R geared
Wiper motor · front	Lucas 28W, 2-speed
· rear	Imos
Fuses	Autofuse (blade type) blow ratings to suit individual circuits

Replacement bulbs

Headlamps	12V 60/55W (Halogen)
Headlamps - France amber	12V 60/55W (Halogen)
Auxiliary driving lamps	12V 55W H3 (Halogen)
Sidelamps	12V 4W bayonet fitting
Stop/tail lamp	12V 5/21W bayonet fitting
Reverse lamps	12V 21W bayonet fitting
Rear fog guard lamps	12V 21W bayonet fitting
Direction indicator lamps	12V 21W bayonet fitting
Direction indicator repeater lamps	12V 4W bayonet fitting
Number plate lamps	12V 5W capless
Door edge/puddle lamps	12V 5W capless
Instrument panel lamps and warning lamps	12V 1.2W bulb/holder unit
Ignition warning lamp (instrument panel)	12V 2W capless
Interior roof lamps	12V 10W festoon
Clock illumination	12V 2W bayonet fitting
Cigar lighter illumination	12V 1.2W capless
Auxiliary switch panel illumination (green)	12V 1.2W capless
Heated rear screen warning lamp (amber)	12V 1.2W capless
Hazard warning lamp (red)	12V 1.2W capless
Heater automatic graphics illumination	24V 5W capless
Air conditioning graphics illumination	12V 1.2W capless
Differential lock warning lamp	12V 2W bayonet fitting
Column switch illumination (fibre optic)	12V 1.2W capless
Rear fog warning lamp (amber)	12V 1.2W capless

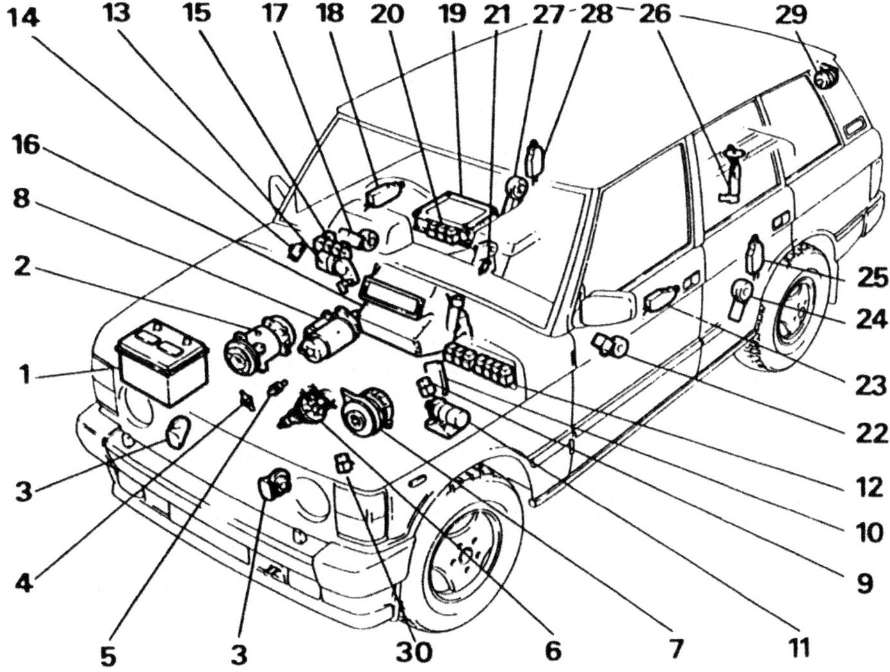

1. Battery
2. Air conditioning compressor (if fitted)
3. Horns
4. Oil pressure switch
5. Water temperature switch
6. Distributor
7. Alternator
8. Starter motor
9. Over-run fuel shut-off relay (fuel injection models only)
10. Power resistor (fuel injection models only)
11. Coil and amplifer assembly
12. Relays
13. Front windscreen wiper motor
14. Choke warning light switch (carburetter versions only)
15. Relays
16. Heater
17. Window lift motor
18. Door lock actuator
19. Electronic control unit (fuel injection models only)
20. Relays (fuel injection models only)
21. Handbrake warning light switch
22. Window lift motor
23. Door lock actuator
24. Window lift motor
25. Door lock actuator
26. Electrical fuel pump
27. Window lift motor
28. Door lock actuator
29. Rear screen wiper motor
30. Fuel shut-off relay (carburetter only)

Note: Right-hand drive vehicles illustrated - certain electrical components may change position on left-hand drive vehicles but can be found within a similar location on the opposite side of the vehicle.

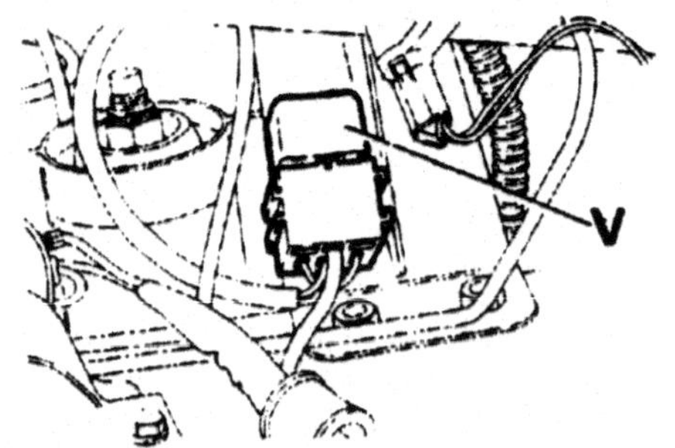

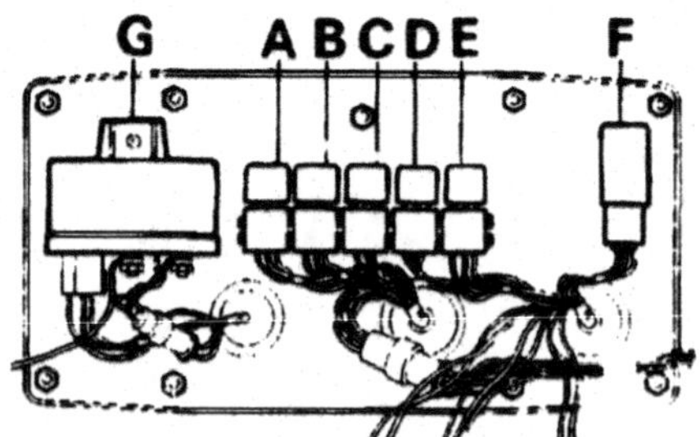

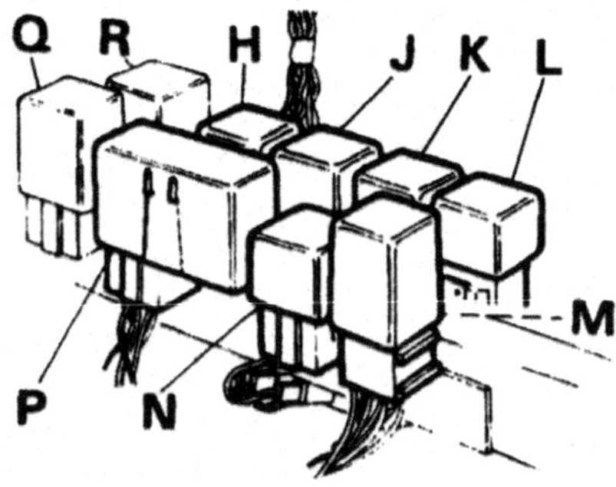

9 Over-run fuel shut-off relay (fuel injection only)

V   Over-run fuel shut-off

12 Relays

A	Air conditioning/heater
B	Condenser fan
C	Compressor clutch
D	Starter solenoid
E	Heated rear window
F	Headlamp wash timer unit
G	Glow plug timer (diesel)

15 Relays

H	Hazard/flasher unit
J	Voltage sensitive switch
K	Interior lamp delay
L	Auxiliary driving lamps
M	Front wiper delay
N	Ignition load relay
P	Rear wiper delay
Q	Overspeed monitor (Saudi only)
R	Overspeed buzzer (Saudi only)

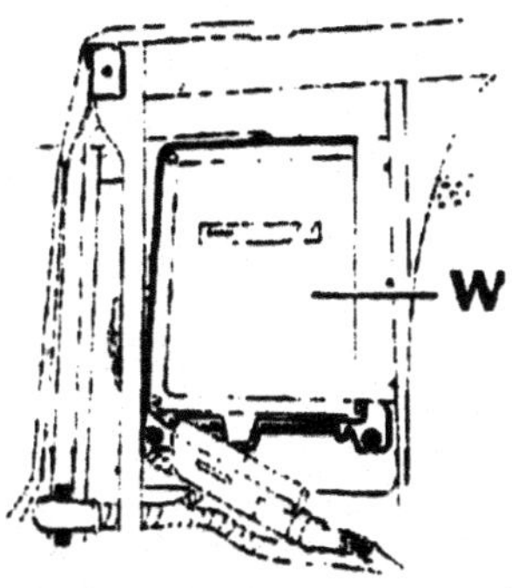

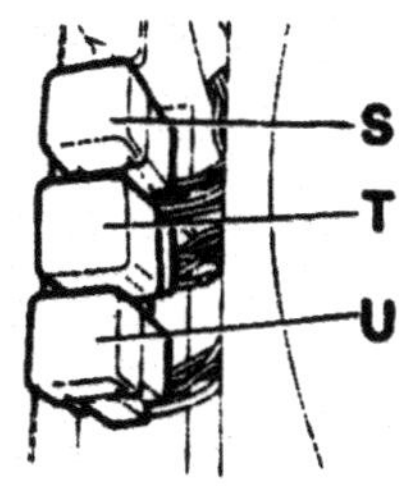

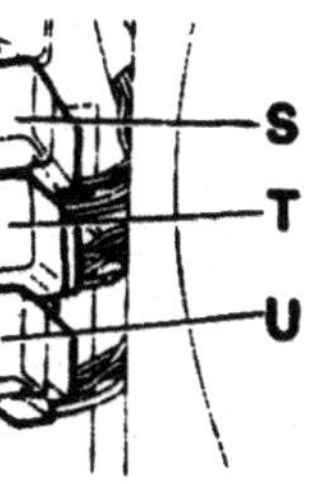

19 Electronic control unit (fuel injection only)
W   Electronic control unit

20 Relays (fuel injection only)
S   Fuel pump
T   Steering module (red case)
U   Main

30 Fuel shut-off relay (carburetter only)
X   Fuel shut-off

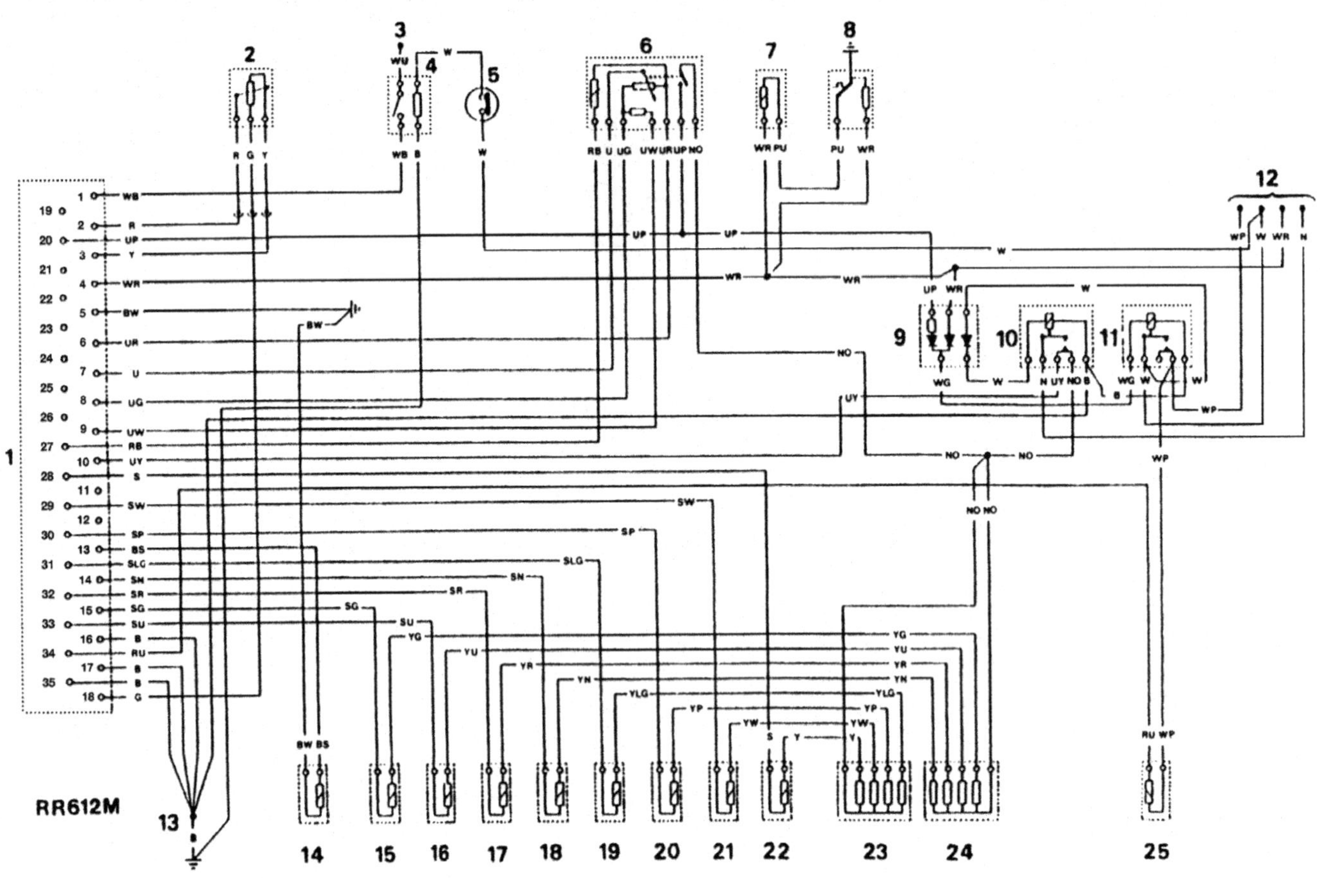

RR612M

Circuit diagram — fuel injection — Fig. RR612M

 1 Electronic control unit (ECU)
 2 Throttle potentiometer
 3 Ignition pick up point (142 on main circuit diagram)
 4 Over run fuel shut off relay
 5 Vacuum switch
 6 Airflow meter
 7 Cold start injecctor
 8 Thermotime switch
 9 Steering module for fuel injection relays
10 Main relay
11 Fuel pump relay
12 Pick up point fuel injection circuit (111 main circuit diagram)
13 Clinch
14 Temperature sensor
15 Injector (No 1 cylinder)
16 Injector (No 3 cylinder)
17 Injector (No 5 cylinder)
18 Injector (No 7 cylinder)
19 Injector (No 2 cylinder)
20 Injector (No 4 cylinder)
21 Injector (No 6 cylinder)
22 Injector (No 8 cylinder)
23 Power resistors
24 Power resistors
25 Extra air valve

Key to cable colours

B — Black	G — Green
K — Pink	L — Light
N — Brown	O — Orange
P — Purple	R — Red
S — Slate	U — Blue
W — White	Y — Yellow

The last letter of a colour code denotes the tracer colour

Connectors via plug and socket

Snap connectors

Permanent in-line connections

Earth connections via cables

Earth connections via fixing bolts

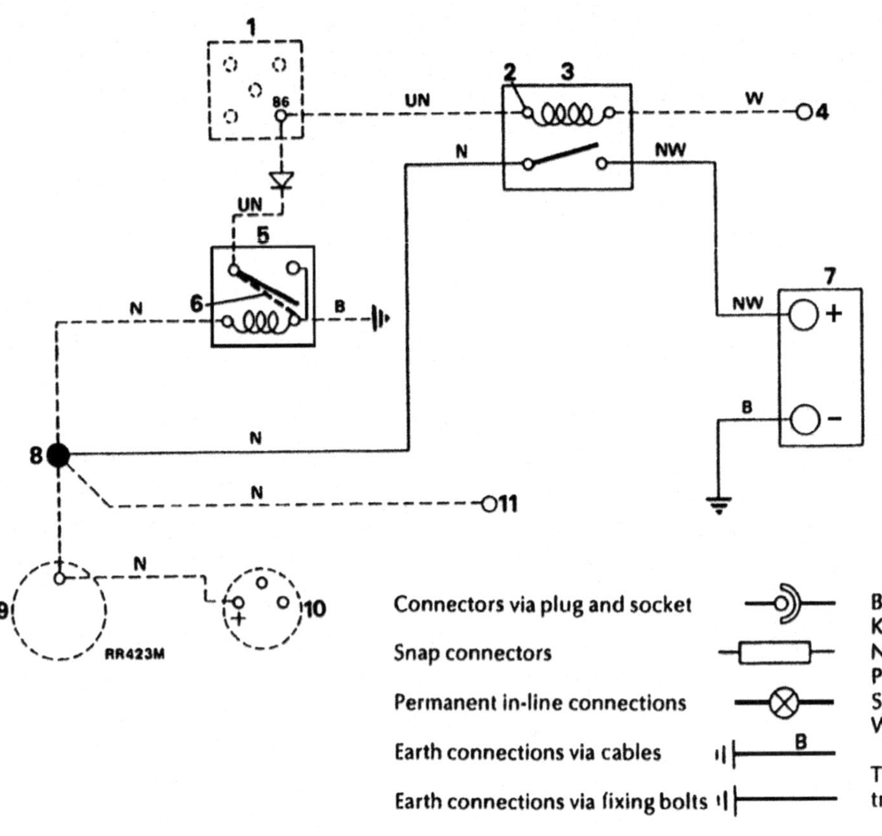

Optional electrical equipment — Range Rover 2
and 4 door models
Split charge circuit diagram — Fig. RR423M
 1 Heated rear window relay
 2 Pick-up point for split charge relay (item
    125 or 106 on main circuit diagram)
 3 Split charge relay
 4 Fuse box
 5 Voltage sensitive switch
 6 Link wire (removed from plug when
    voltage sensitive switch is fitted)
 7 Terminal box auxiliary battery
 8 Terminal post
 9 Starter motor
10 Alternator
11 Vehicle battery

*Note: Chain dotted lines indicate existing
parts.*

Key to cable colours

Connectors via plug and socket		B — Black	G — Green
		K — Pink	L — Light
Snap connectors		N — Brown	O — Orange
		P — Purple	R — Red
Permanent in-line connections		S — Slate	U — Blue
		W — White	Y — Yellow
Earth connections via cables	B		
Earth connections via fixing bolts			

The last letter of a colour code denotes the
tracer colour

1 Clinch
2 Main cable connections (item 75 on main
  circuit diagram)
3 Mirrors
4 Mirror switches

**Optional electrical equipment — Range Rover 4
door models
Electric mirrors circuit diagram — Fig. RR424M**

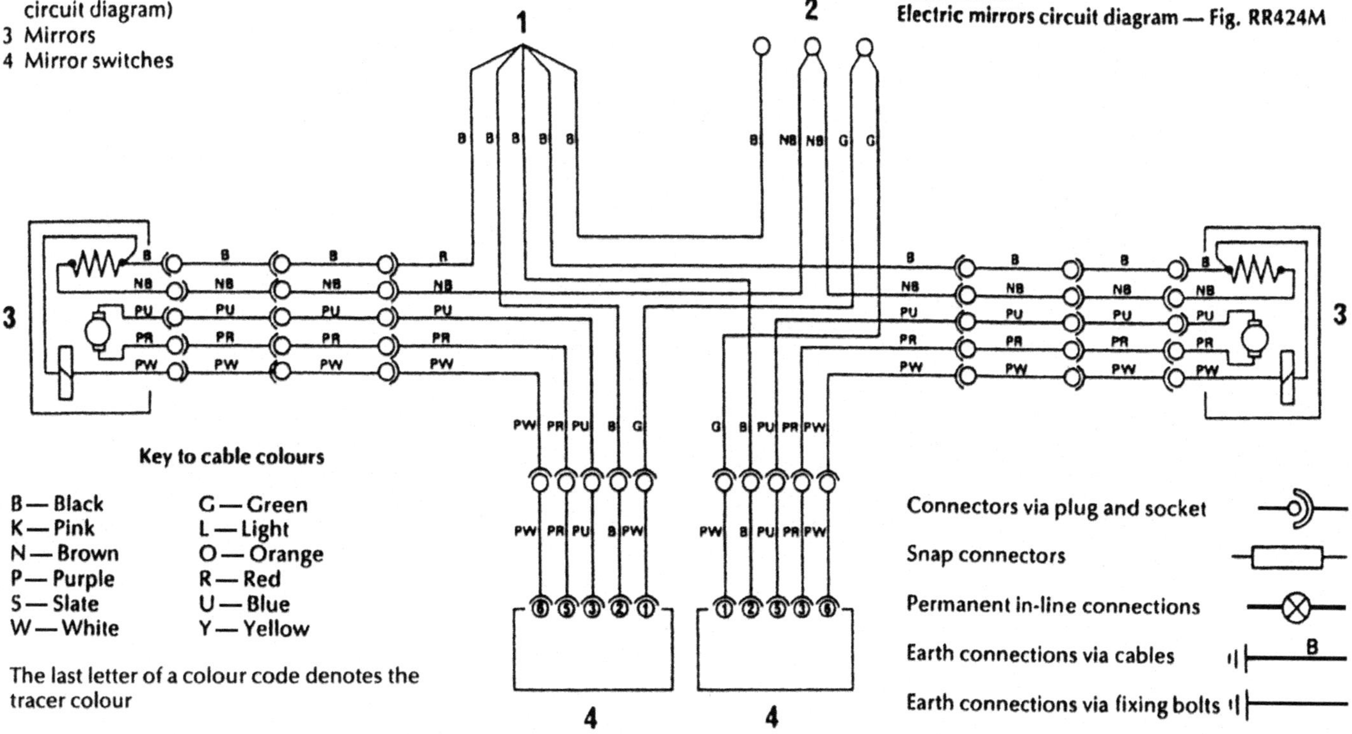

Key to cable colours

B — Black   G — Green
K — Pink   L — Light
N — Brown   O — Orange
P — Purple   R — Red
S — Slate   U — Blue
W — White   Y — Yellow

The last letter of a colour code denotes the
tracer colour

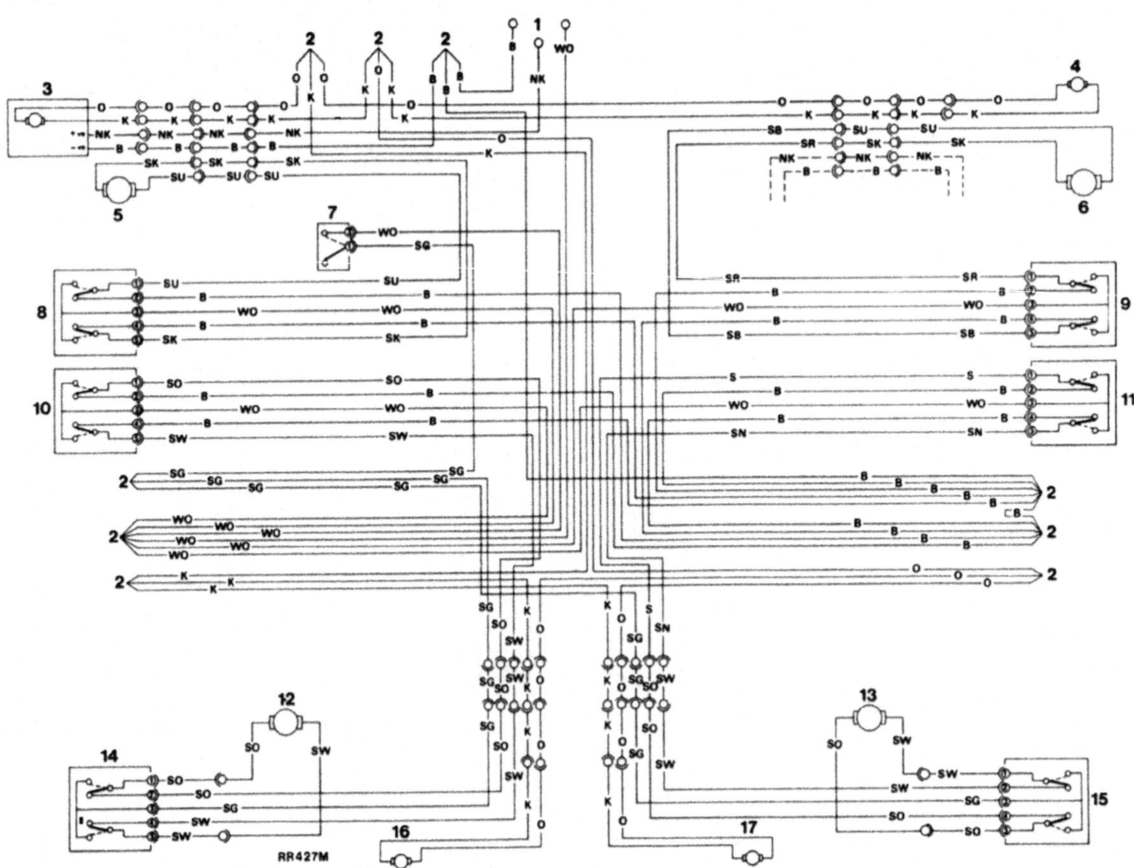
RR427M

Optional electrical equipment — Range Rover 4-door models

Window lifts and door locks circuit diagram — Fig. RR427M

1 Main cable connections (item 107 on main circuit diagram)
2 Clinches
3 Switch unit central door locking (drivers door)
4 Lock unit central door locking (front passenger door)
5 Window lift motor left hand front
6 Window lift motor right hand front
7 Isolator switch
8 Window lift switch left hand front
9 Window lift switch right hand front
10 Window lift switch left hand rear
11 Window lift switch right hand rear
12 Window lift motor left hand rear
13 Window lift motor right hand rear
14 Window lift switch left hand rear door
15 Window lift switch right hand rear door
16 Lock unit central door locking left hand rear
17 Lock unit central door locking right hand rear

Key to cable colours

B — Black	G — Green
K — Pink	L — Light
N — Brown	O — Orange
P — Purple	R — Red
S — Slate	U — Blue
W — White	Y — Yellow

The last letter of a colour code denotes the tracer colour

Connectors via plug and socket 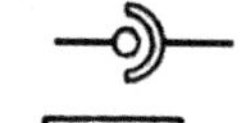

Snap connectors 

Permanent in-line connections 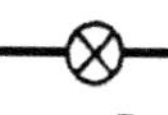

Earth connections via cables

Earth connections via fixing bolts 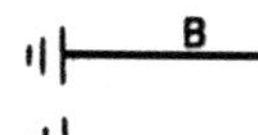

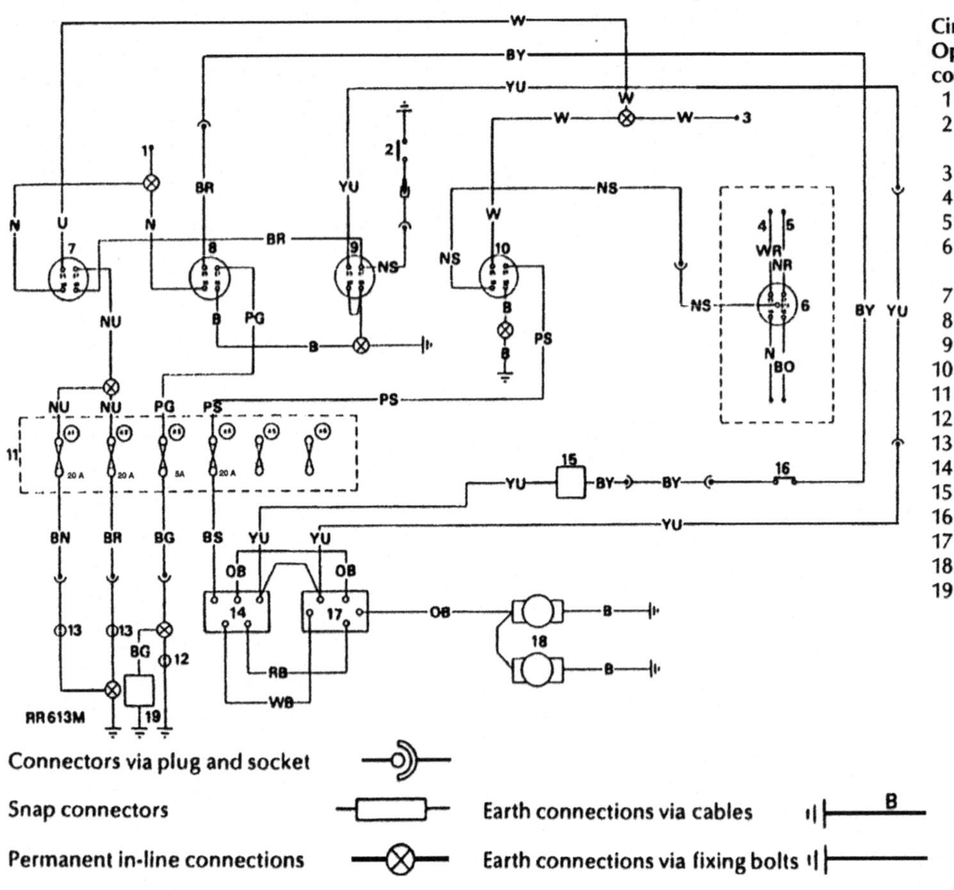

Circuit diagram — Fig. RR613M
Optional electrical equipment recirculating air/conditioning

1 Terminal post
2 Engine water temperature switch (automatic only)
3 Ignition feed
4 Crank feed
5 Starter solenoid
6 Starter relay (item 122 on main circuit diagram)
7 Fan relay
8 Compressor clutch relay
9 Air conditioning controlled fan relay
10 Air conditioning relay (ignition controlled)
11 Auxiliary fuse box
12 Compressor clutch
13 Fans
14 Control switch
15 Thermostat
16 High pressure switch
17 Resistor
18 Blower motors
19 Solenoid-operated air valve

Key to cable colours

B — Black	G — Green
K — Pink	L — Light
N — Brown	O — Orange
P — Purple	R — Red
S — Slate	U — Blue
W — White	Y — Yellow

The last letter of a colour code denotes the tracer colour

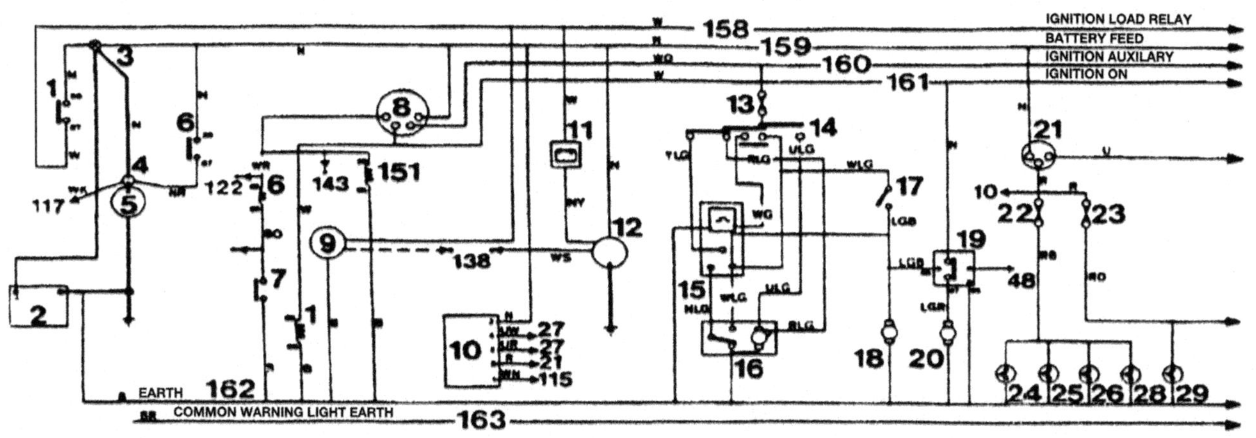
IGNITION LOAD RELAY
BATTERY FEED
IGNITION AUXILARY
IGNITION ON
158
159
160
161
EARTH
COMMON WARNING LIGHT EARTH
162
163

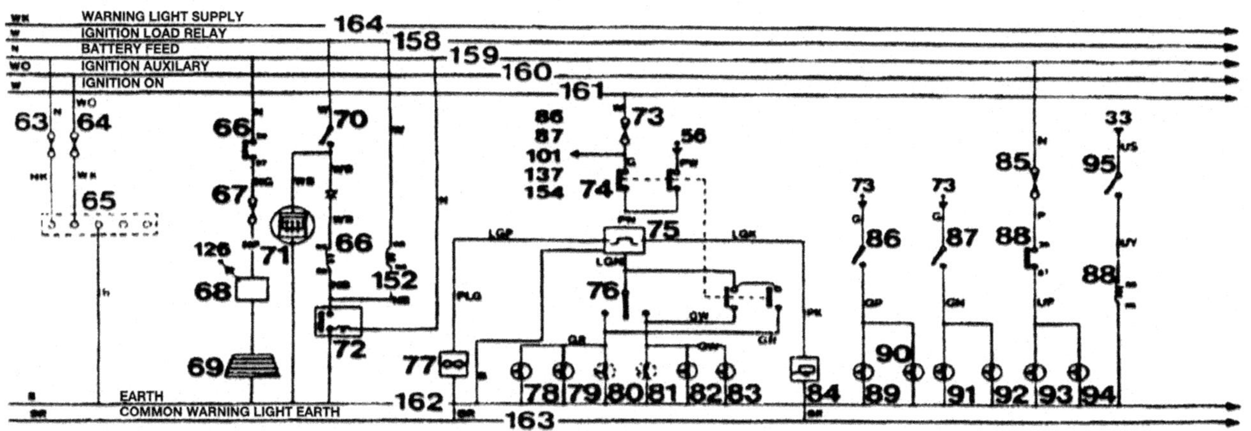
WARNING LIGHT SUPPLY
IGNITION LOAD RELAY
BATTERY FEED
IGNITION AUXILARY
IGNITION ON
164
158
159
160
161
EARTH
COMMON WARNING LIGHT EARTH
162
163

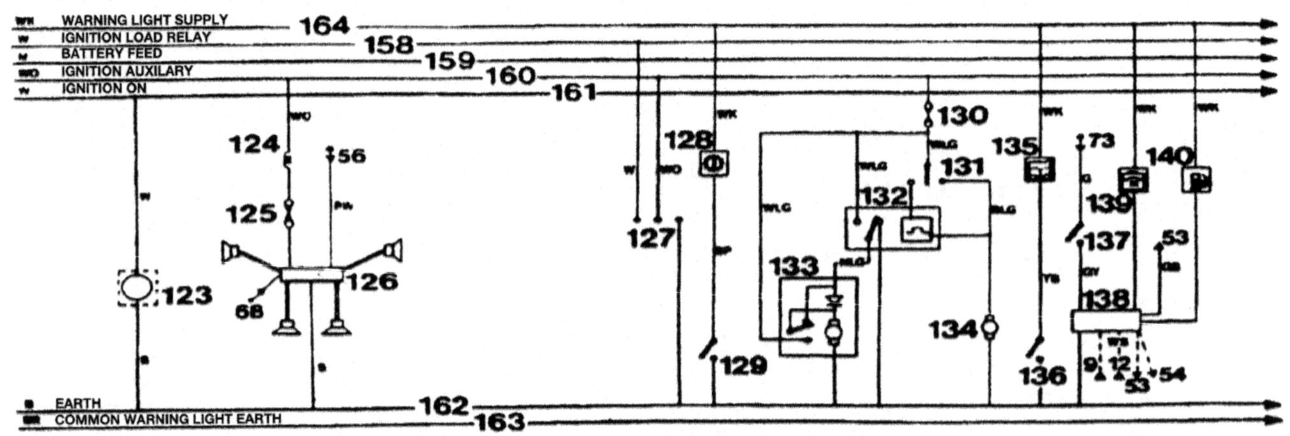

WARNING LIGHT SUPPLY
IGNITION LOAD RELAY
BATTERY FEED
IGNITION AUXILARY
IGNITION ON
164
158
159
160
161
124
125
126
123
68
56
127
128
129
130
131
132
133
134
135
136
137
138
139
140
73
53
9 12
53 54
EARTH
COMMON WARNING LIGHT EARTH
162
163

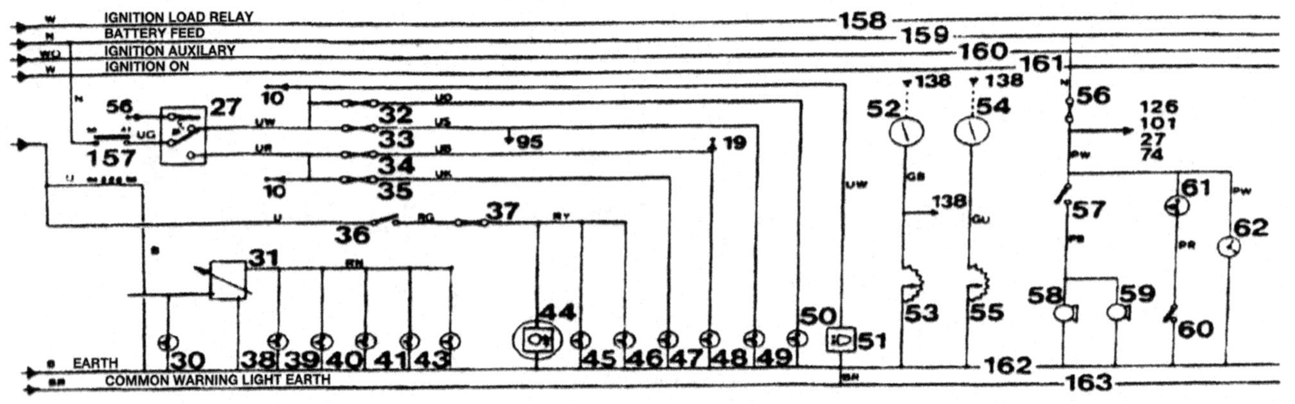

IGNITION LOAD RELAY
BATTERY FEED
IGNITION AUXILARY
IGNITION ON
158
159
160
161
56
27
157
10
32
33
34
35
10
36
37
95
19
31
30
38 39 40 41 43
44
45 46 47 48 49
50
51
52
54
138
138
138
56
126
101
27
74
57
61
62
58
59
60
53
55
EARTH
COMMON WARNING LIGHT EARTH
162
163

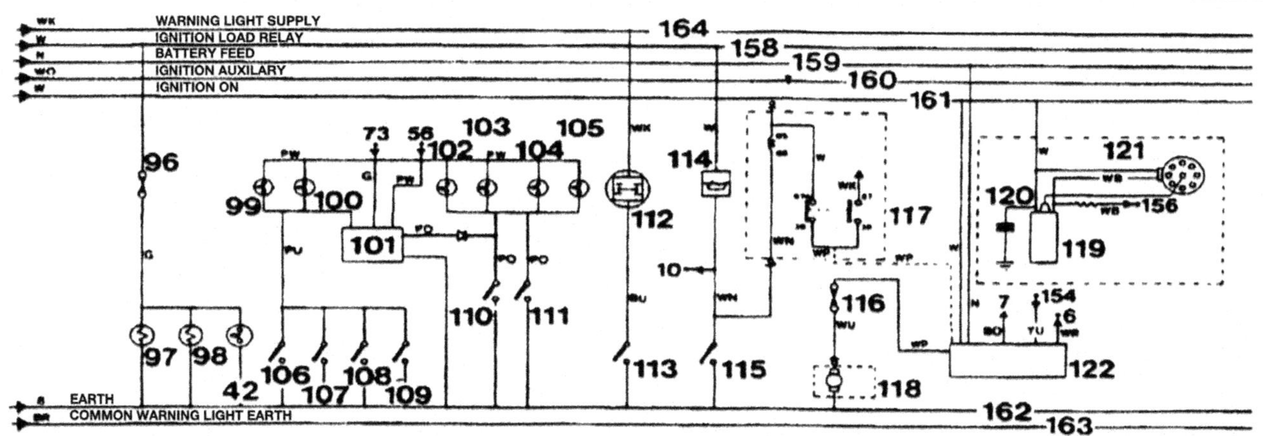
WARNING LIGHT SUPPLY
IGNITION LOAD RELAY
BATTERY FEED
IGNITION AUXILARY
IGNITION ON
164
158
159
160
161
EARTH
COMMON WARNING LIGHT EARTH
162
163

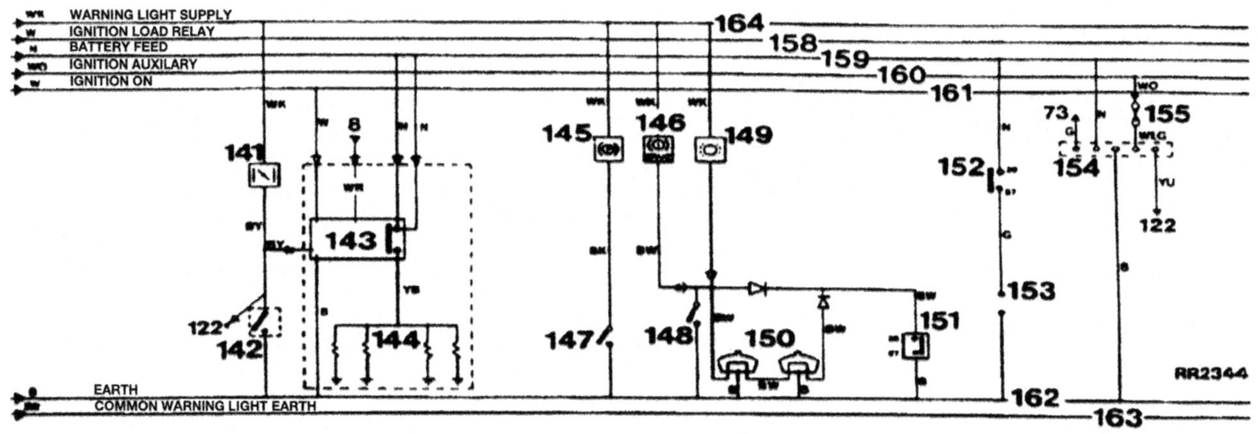
WARNING LIGHT SUPPLY
IGNITION LOAD RELAY
BATTERY FEED
IGNITION AUXILARY
IGNITION ON
164
158
159
160
161
EARTH
COMMON WARNING LIGHT EARTH
162
163
RR2344

MAIN CIRCUIT DIAGRAM   Right Hand Steering - RR2343M & RR2344M

1	Ignition load relay	33	Fuse 4	64	Fuse 20
2	Battery	34	Fuse 1	65	Pick-up point central locking/
3	Terminal post	35	Fuse 2		window lift (option)
4	Starter solenoid	36	Rear fog switch	66	Heated rear window relay
5	Starter motor	37	Fuse 12	67	Fuse 9
6	Starter relay	38	Switch illumination (2 off)	68	Radio aerial amplifier
7	Starter inhibit switch (Automatic)	39	Cigar lighter illumination (2 off)	69	Heated rear screen
8	Ignition switch	40	Heater illumination (4 off)	70	Heated rear screen switch
9	Tachometer	41	Clock illumination	71	Heated rear screen warning lamp
10	Voltage transformer(dim dip)	42	Automatic gear selector	72	Voltage sensitive switch
11	Ignition warning lamp		illumination (2 off)	73	Fuse 13
12	Alternator	43	Instrument illumination (6 off)	74	Hazard switch
13	Fuse 7	44	Rear fog warning lamp	75	Flasher unit
14	Front wipe/wash switch	45	LH rear fog	76	Direction indicator switch
15	Front wipe delay unit	46	RH rear fog	77	Hazard/indicator warning lamp
16	Front wiper motor	47	LH dip beam	78	LH rear indicator lamp
17	Front wash switch	48	RH dip beam	79	LH front indicator lamp
18	Front wash pump	49	LH main beam	80	LH side repeater lamp
19	Headlamp wash timer unit (option)	50	RH main beam	81	RH side repeater lamp
20	Headlamp wash pump (option)	51	Main beam warning lamp	82	RH front indicator lamp
21	Main lighting switch	52	Fuel gauge	83	RH rear indicator lamp
22	Fuse 6	53	Fuel gauge sender unit	84	Trailer warning lamp
23	Fuse 5	54	Water temperature gauge	85	Fuse 15
24	LH side lamp	55	Water temperature sender unit	86	Stop lamp switch
25	LH tail lamp	56	Fuse 11	87	Reverse lamp switch
26	Number plate lamp(2 off)	57	Horn switch	88	Auxiliary lamp relay (option)
27	Main beam dip/flash switch	58	RH horn	89	LH stop lamp
28	Radio illumination	59	LH horn	90	RH stop lamp
29	RH side lamp	60	Under bonnet illumination switch	91	LH reverse lamp
30	RH tail lamp	61	Under bonnet light	92	RH reverse lamp
31	Rheostat	62	Clock	93	LH auxiliary lamp (option)
32	Fuse 3	63	Fuse 19	94	RH auxiliary lamp (option)

95	Auxiliary lamp switch (option)
96	Fuse 17
97	Dash cigar lighter
98	Cubby box cigar lighter
99	LH interior lamp
100	RH interior lamp
101	Interior lamp delay unit
102	LH door edge lamp
103	RH door edge lamp
104	LH puddle lamp
105	RH puddle lamp
106	Interior lamp switch
107	LH rear door switch
108	RH rear door switch
109	Tailgate switch
110	LH front door switch
111	RH front door switch
112	Differential lock warning lamp
113	Differential lock switch
114	Oil pressure warning lamp
115	Oil pressure switch
116	Fuse 18
117	Fuel cut off relay (carburetter models)
118	Fuel pump (petrol models)
119	Ignition coil
120	Capacitor
121	Distributor
122	EFI Harness plug
123	Fuel shut off solenoid (Diesel)
124	Radio choke
125	Radio fuse
126	Radio and four speakers
127	Ignition pick up points
128	Automatic transmission oil temperature warning lamp
129	Automatic transmission oil temperature switch
130	Fuse 16
131	Rear wash wipe switch
132	Rear wipe delay unit
133	Rear wiper motor
134	Rear screen wash pump
135	Low screen wash fluid level warning lamp
136	Low screen wash switch
137	Low coolant switch
138	Multi-function unit in binnacle
139	Low coolant level warning lamp
140	Low fuel level warning lamp
141	Cold start/diesel glow plug warning lamp
142	Cold start switch - carburetter
143	Glow plug timer (diesel)
144	Glow plugs (diesel)
145	Handbrake warning lamp
146	Brake fail warning lamp
147	Handbrake warning switch
148	Brake fail warning switch
149	Brake pad wear warning lamp
150	Brake pad wear sensors
151	Brake check relay
152	Split charge relay (option)
153	Split charge terminal post (option)
154	Heater/air conditioning connections
155	Fuse 8
156	Coil negative (engine RPM input to ECU.)

CABLE COLOUR CODE

B	Black	G	Green	K	Pink	S	Slate
U	Blue	L	Light	P	Purple	W	White
N	Brown	O	Orange	R	Red	Y	Yellow

163

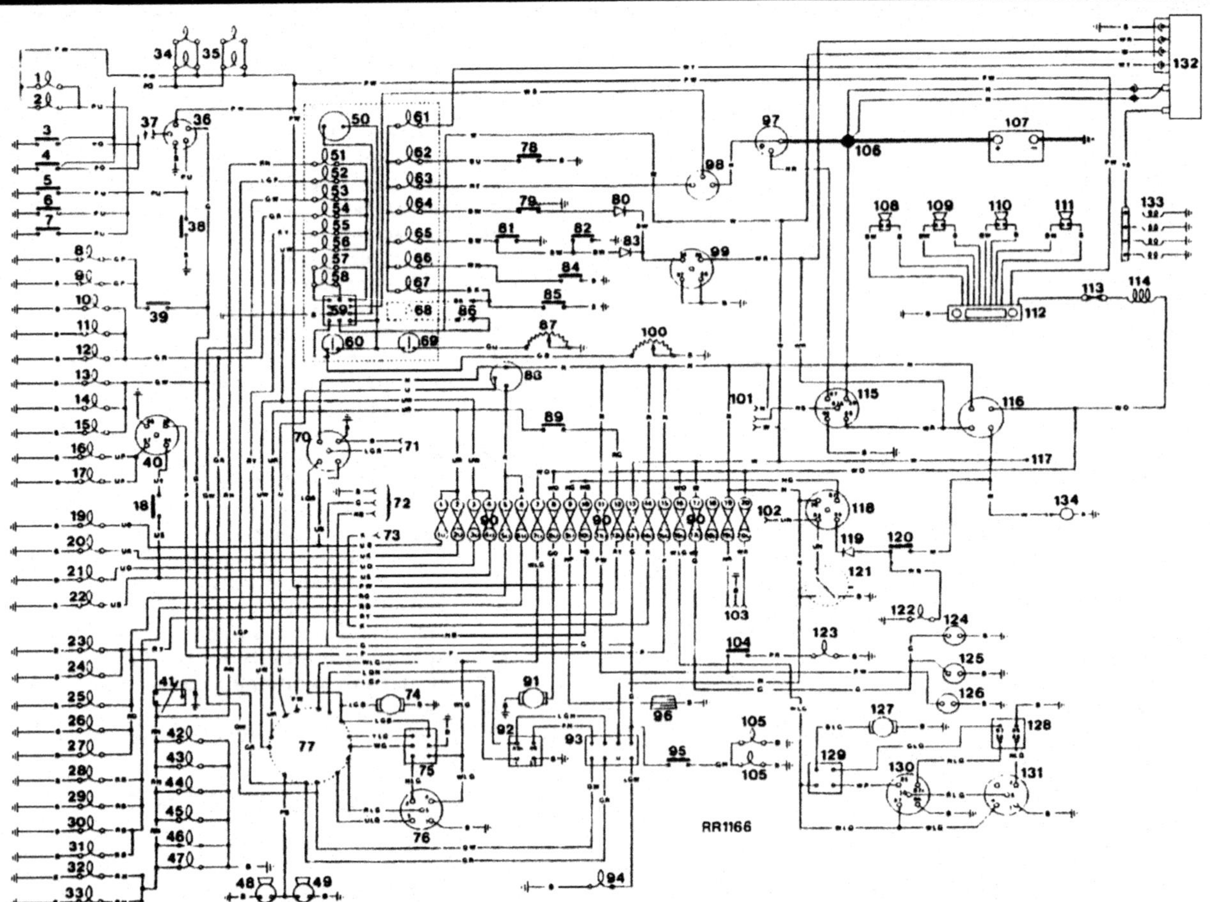
RR1166

KEY TO CIRCUIT DIAGRAM - Fig. RR1166

No.	Description
1	Front interior lamp
2	Rear interior lamp
3	LH front door switch
4	RH front door switch
5	Tailgate switch
6	LH rear door switch
7	RH rear door switch
8	RH stop lamp
9	LH stop lamp
10	LH front indicator lamp
11	LH rear indicator lamp
12	LH side repeater lamp
13	RH front indicator lamp
14	RH rear indicator lamp
15	RH side repeater lamp
16	RH auxiliary driving lamp
17	LH auxiliary driving lamp
18	Auxiliary driving lamp switch
19	RH headlamp dip
20	LH headlamp dip
21	RH headlamp main
22	LH headlamp main
23	RH rear fog lamp
24	LH rear fog lamp
25	RH number plate lamp
26	RH side lamp
27	RH tail lamp
28	LH number plate lamp
29	LH side lamp
30	LH tail lamp
31	Radio illumination
32	Switch illumination
33	Switch illumination
34	LH door lamps
35	RH door lamps
36	Interior lamp delay
37	Diode
38	Interior lamp switch
39	Stop lamp switch
40	Auxiliary lamps relay
41	Rheostat
42	Front cigar lighter illumination
43	Clock illumination
44	Heater illumination
45	Heater illumination
46	Heater illumination
47	Heater illumination
48	LH Horn
49	RH Horn
50	Tachometer
51	Instrument illumination (6 bulbs)
52	Trailer warning light
53	RH indicator warning light
54	LH indicator warning light
55	Rear fog warning light
56	Headlamp warning light
57	Not used
58	Low fuel warning light
59	Multifunction unit in binnacle
60	Fuel indicator gauge
61	Cold start warning light (carburetter versions only)
62	Differential lock warning light
63	Ignition warning light
64	Brake failure warning light
65	Brake pad wear warning light
66	Oil pressure warning light
67	Park brake warning light
68	Park brake warning light (Australia)
69	Water temperature gauge
70	Headlamp washer timer (option)
71	Headlamp wash pump (option)
72	Heated electric mirrors (option)
73	Trailer socket (option)
74	Front screen wash
75	Front wiper delay
76	Wiper motor
77	Steering column switches
78	Differential lock switch
79	Brake failure switch
80	Diode
81	Front brake pad wear
82	Rear brake pad wear
83	Diode
84	Oil pressure switch
85	Park brake switch
86	Pick up point - park brake warning light (Australia)
87	Water temperature transducer
88	Light switch
89	Rear fog lamp switch
90	Main fuse box
91	Heater motor and switch unit
92	Flasher unit
93	Hazard switch
94	Hazard warning lamp
95	Reverse lamp switch
96	Heated rear screen
97	Starter solenoid
98	Alternator
99	Brake failure warning lamp check relay
100	Fuel tank unit
101	Air conditioning (option)
102	Split charge relay (option)
103	Electric windows and central door locking (option)
104	Under bonnet illumination switch
105	Reverse lamps
106	Terminal post
107	Battery
108	LH rear speaker (option)
109	RH rear speaker (option)
110	LH front speaker
111	RH front speaker
112	Radio (option)
113	Radio fuse
114	Radio choke
115	Starter solenoid relay(on)
116	Ignition heat start switch
117	Split charge relay (option)
118	Heated rear windows relay
119	Diode
120	Heated rear window switch
121	Voltage switch (option)
122	Heated rear window warning lamp
123	Bonnet lamp
124	Cigar lighter (dash)
125	Cigar lighter (cubby box)
126	Clock
127	Rear screen wash motor
128	Rear wiper delay
129	Rear wash wipe switch
130	Rear wiper relay
131	Rear wiper motor
132	Timer for glow plugs
133	Glow plugs
134	Fuel shut off solenoid

KEY TO CABLE COLOURS

B -	Black	N -	Brown	G -	Green	O -	Orange	U -	Blue	S -	Slate
K -	Pink	P -	Purple	L -	Light	R -	Red	Y -	Yellow	W -	White

LAND ROVER OFFICIAL FACTORY PUBLICATIONS

Land Rover Series 1 Workshop Manual	4291
Land Rover Series 1 1948-53 Parts Catalogue	4051
Land Rover Series 1 1954-58 Parts Catalogue	4107
Land Rover Series 1 Instruction Manual	4277
Land Rover Series 1 & II Diesel Instruction Manual	4343
Land Rover Series II & IIA Workshop Manual	AKM8159
Land Rover Series II & Early IIA Bonneted Control Parts Catalogue	605957
Land Rover Series IIA Bonneted Control Parts Catalogue	RTC9840CC
Land Rover Series IIA, III & 109 V8 Optional Equipment Parts Catalogue	RTC9842CE
Land Rover Series IIA/IIB Instruction Manual	LSM64IM
Land Rover Series 2A and 3 88 Parts Catalogue Supplement (USA Spec) ✱	606494
Land Rover Series III Workshop Manual	AKM3648
Land Rover Series III Workshop Manual V8 Supplement (edn. 2)	AKM8022
Land Rover Series III 88, 109 & 109 V8 Parts Catalogue	RTC9841CE
Land Rover Series III Owners Manual 1971-1978	607324B
Land Rover Series III Owners Manual 1979-1985	AKM8155
Military Land Rover (Lightweight) Series III Parts Catalogue	61278
Military Land Rover Series III (L.W.B.) User Handbook	608179
Military Land Rover (Lightweight) Series III User Manual	608180
Land Rover 90/110 & Defender Workshop Manual 1983-1992	SLR621ENWM
Land Rover Defender Workshop Manual 1993-1995	LDAWMEN93
Land Rover Defender 300 Tdi & Supplements Workshop Manual 1996-1998	LRL0097ENGBB
Land Rover Defender Td5 Workshop Manual & Supplements 1999-2006	LRL0410BB
Land Rover Defender Electrical Manual Td5 1999-06 & 300Tdi 2002-2006	LRD5EHBB
Land Rover 110 Parts Catalogue 1983-1986	RTC9863CE
Land Rover Defender Parts Catalogue 1987-2006	STC9021CC
Land Rover 90 • 110 Handbook 1983-1990 MY	LSM0054
Land Rover Defender 90 • 110 • 130 Handbook 1991 MY - Feb. 1994	LHAHBEN93
Land Rover Defender 90 • 110 • 130 Handbook Mar. 1994 - 1998 MY	LRL0087ENG/2
Military Land Rover 90/110 All Variants (Excluding APV & SAS) User Manual	2320-D-122-201
Military Land Rover 90 & 110 2.5 Diesel Engine Versions User Handbook	SLR989WDHB
Military Land Rover Defender XD - Wolf Workshop Manual - 2320D128 -	302 522 523 524
Military Land Rover Defender XD - Wolf Parts Catalogue	2320D128711
Discovery Workshop Manual 1990-1994 (petrol 3.5, 3.9, Mpi & diesel 200 Tdi)	SJR900ENWM
Discovery Workshop Manual 1995-1998 (petrol 2.0 Mpi, 3.9, 4.0 V8 & diesel 300 Tdi)	LRL0079BB
Discovery Series II Workshop Manual 1999-2003 (petrol 4.0 V8 & diesel Td5 2.5)	VDR100090/6

Discovery Parts Catalogue 1989-1998 (2.0 Mpi, 3.5, 3.9 V8 & 200 Tdi & 300 Tdi)   RTC9947CF
Discovery Parts Catalogue 1999-2003 (petrol 4.0 V8 & diesel Td5 2.5)   STC9049CA
Discovery Owners Handbook 1990-1991 (petrol 3.5 V8 & diesel 200 Tdi)   SJR820ENHB90
Discovery Series II Handbook 1999-2004 MY (petrol 4.0 V8 & Td5 diesel)   LRL0459BB

Freelander Workshop Manual 1998-2000 (petrol 1.8 and diesel 2.0)   LRL0144
Freelander Workshop Manual 2001-2003 ON (petrol 1.8L, 2.5L & diesel Td4 2.0)   LRL0350ENG/4

Land Rover 101 1 Tonne Forward Control Workshop Manual   RTC9120
Land Rover 101 1 Tonne Forward Control Parts Catalogue   608294B
Land Rover 101 1 Tonne Forward Control User Manual   608239

Range Rover Workshop Manual 1970-1985 (petrol 3.5)   AKM3630
Range Rover Workshop Manual 1986-1989   SRR660ENWM &
    (petrol 3.5 & diesel 2.4 Turbo VM)   LSM180WS4/2
Range Rover Workshop Manual 1990-1994
    (petrol 3.9, 4.2 & diesel 2.5 Turbo VM, 200 Tdi)   LHAWMENA02
Range Rover Workshop Manual 1995-2001 (petrol 4.0, 4.6 & BMW 2.5 diesel)   LRL0326ENGBB
Range Rover Workshop Manual 2002-2005 (BMW petrol 4.4 & BMW 3.0 diesel)   LRL0477
Range Rover Electrical Manual 2002-2005 UK version (petrol 4.4 & 3.0 diesel)   RR02KEMBB
Range Rover Electrical Manual 2002-2005 USA version (BMW petrol 4.4)   RR02AEMBB
Range Rover Parts Catalogue 1970-1985 (petrol 3.5)   RTC9846CH
Range Rover Parts Catalogue 1986-1991 (petrol 3.5, 3.9 & diesel 2.4 & 2.5 Turbo VM)   RTC9908CB
Range Rover Parts Catalogue 1992-1994 MY & 95 MY Classic
    (petrol 3.9, 4.2 & diesel 2.5 Turbo VM, 200 Tdi & 300 Tdi)   RTC9961CB
Range Rover Parts Catalogue 1995-2001 MY (petrol 4.0, 4.6 & BMW 2.5 diesel)   RTC9970CE
Range Rover Owners Handbook 1970-1980 (petrol 3.5)   606917
Range Rover Owners Handbook 1981-1982 (petrol 3.5)   AKM8139
Range Rover Owners Handbook 1983-1985 (petrol 3.5)   LSM0001HB
Range Rover Owners Handbook 1986-1987 (petrol 3.5 & diesel 2.4 Turbo VM)   LSM129HB

Engine Overhaul Manuals for Land Rover & Range Rover
300 Tdi Engine, R380 Manual Gearbox & LT230T Transfer Gearbox Overhaul Manuals   LRL003, 070 & 081
Petrol Engine V8 3.5, 3.9, 4.0, 4.2 & 4.6 Overhaul Manuals   LRL004 & 164

Land Rover/Range Rover Driving Techniques   LR369
Working in the Wild - Manual for Africa   SMR684MI
Winching in Safety - Complete guide to winching Land Rovers & Range Rovers   SMR699MI

Workshop Manual Owners Edition
Land Rover 2 / 2A / 3 Owners Workshop Manual 1959-1983
Land Rover 90, 110 & Defender Workshop Manual Owners Edition 1983-1995
Land Rover Discovery Workshop Manual Owners Edition 1990-1998
★ These books only available direct from Amazon

www.brooklandsbooks.com

<u>**FORECOURT DATA.**</u>

		9.35:1	**8.13:1**	**Diesel.**
		compression ratio		gas oil or derv to
FUEL	Grade - UK rating	4 star **** 97 minimum	2 star ** 90 minimum	BSI 2869, Class A1
	Tank capacity	79 - 5 litres (17 -5 gallons)		
Engine Oil		Dependant on engine type and operating conditions. see pages 143 - 147.		
Tyre pressures	Normal on and off road use all speeds and loads	Front. 1.9 bar (28 lbs per sq in) Rear. 2.4 bar (35 lbs per sq in)		

If in doubt or for specific conditions see page 139.

Brooklands Books Ltd., PO Box 904, Amersham, Bucks, HP6 9JA, England
E-mail: sales@brooklandsbooks.com   www.brooklandsbooks.com

ISBN: 9781855202900   Part No. LSM129 HB EDITION BB   Ref: RR86HH   2W0/2431

Printed by Printforce, United Kingdom